Against the Odds

AGAINST THE ODDS

An Autobiography

Bobby Robson
with Bob Harris

STANLEY PAUL
London Sydney Auckland Johannesburg

To our mutual friends Joe Sanchez and Jonny Dexter

Stanley Paul & Co. Ltd

An imprint of the Random Century Group

20 Vauxhall Bridge Road, London SW1V 2SA

Random Century Australia (Pty) Ltd
20 Alfred Street, Milsons Point, Sydney, NSW 2061

Random Century New Zealand Limited
191 Archers Road, PO Box 40–086, Glenfield, Auckland 10

Century Hutchinson South Africa (Pty) Ltd
PO Box 337, Bergvlei 2012, South Africa

First published 1990
Reprinted 1990
New paperback edition 1991

Photoset in Bembo

Printed in England by Cox and Wyman Ltd, Reading, Berks

British Library Cataloguing in Publication Data

Robson, Bobby *1933–*
Against the Odds
1. Association football. Clubs. Association football
clubs. Management. Robson, Bobby – Biographies
I. Title II. Harris, Bob *1944–*
338.76179633463092

ISBN 0 09 174878 X

The authors and publisher would like to thank the following
for allowing the reproduction of copyright photographs:
Action Images, AllSport, Simon Bruty/AllSport, David Cannon/AllSport,
Duncan Raban/AllSport, Billy Stickland/Allsport, Colorsport,
Ross Kinnaird/Empics, Phil O'Brien/Empics, Mail Newspapers plc,
Sport and General Press Agency, Sporting Pictures, *Sunday Mirror*,
Bob Thomas, Universal Pictorial Press.

Contents

Thou god of our idolatry, the press . . .
Thou fountain, at which drink the good and wise;
Thou ever-bubbling spring of endless lies;
Like Eden's dread probationary tree,
Knowledge of good and evil is from thee.

William Cowper
(1731–1800)

1

All over, bar the World Cup

It was on Tuesday, 8 May 1990 – a month to the day before Cameroon opened the World Cup in Milan with a spectacular victory over holders Argentina – that I knew the best and probably the hardest job in football was no longer to be mine. England's last World Cup game in Italy would also be my last, after eight years in the roughest, toughest, most prestigious job in the beautiful game of football. That moment of realisation meant that it was one of the saddest days of my entire career.

Despite the pressure this very special job creates; the personal assaults from the media; the strain on my marriage; the continual anguish for my family and the long, lonely hours, I didn't want to go. Despite the relatively modest financial returns in comparison to the game's other top posts I would happily have stayed on. Despite the rock-solid confirmation of financial security guaranteed as coach to top European club PSV Eindhoven of Holland, I walked into the Football Association's headquarters at 16 Lancaster Gate, London W2 hoping that the chairman Bert Millichip and his International Committee had changed their minds and would ask me to remain in charge for at least another two years. Mr Millichip hadn't changed his mind, neither had the International Committee.

It was all over . . . or at least nearly all over. There was still that little matter of the World Cup, a competition I believed my England team, the country's England team, had every chance of winning. How close we went, closer even than four years earlier when the eventual winners Argentina put us out of the quarter-finals, thanks to a blatant handled goal from the world's best player of the time, Diego Maradona, which changed the course of the game.

1

Again it was the eventual winners, this time West Germany, who put us out of the competition. They had been the best team in the tournament but they couldn't beat us, not over 90 minutes, nor extra time, and I had to watch in mental turmoil as all our hopes and dreams vanished in a sudden–death penalty shoot-out in the semi-final in Turin.

Just my luck! By then so much had changed, so much was different. During the long two years between the traumas of the European Championships in West Germany and this fateful Wednesday, 4 July, the team had gained its independence and evolved into a quality, world–class machine capable of taking on and beating the best in the world. How close they came to doing that! And I am as certain as you can be in our unpredictable game that had we beaten the Germans we would have won the World Cup against Argentina in the Final in Rome.

It was obvious, not just to me but to everyone in football, that England had a team of which they could be proud. The public back at home in England, those who had followed us on our long trail through Italy and even the media who had cruelly written us off after our opening 1–1 draw with the Republic of Ireland, had come together to back us. My popularity, for the first time in eight years, knew no bounds. PSV Eindhoven couldn't believe their good fortune. I was already theirs while the Football Association were still haggling over compensation terms for my replacement.

I now know that the cards fate dealt me were probably the right ones: it was time for me to go. All the same, I wondered what might have happened with the job I loved and coveted had nothing been decided at that moment. It would certainly have seemed to be the most inopportune and unlikely time in my entire England career for the Football Association to ask me to pack my bags and go.

Strange to tell, I had not even considered going until I attended a World Cup workshop in Zurich at the end of March. Of course I had considered my options, with only a year of my contract to run. But I had no intention of quitting a job I still loved. Maybe two more years, bringing on a young successor, teaching him the ropes, the vast difference between managing a club and managing a national side and all that goes with it.

2

In fact the work was so much in my blood and the footballing future so much brighter than it had been at any previous time that I would have seriously contemplated and almost certainly accepted another four-year stint had it been offered to me.

Zurich showed that to be an unlikely prospect, as one of the travelling media circus cornered Bert Millichip in a lounge at Heathrow Airport on the way out to Switzerland and told the rest of his colleagues the juicy titbit that Robson would be on his way out if he didn't bring the World Cup back to London five months later and even if he did there would be no guarantee; and those were the headlines of the national newspapers the very next day. Bert and the Chief Executive Graham Kelly, who had joined us in Zurich, tried to explain that it wasn't like that at all and that, as usual, the journalists' own interpretation had been placed on the answers to some loaded questions.

But the upshot was that my job was – once more – on the line, and I had to think about my own future at a time when all I wanted to do was concentrate on the immense task ahead in the World Cup Finals in Italy. That was what really mattered to me at that time, and I wanted those crucial games out of the way before I started to consider my future. Even after the stories from Zurich I was inclined to shrug it off, sit on our growing undefeated record and let things take their natural course. Hadn't I done it before? Riding the criticism and the pressure. That one year remaining on my contract could still become two or even four. That's how confident I was that we were going to do a good job in Italy.

Maybe staying on wasn't the sensible or practical thing to do. I had watched with interest how golfer Tony Jacklin had quit the Ryder Cup job, doing two of them and then passing it on because of the intense pressure of the commitment. Here was a top-class player with a tremendous individual record, a huge storehouse of knowledge, personal panache and a great media image saying he couldn't put up with it again, even though he had twice won the biggest team prize in the sport.

Certainly I had asked myself before whether I could take it all again and stay sane. I did it after the World Cup Finals in Mexico and I did it again after those three defeats in the European

Championships in West Germany when, it seemed, the whole world wanted my head. But this time around I wasn't able to sit on it and get on with my job, because it wasn't going to be allowed to rest there. A football writer, Joe Melling, whom I had no cause to disbelieve, telephoned to tell me that he was going to run a story in his newspaper that weekend saying that the FA had already decided on Graham Taylor of Aston Villa as my successor. It was done and dusted. Did I know?

No I didn't. I was stunned. Not because it was Graham Taylor, as he had long seemed to be one of the obvious and leading contenders, but because of the timing of the whole thing. Joe wouldn't tell me his source but promised that it came from right inside the Football Association – in other words from one of my own bosses. It seemed that everyone except me knew for sure that I would be leaving my job after the World Cup Finals. Clubs, including PSV, had made discreet inquiries as to my availability after the Zurich episode. I had given them all the same answer: Thanks for the interest but I was not prepared to listen or discuss the matter until the World Cup was over. Suddenly it struck me that by then it might be too late! I needed to seek a meeting with the Football Association and I needed to do it damned quickly.

There was no confrontation, no row, no showdown. On Thursday, 3 May I met Bert Millichip at the Football Association offices in Lancaster Gate without any sort of embarrassment. There was no rift between us; there never has been. Bert was genial, friendly and as understanding as he had ever been. Both Zurich and the story in the *Mail on Sunday* were mentioned. He asked me the million-dollar question of how long does a manager carry on in this job. I did not know and neither did he. He held up his hands and said that there could be no guarantees after the World Cup. That I understood; the FA had always stood firmly behind me in the past but could not do so for ever, particularly if we suffered the same fate in our opening World Cup games as we had in the European Championships two years earlier.

Bert had been honest with me and I came clean with him. I told him that I had been approached before our game with Czechoslovakia at Wembley on 25 April by a contact who had

4

told me that PSV were more than a little interested if the stories in the English papers were accurate in their assumption that I would be leaving my international duties.

In fact, I had been told that I was top of a very short list and that the job was mine if I wanted it. At that time my immediate response was that I didn't want to get involved at that stage of the preparations for the World Cup Finals. But I was flattered, and the offer stirred me. First I am a patriot, in love with England, English football and the players; but, after that, Dutch soccer has always fascinated and thrilled me, going back to the days of Johan Cruyff and 'total football' in the 1974 and 1978 World Cup Finals. Holland is only a short hop away from my home in Ipswich, and quite often I would pop over to watch a game while manager of Ipswich; and I eventually built one of my best sides around the talents of two of their players, Arnold Muhren and Frans Thijssen.

PSV were also one of the biggest clubs in the world, former European Champions backed by the electrical giants Philips and as ambitious as any team around. They had lost their title to great rivals Ajax, and not only wanted that back, but also the international glory they had achieved before their stars left them for even richer prizes in Italian football. My contact told me that they had players to buy and others on the move, had season tickets to sell and that a decision would be needed as their fans were becoming impatient, thinking they were dragging their feet. I understood all of that; but until this moment I had felt that it was not right to talk about it, just as I had when Barcelona had come in for me while England were in Uruguay and I was at my lowest ebb. Then I told them I had a contract to honour and a job to do, and suggested that they might like to talk to Terry Venables. The rest is history.

This had now become an entirely different matter. If the stories doing the rounds were true, I was going to be added to the list of unemployed in early July, and that wasn't too far away. I have never been a money-grabber and have no fortune tucked away for my retirement. PSV were offering me security for my latter years and no man in the world ignores that sort of offer in those circumstances.

Mr Millichip understood all of this, and because he could give

5

me no assurances for my future at Lancaster Gate he gave me his full blessing on 4 May to have preliminary discussions with the Dutch club. I immediately telephoned the PSV Chairman Jaques Rutz and the General Manager Kejs Ploegsma and they confirmed their interest and the sort of money that they were offering. It made me blink. It was also giving me the chance to return to coaching, working with top players on a day-to-day routine instead of for a couple of days every month or so. It was tempting – so tempting that I decided that unless the Football Association could offer something concrete I would take it. But, even then, I hoped that Bert had thought things over and was having second thoughts and I would stay on as England manager.

I went back to see Bert on Tuesday, 8 May and told him that if nothing had changed I would leave on the conclusion of the World Cup and accept the two-year appointment I had been offered in Holland. He simply said that was fine by him, and made no attempt to persuade me to change my mind. The die was cast and I was on my way out even before a ball had been kicked in anger in the World Cup Finals.

That's football. There is nothing sinister in it, nothing cynical. It is the way the game operates. I had enjoyed two jobs in 21 years: 13 at Ipswich and 8 with the FA. I was one of the lucky ones and I wasn't about to start moaning or complaining about the cruel world. It was a simple fact of life. The job was over – well, at least, almost over.

In an ideal world I would have liked to finish my commitments with England before making the announcement of leaving and taking the new job. Although this was certainly best for me and for my team, it wasn't an ideal world and there were too many other considerations to take into account. The FA, for one, needed to officially start looking for a replacement, even if the decision had already been made, while PSV were desperate to make the appointment public.

Compromise was the name of the game, as it so often is in this type of dealing. When my financial advisers had talked to PSV and sorted out much of the contract, which would be signed *after* the World Cup, I went back to Bert Millichip and Graham Kelly to tell them that the deal had been worked out and all that remained was how and when it was going to be done, particularly in the light of the growing speculation in the Dutch papers, which was quite naturally being picked up back at home.

I wasn't too concerned then about public and media reaction. After all it was quite a normal matter for international managers to move on after a major competition. West German manager Franz Beckenbauer had already told his Federation that he would be leaving; and Dutch manager Rinus Michels had gone to the West German side Bayer Leverkusen following the Dutch triumph in the European Championships.

Bert and Graham were all for issuing a statement as quickly as possible, as were PSV, but we all agreed it needed to be done in a controlled and dignified manner at the right moment to suit everyone and, in any case, I was not entirely satisfied that my business with PSV was fully complete.

My priority had, in any case, become the upcoming warm-up games at Wembley against Denmark on 15 May and Uruguay exactly a week after that. In fact the i's were not dotted nor the t's fully crossed until a further visit to Amsterdam by my business manager on Thursday, 17 May and confirmation by myself with a telephone call on Sunday, 20 May. We went through the contract the following day – the very day I named my squad of 22 for Italy.

All of this was going on at our regular team headquarters at Burnham Beeches in the heart of the glorious Thames Valley countryside, culminating with a meeting with Graham Kelly there in the afternoon of our defeat against Uruguay. We had succeeded in keeping the whole thing under wraps: not even the senior internationals knew what was going on. The FA were all for making the announcement on Thursday, 24 May to be released in the papers the following day – the very day we were due to leave Luton Airport for Sardinia and therefore, in my opinion, a bad choice. Both the team, who were taking their wives with them, and myself would be besieged, and it was my plan to tell the players privately on the Monday once we had settled into our hotel.

Apart from those actively involved and my ever-patient wife Elsie no one knew what had been going on in the background and I needed those couple of days to tell my staff, particularly my old friends, coach Don Howe and assistant Dave Sexton. They had no inkling that I was even considering my future and as they were so involved it was crucial I should tell them before it all became public knowledge. Some hope! Maybe it was naive of all of us to expect such a big move to stay secret but none of us could have imagined the cruel, messy way the news eventually broke.

There was no indication at all as I spent the day prior to our departure attending a meeting with the Minister for Sport Colin Moynihan and Glen Kirton, the Football Association's Head of External Affairs. He had called us in to see him – in fact insisted – to tell us what was expected of the England team in terms of on-field behaviour during the World Cup. What a waste of time that was! We had always been fully aware of our responsibilities, particularly since the Heysel disaster five years earlier. No international team had a better disciplinary record than England over my eight years, with just the one sending-off in Mexico when Ray Wilkins was unfortunate to have to go after throwing the ball down and a handful of bookings.

Bert Millichip and Graham Kelly had met the Minister the night before, and Glen and I thought it in order to see them after our meeting to report what else had been said. They were at the Great Western Hotel in London for the AGM and we timed our arrival to catch them between meetings at lunch-time.

We quietly arranged that the announcement would be made after training at noon on Monday. No further mention was made of my personal life after I had talked privately to Graham Kelly the day before, thanking him for his support over some difficult personal moments and warning him, in passing, that I feared there could be some more mud hurled at the fan, as I had heard that a woman who had caused me trouble before was trying to resell the story to make a financial killing at an opportune moment. Kelly told me that I had ridden it before and would ride it again, adding that I could anticipate the same backing I had received before, and that if any of it was incorrect and I wanted to sue they would back me in that as well. It was something I had been forced to live with for some weeks; it was just something else to hinder my own mental preparations for the competition ahead, and it was nice to know who was on my side. I returned home to Ipswich to pack and prepare, not solely for two months in Italy but for two years in Holland immediately afterwards.

It was then that the bombshell broke, with a telephone call from a football writer, Steve Curry, of the *Daily Express*, who was already in Sardinia with the advance press corps. He told me that the previously middle-of-the-road newspaper *Today*, who had largely backed me in the past, were running a story next day that I had resigned as England manager because of a threat of my personal life being exposed by the serialisation in another newspaper of a book written by a woman I had known 14 years before.

I was flabbergasted, stunned, appalled and shocked. Curry, who told me he was with the *Today* football writer Rob Shepherd at that moment, added that I had been seen handing envelopes to every member of the International Committee containing a hand-written note with my resignation. I told them that I was packing to leave as planned, and that there was no envelope and they would be well advised to kill any such story because there was not a grain of truth in it. Certainly at no stage of my visit to the Great Western Hotel did I pass around envelopes, and if anyone can produce that hand-written letter I will hand over a million pounds.

I thought that I had killed a very nasty situation, but it soon became evident that I had not, as I took calls to warn me of the storm clouds brewing; and then, at midnight, the vultures began arriving at my front door with photographers, tape recorders and notebooks poised. I couldn't believe it and telephoned my closest journalistic contact to ask what I should do. I took the advice offered: I bolted the door, switched out the lights, went to bed and waited for the explosion.

As sure as day followed night, it happened. I was up after a sleepless night before seven and looked out of the window to see an ever-increasing group of reporters and photographers. At least they had the decency to wait until eight o'clock before they began banging on the front door. I couldn't stay inside for ever. I had a hairdressing appointment at 9.30 that morning and other urgent appointments. I answered the door.

They confirmed what had appeared in the papers as they scrambled to catch up and outdo each other. Some said I had quit already, another, the *Daily Mirror*, which has waged a continual war against me, had both stories — that I had quit because of this woman and that I was to leave to join PSV.

All those carefully laid plans had gone; and, worse, I was accused of being greedy, unpatriotic, a cheat, a liar and of running out on England.

So much for believing that my departure would be accepted in the same fashion that West Germany, Holland and others had accepted pre-tournament announcements from their managers in the past. There was no such sophistication from our tabloids: the very same papers which had been demanding for so long that I quit were now taking me to task for accepting another job, even though they had told their readers that I would not be kept on.

Not once but many times in those seven weeks did I ask myself if our own newspapers really cared whether England did well in the World Cup. At times I even wondered whether there was some sort of conspiracy to undermine any chance we had of doing well. Of course it was not true. I, and my England team, were just victims of the tabloid newspaper war, the battle to sell more papers than their competitors by going more and more over the top. I had watched this cancer spread over the eight years I had been in the job. It was ugly and damaging and, so often, the reports were untrue.

What a way for us to go to Italy! The Football Association, in the face of questions that night, had felt forced to leak the fact that I was, indeed, leaving. To cover both them and me, a full-blooded press conference was called at Lancaster Gate where, not for the first time, the place was besieged by the media, leaving me to handle another nightmare which had so little to do with football and the job in hand. It also crossed my mind that I hadn't signed the contract waiting for me in Eindhoven, and I wondered whether I would have any sort of job waiting for me at the end of this World Cup.

I confess it was a very nervous and disturbed Bobby Robson who joined his squad and officials at the hotel that night prior to their departure to Italy the next day.

The hardest job in football

Was it all worth it? When I signed that first five-year contract back in the summer of 1982 I fully anticipated a four-year stint and a move back to club football immediately after the World Cup Finals in Mexico. I knew the job was going to be hard, I knew the job was going to be tough but I didn't know just how much it would change in the course of the next eight years. No one could have known. In fact it was the most traumatic, dramatic period in the 125-year history of the world's oldest football association: the growth of hooliganism; the shame of the 39 deaths at the Heysel Stadium in Belgium before the European Cup Final between Liverpool and Juventus; the fire at Bradford City; the deaths at the Hillsborough semi-final between Liverpool and Nottingham Forest; the five-year banning of all our English teams from European competition. That ban cost all my home-based players vital international education, destroying the only bridge between club football and competitive international football. The hooliganism and the tragic deaths cost us our reputation and made us unwelcome abroad, as well as losing us fixtures against teams like Italy and Holland in our preparations for European and World Championships. It made football a dirty word at home for the government, whose disaffection with our sport and the image it gave us provided the media with a bandwagon to jump on.

Suddenly it was the bad side of football that much of the media were looking for; they produced degrading, attacking, insulting articles and items. And it suited them as their own industry changed, with a circulation war developing between daily papers like the *Sun*, the *Mirror* and the *Star*, Sunday papers like the *News of the World*, the *People* and the *Sunday Mirror* and even between the middle-of-the-road dailies, the *Express*, the *Mail* and *Today*.

Footballers and football managers had become prime targets, moving from the back pages to the front and to the gossip columns, joining the film and television stars and politicians in the full glare of the spotlight with every failing, every nervous twitch, every mispronounced word and wrong name held against them, and every skeleton in every cupboard not just sought by any means but then fleshed out to suit the paper involved.

Football itself has not been blameless. Far from it. Many of the most vitriolic of the articles aimed at myself and my players were 'signed', if not written, by former international players, like Mick Channon, Alan Ball and Malcolm Macdonald, former England captains like Emlyn Hughes and Kevin Keegan and even an ex-manager, Sir Alf Ramsey, whom you would have expected to have more compassion and to know better. Pieces of silver, it seems, were more important than integrity.

You can certainly say that the job has its headaches, and while I pray it will improve for Graham Taylor and anyone else who takes on the biggest, hardest job in football, it will never go back to the days of Walter Winterbottom or even, for that matter, Ron Greenwood; and that could seriously affect the decision of some bright young manager of the future when the position becomes available again.

It has often been a nightmare, a pain in the backside, an intrusion into the most private recesses of my life, and on two or three occasions I wondered whether the time was right to pack it all in – but never once did I regret giving up what was the game's very best, most comfortable job in football at lovely Ipswich, even to the extent of taking a drop in salary to move from club to country and then watching as managers and even one of their assistants earned more in a season than I did.

I am sad that I could not emulate my Ipswich and England predecessor Sir Alf Ramsey in winning the World Cup for my country but I leave proud of taking England to their first ever Semi-Final away from home soil and in qualifying for three of the four Finals we aimed for in my eight years. I am certainly not bitter. Far from it: I am grateful. I depart a better, more rounded person – better educated, well travelled and, I hope, a more forgiving man than I was when I took on the duty after Ron Greenwood's undefeated run in the 1982 World Cup Finals. In those days the prospect of making after-dinner speeches to some of the country's elite businessmen would have frightened me to death, as would the in-fighting, the policy debates and the battles with club managers and the Schools Football Association.

I went into it for the excitement, because being manager of England is the top job in my profession and a job very few managers can ever hope to attain. It is not a smash-and-grab affair, but a minimum of a four-year cycle in an attempt to beat every other country in the world and win the World Cup, the greatest competition of them all. It was an advantage, a great stimulus, to have played in a World Cup myself in Sweden under Walter Winterbottom and to have travelled to Chile for another, although it never entered my head that I might be going back twice as a manager, not in my wildest dreams. Just imagine what Franz Beckenbauer must feel, having won the World Cup both as a manager and a player – and finishing runner-up as both, as an added bonus.

The first time I even thought about the position really seriously was when Ramsey was dismissed in 1973 after the goalless draw in Portugal. The media linked my name with the vacancy. It was nice, even though I knew that I wasn't in with a shout. Then, when Revie walked out to take an appointment in the United Arab Emirates, I was interviewed for the job along with Lawrie McMenemy, Brian Clough and Ron Greenwood. Again I didn't fancy my chances at all; but the experience did me no harm and I felt, along with Brian Clough, that I had enjoyed a good interview. Once more the FA did the right thing in going for Ron Greenwood, the complete opposite to Revie and therefore the perfect antidote to everything that had happened previously.

The interview with the late Professor Harold Thompson went well, and I thought that if I continued to get it right with Ipswich at Portman Road I would be in with a real chance next time around, especially as Ron Greenwood had stressed that his was a short-term appointment. I knew my best was still to come as a manager, and I needed that experience to be able to do the job at all.

Tommy Docherty claimed he didn't get the job because the Football Association didn't know which club to write to while Brian Clough, equally tongue-in-cheek, suggested that it would be better if the Archbishop of Canterbury went to see Professor Sir Harold because he would only have to kiss his hand!

In between, I had two offers from Barcelona, one from Bilbao and another from Everton and a chance to return to my native North-East with Sunderland. There were one or two other offers which I promised to keep, and have kept, confidential.

The offers came because I had developed two teams, won the FA Cup and earned invaluable experience in Europe, where Ipswich won a hard-fought UEFA Cup. I would have loved the chance to win the First Division title – we finished as runners-up twice – but the chance of the England manager's job came and I doubted whether it would come again if I were foolish enough to pass this up.

I was extremely happy at Ipswich, earned one of the highest salaries in the game, loved where I lived and, in Patrick Cobbold, had the best boss around – who would have readily appointed me to the board, even though I already enjoyed all the privileges of being managing director.

But I had also already had a taste of the 'sweet' life with England. When Ron was appointed to the job he gathered around him several coaches to help, including Brian Clough, Terry Venables, Don Howe, Dave Sexton, Howard Wilkinson and myself. Don and I earned 'brownie points' by being put in charge of the B team, with Terry, Howard and Dave looking after the Under-21s and Brian Clough in charge of the youth set-up. It all worked well, except for Cloughie who wasn't able to give enough of his time to the job. He quit, and I do not believe that did his prospects as a future England manager much good at all, even though he was and remained the so-called 'people's choice'.

Ron took over the reins too late to rescue England from their unhappy qualifying position, but still wanted to go to Argentina to study the 1978 World Cup Final and, because it clashed, he asked me to manage an agreed FA tour to Kuala Lumpur,

Singapore and New Zealand. Coming on top of winning the FA Cup at Ipswich it was a great thrill and honour. For the first time I was given a real opportunity of managing top players from other clubs, travelling with them, observing them, working with them. I was lucky to have Jack Wiseman from Birmingham City and Lionel Smart of Swindon in charge of the trip. They were brilliant and, to this day, it remains one of the finest trips I have ever been on.

The players responded. They were of good quality and we got good results: Joe Corrigan, Viv Anderson, Alan Kennedy, Paul Mariner, Brian Talbot, John Hollins – to name but a few. There was not a single misdeed on a long, end-of-season trip. One such slip can wreck an entire tour. This one was so happy that, in Singapore, all the players dipped into their own pockets and clubbed together to buy Jack and Lionel presents.

After that, I took an England side to Australia on a trip where we set off on Thursday, arrived in Sydney on Friday, played and won on Saturday and flew back on Sunday. I was also a guest of the Football Association at the 1980 European Championships and I took an England team to Iceland when Ron and Don were with the main bulk of the World Cup squad prior to the World Cup in Spain. It was pretty clear, with Ron giving me my head, nominating me, recommending me, that when he left I would be in with a strong chance of taking over.

I had seen some hooliganism in Italy when England played Belgium in Naples and I knew that Ron had come under some very unfair pressure from the media after a defeat and some more hooliganism in Switzerland but, on the whole, I was protected in my position at Ipswich and still saw the England job through rose-tinted glasses. The media pressure was beginning to change but I was hardly aware of it where I was, with an occasional interview and seeing the local guys before and after matches. The press were even invited into the boardroom half an hour after games.

I knew what the England job meant in football terms – but certainly not the rest of it. My visions were interesting in retrospect. It was undoubtedly something of an ego trip, being 'Mr Football', working at the highest possible level with free selection of the best players and, in between, travelling the world, seeing how the rest of the world performed and spying out our opponents. It was a true picture, but only the tip of the iceberg was showing.

Don Revie claimed publicly that I had been approached before he walked out, but the truth is that the first I heard that I was definitely to be offered the England job was when my chairman told me that he had been officially approached by the FA Secretary Ted Croker for permission to speak to me about England. Patrick didn't want me to go but he could not have been more helpful. He said it was entirely up to me. Ron Greenwood had given his approval, having made it clear that when England's interest ended in the World Cup in 1982 he would gracefully retire. I checked that out with Ron myself to ensure that nothing was done behind his back and, as one of his spies, I was able to attend a briefing at West Lodge Park before the team left for Spain. I was there for two days and watched the squad depart. The entire hotel staff and a few more besides came out to watch them go and I found myself being caught up with it all. While I was with the squad Ron took the time to talk to me, telling me that it was a good job, working for good people who let him get on with it without any major interference. That was important.

I hadn't fully made up my mind at that stage, although it was what I was leaving behind rather than what I was going to which made me hesitate. We had just won a European trophy and had been pipped by Liverpool for the title. I wanted that Championship so badly, and honestly believed we could win it next time. Three times I felt we were good enough to win it, only to fail for one reason or another.

The money I was being offered was a bit of an insult. I was prepared to take a cut, but not what they were offering, and I told them quite bluntly that I liked their job but not their salary. Ted Croker was stunned when I told him what I was earning, and he soon made the offer acceptable, if not up to my Portman Road wages. Money was secondary. If it had not been, I would have gone to Barcelona or Saudi Arabia. No, money wasn't the real stumbling-block. It was that damned League title: it grieved me that I had not won it. But what decided me was that winning the World Cup for England was even more important than winning the League Championship for Ipswich. If you want to get to the moon you have to get on the rocket first of all. I believed England had the players to win the World Cup, so I traded one for another: Ipswich and the League title for England and the World Cup. I felt that I had done a good job for Ipswich and was leaving them in good shape with a good staff, making a profit and challenging for the top honours. It saddened me to watch the team slip into the Second Division and the crowds dwindle. But the hard core of supporters is still there, and as for the future, I am delighted to say, as a local (I have kept my house in Ipswich), that the future looks rosy again.

The decision was not one that anyone else could help me with; I had to make it entirely on my own. I suppose that all along there was only one answer and, backed by my wife Elsie, I went back to the FA and told them of my interest. We had a brief meeting before Bert Millichip, Ted Croker and Dick Wragg, the Chairman of the International Committee, left for Spain and arranged a second meeting in Madrid during the second phase of the competition.

I went to Spain on my spying mission for Ron to watch, among others, Austria and West Germany, who were likely to provide Ron Greenwood and his team with opposition later in the tournament. I returned to Madrid to report to Ron, but didn't linger, because the press were increasing their speculation that I was about to take over – and Ron didn't need that added hassle. I then met with Bert Millichip, and everything was agreed to my satisfaction. We shook hands on it and I asked if we could keep it quiet until I had told my chairman and Elsie. We agreed that there would be no announcement until Ron officially retired. (Maybe that's what I had in mind for myself eight years later. I wasn't as lucky as Ron.)

I didn't fully realize what I had let myself in for: the threat to my marriage, my sanity, the quality of life – that was all to come. In those first two years I would sit on the train from Ipswich to London sometimes asking myself what I was doing. It wasn't the way I thought it would be. I couldn't get the players I wanted. I couldn't get them together as much as I wanted. The results weren't that good, and when we had a bad one I would have to sit on it and the pressure for a month or maybe more. In the League, you could have a bad result, talk about it and write it off after three days as you prepared for the next game. With England you have to win every match. It is expected of you, whoever you are playing and whatever the competition. You go in thinking you will experiment in 'friendlies', when it doesn't matter. Then you catch the disease, and they all matter. Every game you play you must win. Ours are the best players in the world when we play – at least, that's how everyone thinks.

As for myself, I felt like public property. You become instantly recognisable. Even on a shopping trip, in those early days, Elsie would nudge me and ask: 'What are they looking at? Have we both got two heads?' Meanwhile the other shoppers are nudging each other and asking what we are doing in Sainsbury's, like them and their neighbours. You are on your own, with no one to talk to.

To make matters worse, we lost out in the European Championships, thanks to a 1–0 defeat against Denmark at Wembley. It was looked on as a disaster, as indeed it was in footballing terms, with one journalist describing the Danes as a bunch of butchers, bakers and candlestick-makers. He, like many unversed observers, had failed to see one of the great emerging teams in world football; he had seen only the fact that England had lost to them – and, of course, it was all down to me.

I even had the *Daily Mirror* demanding my head after we had lost our first game in nine matches against Scotland, conceding only our second goal in that run. That one I could never understand. The journalist who was asked by his publisher Robert Maxwell to write the article had not even attended the game!

Go – I often thought in those first two years that if I could swap the jobs again I would have done it. If a little Irish leprechaun had offered me a wish I would have asked him to give me back my beloved Ipswich. Yet in the middle of all my doubts and fears I turned down a vast offer from Barcelona. Why? Because I had to honour my contract. They honestly believed that they were offering me a way out and that I would jump at it in the same way as Don Revie had done when the Emirates 'rescued' him from the England job. They even told me that managing my country was a thankless job with no future and no reward. I answered: 'You are probably right – but I am staying.'

The chance of a lifetime had come, but I couldn't leave. The allegiance, the honour, they stay with you if you are a man of any substance at all. The England job outweighed everything else. There was no way I could walk out, no way I was going to break my contract. I told myself that I had got to learn to like it. I did, against all the odds.

I had another chance to leave with honour and respectability after the Mexico World Cup. We had recovered from a bad start, amid more demands for my head, to reach the Quarter-Finals and that defeat against Argentina and Diego Maradona's hand-ball and brilliant solo goal. There was no pressure on me. Officially I had another year to run on my contract, even though I knew – and the FA knew – that the fifth year was cosmetic, and designed to give me a decent pay-off should we agree to part. I talked about it to one or two close friends, after our defeat, while I stayed on in Mexico to watch the climax to the competition. But I felt in my mind and body that desire to have another crack. I had tasted the World Cup Finals and had the experience of reaching the last eight knowing that, with a little bit of luck, we could have gone further, much further.

I shall never forget the feeling of walking off the pitch at the Aztec Stadium having beaten Paraguay 3–0 to reach the last eight. I knew we had got to play Argentina, and, if we beat them, the favourites, we could win the World Cup. Then to go so close and lose left me with the burning urge to do it again.

To some who have that bitter experience it spells the end. To me it called for an even bigger effort. I had come through my early problems and was beginning to enjoy the good times. I felt strong enough both mentally and physically. I knew the job and knew I could handle it. I had suffered Heysel and the European ban and I thought there was nothing else they could hit me with. The ban, I assumed, would soon be lifted and I could get on with the job with properly schooled players, conversant with the wider game on the Continent. Little did I know! Heysel was to linger on and on and on. It turned into a monkey on my back, and on the back of English football. It was typical of my luck that the ban was eventually lifted days after I finished in the job – and, so we are told, partly because of the good behaviour of our players, their sportsmanship in the World Cup and the winning of the World Cup Fair Play trophy.

We were already in Mexico for a pre-World Cup curtain-raiser when the dreadful events unfolded in Brussels, and instantly we were tarred with the same brush. We were hooligans and murderers. We were still picking up the grisly details of the deaths in the Heysel Stadium when we held a press conference, and I was acutely aware of how aggressive the Mexican, Italian and West German press were towards us.

Of all teams we were due to play the Italians within days of the European Final and it was only the understanding of the Italian Federation which helped us through that awful time. We met immediately and agreed that bridges had to be built and we needed to play that game on schedule or the damage could be lasting, even permanent. Ted Croker and Bert Millichip were still en route to Mexico City and it needed all Dick Wragg's vast experience and statesmanship to keep us afloat. We were being booed and hissed by people, even in the hotel. But we had to keep the game going, erect those bridges, show the public that Italians and Englishmen were still friends despite what had happened, that it was a tragedy for both countries and that we both wanted to heal the wounds and show the world that both sets of footballers wept for what had happened so far away.

We went into that game knowing we could not afford the slightest flare-up. That meant no fouls, no swearing, no dissent, in short nothing which could be seen as aggressive in any way. We had to play with our hands behind our backs in a game everyone wanted us to lose. The players were all warned individually, by Mr Wragg and by me, that if anyone transgressed they would never wear the England colours again. Each one was asked if he understood. The rules were laid.

We lost, and the decisions ensured we would. It is not sour grapes, but we had a bad penalty awarded against us and failed to win an obvious penalty ourselves. Watching the video replays proves those facts beyond all doubt. But we expected it and were, in fact, resigned to it. The players that day played under phenomenal strain, a strain which never fully went away. It wasn't the fault of the Italians: far from it. They played it straight down the line when they could have taken total advantage. They could have set us up with provocation and intimidation when, not so many years before, that had been the very nature of their game. Maybe they had been warned as well. I don't know, but I do know that I have nothing but respect for them and the way they treated us that day.

That respect will now stay for ever, after the third place play-off game against them in Italy. Both of us were disappointed to have gone out of the competition on penalties in the Semi-Finals, but that game was competitive and still played in the best possible spirit.

England, after Heysel, played every game under the shadow of fear — fear that the world ruling body, FIFA, would follow the UEFA ban on the clubs with a total ban on our national team. We were on the brink of a precipice. It would have meant complete isolation for the players, while for me there would have been nothing, no job, with no team to manage. In Mexico in that summer of 1985 I had the gut feeling we were very close to that total ban. No one confirmed it from FIFA but I knew that trouble on or off the pitch could destroy English football.

Another awful decision cost us the draw against hosts Mexico, and we still had the West Germans to play but, as so often happens in these things, the Mexicans had seen what went on in the first two games and felt some sympathy for us. They didn't exactly turn but at least they were neutral. We won 3–0, won well and averted a third successive defeat and an unwanted entry into the record books.

If you had told me that by the next World Cup our teams would still be absent from Europe and the threat against England's participation would still be hanging over our heads I would not have believed it to be possible. It has been a long sentence, particularly for the innocent people, the players, managers and supporters who have never been involved in violence on or off the field. It was too long to be fair or just, especially as, in hooligan terms, we had mercifully slipped way down the inter-national league table. But I knew at the time that re-entry would not be instant, and I had to try to make the ban work for me and try to cover for the loss of experience and the education of our top players who would suffer from their absence from Europe.

I asked for the free mid-week European dates to be turned

over to the international team. I requested that Saturday League fixtures prior to big international matches should be cancelled. I got no response at all. In fact the powers-that-be even introduced new competitions to fill the blank dates. The one advantage we could have gained was lost to us, and once again it was only lip service paid to international football.

Instead we lost out in every way. Ninety per cent of the squad in Italy had never had the joy and experience of playing in European competition. There were 70 or so who played in Europe every season when we were competing. We lost out with our managers, our coaches, experience, education and financially. Most of all, we missed those white-hot evenings when an English team played one of the top Continental sides with everything at stake. I had nights like that with Ipswich – at Barcelona, for example, in a sense an international match all on its own, a totally different experience from even the biggest domestic match and an essential part of the growing process. It was wonderful even at little Ipswich against the likes of Barcelona, Cologne and Feyenoord, matches played in a supercharged atmosphere. If you didn't wobble on those sort of games you weren't going to be hit by the shakes for your national team. It can make you a player. They were great tests of character, and we lost all that. International football was, for so long, an extension of Europe.

It came home to me before the World Cup in Italy, when I watched PSV Eindhoven play Real Madrid. It was such a marvellous occasion, yet I was so sad because it made me realize what my English players had been missing: the atmosphere, the tactical scene, learning to play sensibly when critical issues develop.

Later I was in Bari, looking at the wonderful stadium where I was to experience my last game in charge of England, when someone asked me which games I was going to watch on television. I was in my room for the rest of the day, starting with Fiorentina playing in the Soviet Union at 2 p.m., Napoli against Werder Bremen at tea-time and AC Milan against the East German champions in the evening. You could feel the atmosphere in the hotel room.

Those were international experiences for the players, and I thought it unfair that the young Italian international Roberto Baggio should be gaining that experience with Fiorentina while

22

Paul Gascoigne was at home with Spurs, being denied the opportunity to mature a little more before the World Cup Finals. It's in games like that, where you might be getting nothing from the referee, fighting against the odds and still getting a result on foreign soil, where application is so important. Friendlies mean nothing. Regardless of what we achieved in Italy, our game in England has been crucially damaged and it will take years to recover.

I remember while I was at Ipswich walking out at St Etienne in France for a UEFA Cup tie against a side led by Michel Platini and rated as one of the very best in Europe. It was still several hours to kick-off, but the stadium was full and you could feel the atmosphere. The place was literally shaking. I turned to my assistant Bobby Ferguson and said that if we didn't absorb the atmosphere and cope with the tension we would be crushed. We went a goal down but won 4–1, and from that side we produced several international players for the home countries.

For five of my eight years I was left only with what clubs gave me from our frenetic, 100–miles-per-hour domestic game.

Even when we were in Europe we heard constant criticism that our game was outdated and out of step with our main Continental rivals. How could that be, when we won a trophy for 17 consecutive years and dominated the European Cup with Liverpool, Nottingham Forest and Aston Villa?

Those were great nights, and with top games on their own doorsteps English managers would come and watch without missing anything at their own club. At Ipswich we always made sure we got those young managers and coaches into Portman Road no matter how full we were. My instructions were to let the workers, the technical people in.

Football worked hard from within to right the wrongs; but then came the next tragedy – at Hillsborough, when all those young people were crushed at the start of the FA Cup semi-final between Liverpool and Forest. The irony was that it was not down to hooliganism. I was there in the front row of the directors' box and I could see that for myself; but, naturally, people abroad heard the reports and assumed the worst – even top UEFA official Jacques George, an educated man who should have known better than to jump to conclusions before he knew the facts.

Even though it was proved that hooliganism was not to blame I have no doubts that it again delayed our re-entry into Europe. All in all I couldn't have picked a worse decade in which to manage England. We have not only done well to qualify for every major final in that time, we have done well just keeping our game alive in the face of opposition from government, disenchanted sponsors and spectators frightened to go to games. Fortunately there have been enough people in love with the Beautiful Game to cherish it, keep it going until the moment arrived in Italy to set it back on the upwards trail again. It is a great tribute to the players of our game that they have continued to do so well, and will do even better now we are back into Europe and accepted again.

3

The making of an England manager

I don't know about the five who went before me but this one was born Robert William Robson in the mining village of Sacriston, County Durham in the North-East of England on 18 February 1933.

I came from mining stock and my father Philip went down the pits the day after he left school at the age of 14 and missed only one shift in fifty-one years before his retirement. He couldn't afford to miss them because if you did you weren't paid and there would be someone waiting to step into your boots. Seven of us lived in our little two-bedroomed, terraced house in Langley Park where we had moved a few months after I was born. There was dad, my mom Lillian, and we five boys, Tom, Philip, Ronald, Keith and myself.

There wasn't a lot of money to go round in those days and many of our clothes were passed down from the elder brothers but we didn't know any different as it was the same for all the families around us. Entertainment was simple for the kids, football in the winter and cricket in the summer and I kicked my way through more pairs of shoes than my mom could afford to replace. The street was our pitch and the outside toilets our goals.

My competitive football was limited, because the headmaster at Waterhouses Modern Intermediate School wasn't too keen on the game and wouldn't enter a team in the League. The only organized football I played was in the odd game arranged by the PE master. In many ways it didn't hurt my career at all because it gave me more time to work on my skills, an area that is neglected these days as kids play matches all the time with no time to practise.

Apart from the street my interest in the game was heightened when my dad took us the 17 miles into Newcastle for Newcastle United's home games at St James' Park. Often we were the first in the queue, hours before the kick off, to watch Len Shackleton, Albert Stubbins, Jackie Milburn, Charlie Wayman, Bob Cowell and Alf McMichael. Watching them made me want to play but it wasn't until I left school that I began playing for Langley Park Juniors, an under-18 side.

In those days the scouts would flock to the North-East looking for players and there were plenty at our games. I was invited to Middlesbrough and Southampton for trials. I thought I did quite well at Ayresome Park but I left without anyone saying anything to spend a month at the Dell before being released. Clubs couldn't sign boys until they were seventeen and when I reached that birthday both Middlesbrough and Southampton came back along with Newcastle, Lincoln, York, Blackpool, Huddersfield and Fulham.

My earlier experiences with Middlesbrough and Southampton put me off them while my favourites at Newcastle signed too many big name players to encourage youngsters to join them. Few locals made it to their first team in those days. I chose Fulham, manager Bill Dodgin and seven pounds a week, the maximum they were allowed to pay me. But Dad would only agree to let me go to London if I kept up my apprenticeship as an electrical engineer and carried on at nightschool.

It was manager Bill Dodgin who persuaded me that I had to make a decision and I became a full-time footballer with the happy-go-lucky London club, their kindly manager and comedian-chairman Tommy Trinder. I stayed with them for five years, learning my trade, playing 152 games and scoring 68 goals, playing with people like Johnny Haynes, Bedford Jezzard, Jimmy Hill, Charlie Mitten, Tony Macedo, Jimmy Langley, Bobby Keetch, Tom Wilson and many other characters.

In terms of my England future it was at Craven Cottage that I became interested in coaching. Jimmy Hill was one of Walter Winterbottom's FA Full Badge Coaches and he was always trying to get things altered at our coaching sessions. The other influence was a central defender named Ron Greenwood, eventually to become England manager immediately before me. Both were clearly managerial material although vastly different in attitude and approach. Ron was a deep thinker, listened to and respected whenever he discussed football.

Another strong influence upon me was the Hungarian performance at Wembley on 25 November 1953. A group of us went from Craven Cottage to watch the undefeated Hungarians take on the challenge of England's unbeaten record at Wembley. The Hungarians won 6–3 that day and their performance had a profound effect on me. It was not long afterwards that I began attending the FA Coaching courses at Paddington Street with Ron Greenwood, Jackie Goodwin, Jimmy Hill and others.

The English complacency had been well and truly shattered. We were no longer the masters. It changed a lot of us in our thinking and approach to the game. It was also after that defeat that the Football Association's International Committee allowed Walter Winterbottom to make recommendations about selection – although the Committee still had the last word on the team.

My own international career began when I left Fulham to join West Bromwich Albion. I went to the Midlands in March 1956. Bill Dodgin had left Fulham and Vic Buckingham was persuasive in his efforts to move me to the Midlands. The Baggies, as they were known, had offered £25,000, a great deal of money to a hard-up Second Division club as Fulham were in those days. The record was only £34,000.

It wasn't all I had imagined and I was lonely in my digs, away from my wife Elsie, until I became friendly with the Albion's full back Don Howe, the man with whom I was to share my England career, not only as a player but as coach throughout my eight years with the FA. He was there when my former team-mate Ron Greenwood was in charge and resigned soon after I had left to join PSV Eindhoven, saying that he wanted to concentrate on his work with Queens Park Rangers. The coincidences do not end there, for one of the biggest shareholders was a man named Bert Millichip, eventually to become Chairman of WBA and who, as Chairman of the FA, was my boss when I became England manager. It was Bert, a solicitor, who did the conveyancing on my first house which I bought in 1958 for £2,425 – soon after I began my international career with England.

I made my debut on 27 November 1957, having made my first Under-23 appearance a year earlier against France and I went on to win 20 caps, scoring four goals. Over a similar period nowadays a regular player would win around 50. With so few games at international level and only the League and FA Cup to occupy the clubs there was little sign of the club versus country controversy. Wolves, who won the title that season, played only 42 League games and four in the FA Cup, barely two-thirds of today's programme for a successful team.

Walter Winterbottom was still the manager and he was still hindered by interference from the International Committee. Despite the time available, little of it was spent in preparing the national side and we made little impact on the World Cup in either 1958 or 1962. It was also worth more to play for England then, for I was paid the princely sum of £20, the equivalent of a week's wages. But the honour of playing for England then, as now, was far more important than the money involved.

Just as outside factors like Heysel and Sheffield affected my career as England manager, there was also a tragedy which took its toll on my playing career. We won that first game against France 4–0. I scored two of the goals and Manchester United centre forward Tommy Taylor the other two. It turned out to be the last time Tommy, Duncan Edwards and Roger Byrne were to play for England, for the Munich air disaster took them away from us before the next game. Who can say where we would have gone from there with three such good players who had so much to contribute?

I was nervous about that first game and the great Tom Finney warned me that the gulf between League and international football was huge. Instead of three or four good players they were all good! But despite my two-goal start and the loss of the United players I found myself left out of the next game. Not that it made any difference as we won 4–0 again, this time against Scotland at Hampden.

My taste of the World Cup came in Sweden in 1958 when the FA decided to cut the squad from 22 to 20 – and left behind Stanley Matthews and Nat Lofthouse. We were expected to go through our group but we drew with the Soviet Union, Brazil and Austria and went out of the competition 1–0 in a play-off against the Soviet Union.

My luck wasn't too good in those days either. I had 'goals' disallowed against both the Soviet Union and Austria. Had either of them counted we would have gone through. I was left out of the play-off game and didn't play again for two years, by which time I had switched from being an attacking wing half to play-maker.

I was in and out of the side and played my last game in a 3–1 win over Switzerland on 9 May 1962. I went to Chile for the World Cup that summer but was injured in a warm-up game in Peru, lost my place to a promising young player named Bobby Moore and never got back in again.

We had our problems with the press even then, although it was quite harmless. Peter Swan had his picture taken with a local lady at a function which was wired back and used in England. His wife, who was having a baby, did not like what she saw and she wrote telling him so. But by the time he received it he was laid up in hospital with bad tummy trouble. It was a case of keep taking the tablets – and he hadn't.

My room-mate on that trip, Jimmy Adamson, was being groomed to take over from Walter Winterbottom but when the time came he turned it down and the FA then went to Ipswich for Alf Ramsey. His arrival from the professional ranks changed many things, not least of all picking the team himself. He knew what he wanted and was single-minded in going out to get it. The reward was the World Cup in 1966.

My learning at club level took me back to Fulham in 1962. We had some excellent players in Johnny Haynes (then the first £100 a week footballer), Alan Mullery, George Cohen, Graham Leggat and Eddie Lowe, but we were always two or three players short to go all the way and win something. It didn't help when Fulham sold Mullery to Spurs, saying they needed the money. We were convinced then that the club had no ambition.

In 1967, with my playing career coming to an end, my mind turned to what I was going to do next. I was well into coaching by then and had decided I wanted to stay in the game either as a coach or a manager. Even though I was then 34, Arsenal wanted me as a player while the cricketer Trevor Bailey interviewed me for the player-manager job at Southend where he was a director.

Managing England couldn't possibly have been further from my mind at that formative stage of my life. I was more interested in an unexpected inquiry from Vancouver in Canada, a city that had impressed me while on a visit with West Bromwich Albion. The £7,000 a year I was offered to manage a new team called the Royals was twice my Fulham salary, and after persuading my wife Elsie that we should take our three sons out of school we sailed off in the SS *Oriana* to a new life and a new career.

It should have been a good learning experience as I had to build a side from scratch with a limited budget, but four months before the start of the season we still had no team and, worse, my salary cheques failed to arrive. The club were struggling to keep their heads above water even before a ball had been kicked. Inevitably, their franchise was taken over, by a man who promptly appointed Ferenc Puskas as a coach and began to form a team in Madrid. I went over there and it was chaos. Puskas may have been a great player but he wasn't much of a coach and we couldn't discuss anything at all because neither of us spoke the other's language.

It became increasingly depressing and I eventually went back to Vancouver and my family to spend a miserable Christmas setting the legal wheels in motion in an attempt to gain some satisfaction and recompense through the courts. But while I was waiting Fulham came back for me, this time as a manager, and I took an almost 50 per cent drop to return to Craven Cottage for the third time in my career. I have never been so glad. The Royals went bankrupt so had I sat on my hands and waited, I would never have received my money.

Not that I lasted long at Fulham. Nine months to be exact before I was sacked. It was a shattering experience, particularly as the papers knew about it before I did. The Chairman Sir Eric Miller, who later shot himself, wanted to interfere not only in the buying and selling of players but in team selection as well. I fought against it and got sacked for my trouble. Johnny Haynes was made manager in my place. I felt no resentment.

I was unemployed for three months in that winter of 1968-9. It was a new experience. So was standing in the dole queue, which I eventually forced myself to do, joining not layabouts and ne'er-do-wells as I thought, but bank managers, professional people and even an army major.

The only club to come in for me was from Norway. I didn't fancy that and I was only too grateful when Dave Sexton telephoned to offer me a part-time scouting job. My first game was Ipswich against Forest and I suddenly realised that both sides were without managers and that they might think I was touting for a job. All the same, I wrote off next day applying to Ipswich. It was probably one of the most important and certainly the most productive letter I ever wrote.

Frank O'Farrell and Billy Bingham were favourites for the job but Frank said he would only leave Torquay for a club with potential while Billy preferred to remain at Plymouth. I took the job without a contract but with the promise of at least two years from their wonderful chairman, the late John Cobbold.

It was the start of the happiest time of my life. I turned down clubs from England and Spain to stay with little Ipswich and it was only the offer from England which eventually shifted me after 13 wonderful years. In that time we twice finished as runners-up, won the FA Cup in 1978 and the UEFA Cup in 1981.

I wasn't even sure I would last those initial two years as I fought some of the senior players to establish my control and authority. The crowd also had a go at me, chanting 'Robson Out, Robson Out', much to the distress of my wife who was sitting in the stand watching a little Irishman named George Best tear us apart.

The Board called me in next day for the regular meeting and I feared the worst. I need not have worried as John Cobbold began the meeting by saying; 'Gentlemen, the first business of the day is to officially record in the minutes the apologies of this board to our manager for the behaviour of the fans last night. Agreed? If it ever occurs in this ground again, I will resign as Chairman. Right, on to the next business.'

That's how they were at Portman Road, very civilised. When we were bottom of the table they called me in and offered me a new contract!

Mr John's idea of a boardroom crisis was when they ran short of white wine after a game. That's why they were such a good club to work for and I would have loved to give them the First Division title before I left.

But when I went off to work at Lancaster Gate I left behind a good team, a solvent club and a beautiful new stand with enough supporters going every other Saturday to make it financially viable. It was a mutual admiration society. I was sorry to leave and, on occasions, I regretted what I had left behind. But it all helped me to grow as a football manager and prepare for the eight years which followed.

4
The first eight years are the worst

The test of Graham Taylor, or any England manager these days, is qualification for the two major international titles, the European Championships and the World Cup which are nicely spaced out with two years in between. Obviously the World Cup is the premier event but, because 24 nations now compete in the Finals, it is often easier to reach than the European Finals which have only eight qualifiers, just one from each group. This leaves no margin at all for error as I discovered in my very first competition when we lost to Denmark at Wembley, the only qualifying game defeat of any sort in my eight-year international managerial career, and it cost us our place in the Finals in France.

Those first two years were hard and I often wondered to myself why I had quit the cosy world of Ipswich Town where I had enjoyed 13 fabulous years of success and happy times with little or no interference from either the press or my board of directors.

Even before England kicked a ball under my management I found myself plunged into a new controversial world when I decided for my first game in charge, an away European Championship game in Denmark, to start without the services of a player I admired greatly, Ron Greenwood's skipper Kevin Keegan. It was a carefully considered decision reached after discussions with a number of people. Keegan had opted for the Second Division with Newcastle and I wanted to see where we could go without him. It led to me being spat at and abused by my fellow Geordies at St James' Park. That was a little taste of

33

what was to come over the next eight years. The job was going to be anything but easy, on or off the pitch.

Any doubts over the difficulties of the task ahead were then dispelled in that first game in Copenhagen on 22 September 1982. Sitting on the bench that night I realised the frightening responsibility of the task I had assumed and what it meant to the country. This was vastly different from playing in the international team, there you shared the responsibility. This time I felt on my own. The short hairs stood up on the back of my neck as the realisation sunk in.

Not for the only time in my eight-year reign a goalkeeper named Peter Shilton saved my bacon that night in Denmark, for the game had Danish written right through it. They were just emerging as a great team and that night they slaughtered us. They were much the better team and deserved to win. Unknown winger Jesper Olsen, later to make a name with Manchester United, took apart our experienced Liverpool full back Phil Neal. It was my fault as much as Phil's, for I underestimated the little blond flyer having seen Ipswich's George Burley contain him with consummate ease when my club beat Ajax in a UEFA Cup tie. That night in Copenhagen little Jesper began to carve out his career.

That was one of three errors I made that night. Tony Morley, the winger Ron Greenwood had left behind that summer in Spain, did not provide the cutting edge I hoped for, while my former Ipswich central defender Russell Osman looked out of his depth as he failed to contain Preben Elkjaer, another who was to go on and make a massive international career for himself.

Even so, we twice took the lead through the sharpness of Trevor Francis and might have won thanks to the outstanding goalkeeping of Peter Shilton, then a sprightly 32-year-old and, some said, heading for the end of his international career. Hansen equalised our first goal from the penalty spot after Osman had upended Olsen who was to score the second equaliser himself when he dribbled through the defence, past Robson, Osman and Butcher, before beating Shilton in the dying moments of the game. That goal was to have a major effect but not so much as the goal the Danes scored at Wembley in the first match of the following season.

It was 21 September 1983 and it remains one of the blackest days of my international management. Since that first game we had gone along fitfully as I learned the pitfalls of the new job: trying to get used to the absence of the day-to-day involvement with the players; not being able to discuss the previous match for weeks on end; not always being able to get the players I wanted; not to mention learning to live at this new level.

The West Germans had beaten us 2–1 in my second game in charge with two super goals from Karl-Heinz Rummenigge to give me the first taste of what a downer a defeat at Wembley was. And when Greece came with a packed defence and held us to a goalless draw it didn't make me any happier. But it was something of a roller coaster ride going towards the Danish match with a record-breaking 9–0 win over little Luxembourg and a good 2–0 win over Hungary. In fact we had built a nice little run of ten undefeated games, conceding only a couple of goals on the way.

I had watched the Danes and knew that they were developing into a fine side, improving from when they had outplayed us a year earlier. I was worried. That was fair enough, but the mistake I made was to allow that concern to be transmitted to the players. I exaggerated the Danes' ability in my mind and felt that we would be in trouble if I did not outline the main aspects of the danger and emphasise what a difficult match it was going to be for us. I mistakenly thought it would increase their determination but instead it sowed seeds of doubt in my players' minds and they thought that I believed we were not good enough to beat the Danes. I put our rivals up on a pedestal and knocked our own confidence so that we did not challenge or work as a unit that night.

The great irony was that they came to Wembley scared of us and we only needed to have played reasonably well to have won by a couple of goals. As it was we went down to a single goal, an unlucky penalty conceded by Phil Neal when the ball bounced up awkwardly and hit his hand. But it was enough to end our hopes in the European Championships, even though we continued to make a fight of it by beating Hungary and Luxembourg in our final two games. Even then the gloss was taken off by the lunatic fringe of supporters who wrecked the beautiful Duchy of

Luxembourg for the second time in successive visits. I was to get used to apologising for those animals who called themselves England supporters but no one could have known then the dramatic effect they were to have on the game in general and the England team in particular.

Going out hit us badly. We lost to a couple of Platini goals in France, lost horribly in Wales and crumbled to a two-goal defeat at Wembley to the Soviet Union before heading out for, of all places, Brazil, with what was a young and inexperienced team. It was a fixture I needed like a hole in the head at that stage of my international career with the newspapers screaming for Brian Clough to replace me.

One tabloid newspaper – no prizes for guessing which one – had even been offering lapel badges saying 'Robson Out' and 'Clough In'. It was during this low point that Barcelona came in for me again, sure this time that I couldn't possibly say no in view of what was happening in my own country. I told them I had three years of my contract left and I was running nowhere. To cut a long story short I recommended Terry Venables and the rest is history.

The revival began unexpectedly when, with a bunch of kids and playing two black wingers, John Barnes and Mark Chamberlain, we bounced back against all expectations and predictions to beat the South Americans 2–0 in their own giant Maracana Stadium with the young John Barnes running half the length of the pitch to score a spectacular solo goal while another youngster, Mark Hateley, headed a picture-book second.

It was a wonderful lift, especially as the great soccer pundit Jimmy Hill had asked me was it even worth going to South America given our form and the players at my disposal. We had won in Brazil for the first time in history and had launched two players from international obscurity towards their destiny. Hateley was almost immediately transferred from Second Division Portsmouth to AC Milan for £1 million.

Strangely, Barnes had to live with that goal from then on as everyone expected him to repeat it every time he pulled on an England shirt and they were disappointed when he didn't.

Although we lost 2–0 in Uruguay and drew 0–0 in Chile, the result against Brazil had taken the pressure off, as had the World

Cup draw back in December when the threat of hooliganism had diminished as we were pitched in with Finland, Northern Ireland, Turkey and Romania. For a variety of reasons severe acts of hooliganism were unlikely in the away matches while a five-team group meant that the top two would go on to the Finals in Mexico.

We took off that next season, making a sprint start to our bid for a place under the sun in Mexico. We warmed up against the East Germans in September, instead of taking on a competitive match too early in the season, and reaped the benefits as we hammered Finland 5–0 at Wembley and Turkey 8–0 in Istanbul, a staggering result by any standards.

When we beat Northern Ireland in Belfast with a late Hateley goal we really were on our way but, despite maximum points and 14 goals from three matches, we were hammered by our own newspapers next day for our battling performance against a desperate Irish side. Draws in Romania and Finland meant that we only had to keep our heads against Romania, Turkey and Northern Ireland and we were home and dry. But it never does to look too far ahead in our game.

After seven games without defeat that season we finally lost our unbeaten record to, of all people, the Scots, in a game switched from Wembley to Hampden because of the hooligan threat on a Bank Holiday in London when police resources would be stretched. It wasn't a bad game and we had 20 shots at goal only for a Graeme Souness-inspired Scotland to win with Richard Gough's header from Jim Bett's cross.

No Englishman likes losing to the Scots but I was unprepared for what followed on the Monday morning when the *Daily Mirror* carried a front-page story that I must be sacked. It was hardly a front-page item to my mind but they were soon to have football on the front page again when the Heysel Stadium disaster rocked the football world, with far-reaching effects for our entire game both at club and international level. At the time we were in Mexico City waiting to play World Champions Italy, hosts Mexico and runners-up West Germany in a tournament organised to test the World Cup machinery for a year later.

The true horror of the night in Brussels gradually unfolded as we learned that 39 spectators, mainly Italians, had died in crowd violence before the European Cup Final between our own great champions Liverpool and Juventus. The repercussions were immediately obvious as English clubs were withdrawn from Europe, and we waited and wondered whether FIFA would follow up and ban the English team after the troubles which had followed us around the world over the past few years.

Not least of the problems was the fact that our opening fixture was against the aggrieved Italians in the Aztec Stadium. Fortunately the relationship between the two countries is so strong that the game went on, played in a subdued spirit, with England never, ever going to win. Had the two countries pulled apart at that moment and cancelled the game I dare not think what might have happened to our football.

The pressures on our players in those weeks were enormous, but to their immense credit they worked hard to keep it together even after we lost again to Mexico by a goal from Flores, with a perfectly good equaliser from Viv Anderson disallowed. We were unpopular and this was the third major decision to go against us in two games. We expected it. The upshot was that we faced our old enemies the Germans knowing that another defeat would constitute the worst-ever losing run by an England manager in history.

We need not have worried. The Germans had arrived late and paid for it as we scored our biggest victory over them for 50 years. We won 3–0 with Peter Shilton saving a penalty from Brehme. What a pity it was he couldn't have waited a few more years to have done that when it really mattered in the shoot-out in Turin!

We rounded off that mixed tour with a five-goal thrashing of the United States in Los Angeles, but it was typical of the buffeting we were taking that the gloss was taken off when we arrived back at our hotel to find that some sneak thief had made a sweep of the players' rooms, stealing money and other valuables. I just hoped that was all we were going to lose. Would we lose our international status as well? Would we be returning to Mexico next summer?

Fortunately the answers to both questions were the right ones. We made light of the problems as we went through the season undefeated, with draws against Romania and Northern Ireland and a five-goal romp against Turkey clinching our place at the top of the group, while the Mexico City World Cup draw gave us Portugal, Morocco and Poland. We warmed up with wins in Israel, Egypt, the Soviet Union, Scotland, Mexico and Canada for a nice little 11-match undefeated run on the way to Mexico.

It wasn't long before it was falling apart and the papers were screaming for my head again as we lost our opening game in Monterrey 1–0 to unfancied and squabbling Portugal.

As if that wasn't bad enough, worse was to follow against group outsiders Morocco when, under blazing sun and in 100 degrees of heat, our world collapsed. In the few remaining minutes before half-time, our skipper Bryan Robson dislocated his shoulder yet again and his deputy Ray Wilkins was sent off for tossing the ball back towards the referee after a silly offside decision. Ten men in that heat. Morocco had shown in the first half that they were no mugs and they had opened with a draw against the admired Poles. How could we salvage a point from this nightmare? The Moroccans solved it for us. With a great victory theirs for the taking, they retreated and, with Glenn Hoddle pulling the strings, we dominated the second half. They were so timid that they would not even come out to play when they won free-kicks in our half. It was a priceless point and kept us in the hunt even though we were without Robson for the remainder of the tournament and Wilkins who was suspended for the next two games.

With Poland beating Portugal it was all up for grabs again. Nerves were twanging at the start of our match against Poland, but a super Gary Lineker goal after seven minutes settled us down and he went on to notch a spectacular hat-trick to establish himself as one of the tournament's top players. Stories of our death were premature. We were still very much alive and kicking and heading for Mexico City and a date with the South Americans, Paraguay.

Peter Shilton kept us on terms against the speedy South Americans in the first half until Lineker popped up once more to stab home Steve Hodge's unselfish pass. That goal settled us and we were on our way. Paraguay didn't like it and began to get physical with Delgardo elbowing Lineker in the throat. Our top goalscorer was carried off but they paid the penalty as Peter Beardsley added a second while Gary was receiving treatment and then he recovered and came back to score the third – his fifth in two matches.

Our run of good fortune came to an abrupt halt in the same Azteca Stadium only four days later. A flat game was lifted when Maradona the Argentine captain, challenged Peter Shilton for a ball and knocked it past him with his fist. I waited for the Tunisian referee to sort out this obvious handball. He didn't and we were a goal down despite Shilton's furious protests.

The players didn't need my warning that Maradona could change a game in the space of five minutes and there was little they could do about it when he took on our entire team before scoring the second goal. It should have killed us off but it didn't. It took the officials ages to let us put substitutes Barnes and Waddle on, but once we had managed it we took the opposition apart. With ten minutes left Barnes went past two defenders and crossed for Lineker to score his sixth goal of the World Cup. Barnes did it again with three minutes left, but somehow it was Lineker who finished in the net with the ball the wrong side of the upright. The referee gave us no added time to compensate for the Argentinians' time wasting and we were out of the World Cup, losing to the eventual winners.

I decided to stay on, if the FA would have me. The draw for the European Championship qualifying tournament had again been kind in terms of where we were playing, for Yugoslavia plus return visits to Northern Ireland and Turkey were not likely to attract the hooligans. I would be disappointed if we failed to make it this time. I was already looking forward to pitting my wits against the best again in West Germany.

In the two years between Mexico and the European Championships we lost only two games, one away to Sweden and the other in West Germany, neither of them competitive games. In between we had unbeaten runs of seven and eight games, qualifying in spectacular style by dropping only one point while scoring 19 goals and conceding just one – and that in our best performance of all in Yugoslavia where we won 4–1.

That was one of the best displays and results in my entire eight years but, sadly, it was underestimated by the critics who wrote off the Yugoslavs as a bad team. They were never that, as they subsequently proved. For 25 minutes we were unplayable. Beardsley, Barnes, Robson and Adams all scored in that glorious opening spell. Katanec pulled one back with ten minutes to go but it was over long before that.

During our run into that game we also proved that lightning does strike twice when we beat poor old Turkey by eight goals for a second time in three years. It made the goalless draw in Izmir six months earlier even more baffling in view of our 21 goals in the three other games against them. We also beat the Irish home and away while Yugoslavia had their chances to beat us at Wembley only to lose to goals from Mabbutt and Anderson.

We had drawn with Brazil and Holland while beating Spain in Madrid with a four-goal blast from Gary Lineker who carried on where he had left off in the World Cup despite a move from Everton to Barcelona. It was a great build-up coming off the back of our last-eight place in Mexico. We had developed, improved and maintained the continuity while looking at new players here and there. We had qualified in style and we didn't appear to have too many weaknesses in the team.

Even the critical English press were saying it was the best side the country had boasted for 22 years. I didn't dispute that, for to have done so would have destroyed the confidence that we had built up. I was pleased that the press had taken that line because they were putting pressure on themselves not on the team. It was nice for the players to see pleasant things written about them for a change.

At no stage did I say we would win it, although I firmly believed we could. I thought that we had the best forward line in Europe at that time. Lineker was going well at Barcelona and had scored 20 goals in a sensational 17-match burst for England. John Barnes and Peter Beardsley had both enjoyed tremendous first seasons with Liverpool, while Spurs had done me a great turn with Chris Waddle.

Remember when Manchester United refused to allow Bryan Robson to have an operation before Mexico? Terry Venables and Tottenham went the opposite way with Chrissie. A hernia had been diagnosed which explained why he had lost his explosive pace and his inherent sharpness. He had been playing in pain. Terry had told him that the most important thing was to get fit for the European Championships and told him to get the operation done even though it would mean a two-month slice out of his domestic season. He came back fit and ready – at least so both he and I thought!

In the meantime I had lost Terry Butcher with a broken leg. He and Glasgow Rangers made a valiant effort to get him ready in time but, in the end, he was too big a risk. He was almost fit but another kick could have ended his career. We were only allowed 20 players and I had no cover for Tony Adams, Mark Wright or Dave Watson who was injured for most of the time out there.

But no one disputed that we had the best 20 players available, and the only contentious issue lay with Hoddle, whom we had been using successfully as a substitute for the last 20 minutes of each game. But suddenly my outstanding forwards began to dry up. We failed to score against Hungary and could only score once in each of the games against Scotland, Colombia and Switzerland. The writing was on the wall if we could have seen it.

Our opening game was against Jack Charlton's Republic of Ireland side in Stuttgart and although we respected them, we more than fancied our chances. But aerial errors by, first Garry Stevens, and then Kenny Sansom let in Ray Houghton for a fifth-minute goal and we were left to chase the match. It shouldn't have been a problem, only a set-back. It shouldn't have made a scrap of difference, the number of chances we made but a combination of misses, good saves by Pat Bonner and shots which hit the woodwork, conspired to frustrate us as we totally dominated the second half.

Lineker did everything but score; Beardsley side-footed wide from in front of goal and a shot from substitute Hoddle slipped through Bonner's hands only to run wide of the post.

It was a bad result but, at that stage, not a disaster. There was no need to panic. Holland, who had lost to the Soviet Union in their opening match, were up next and after a 2–2 draw with them at Wembley we knew we could get the measure of them this time. I decided to start with Hoddle as he would directly confront Arnold Muhren. They would never kick each other; it

A young Bobby Robson at Fulham in 1968

Looking anxious as I wait for the final whistle of the UEFA Cup Final against AZ '67 Alkmaar in 1981

Wonderful, wonderful Copenhagen before my first game as England manager in Denmark

My turn for the hard work helped by Kenny Sansom

A tragic and worrying time in Mexico immediately after the Heysel disaster

Pleased? I should say so! We have beaten Paraguay and are in the last eight to play Argentina

Gary Lineker strikes again as he scores twice to beat Paraguay in 1986

Under siege after our shock 1–0 defeat to Portugal in our opening 1986 game in Mexico

Bryan Robson, myself, former FA Secretary Ted Croker and Peter Shilton looking official

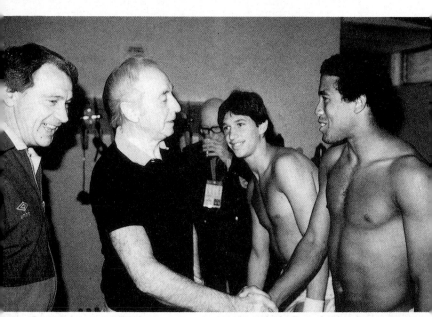

The legendary Sir Stanley Matthews meets Gary Lineker and John Barnes in Mexico

would be skill versus skill with the physical duel taking place between Robson and Wouters.

Again I thought that, as a team, we played quite well but we couldn't take our chances. It was Marco van Basten, a substitute against the Soviets, who showed us how to do it with a super hat-trick. In the end it was not about tactics, phobias or hang-ups. It was about scoring. They took their chances and we again missed ours, scoring once through Robson and hitting the wood-work twice before van Basten notched his first after Gary Stevens had dwelt on the ball instead of knocking it into touch. He didn't know what to do and Gullit robbed him and provided the chance for van Basten to turn Adams and beat Shilton.

It was Robson's courage which put us back into this high-quality match, with the midfield player literally forcing the ball over the line as goalkeeper Van Breukelen bowled him over. It was sheer bravery, the sort of challenge that breaks bones although, I hasten to add, it was not deliberate.

Any gambling money would have had to go on us at that stage. We were exhilarated and lifted. We had the impetus and we were going to win it. For either of us to lose meant a rapid exit. Waddle had just replaced Steven when they scored out of the blue as a miss-hit shot flew straight to van Basten who controlled it beautifully before scoring.

I threw on Hateley for Beardsley as we tossed everything forward to try and salvage something from a match where we had been the better team for much of the time. Van Basten finished us off with a third goal and we had lost. We were on our way home. I couldn't believe it.

We were really despondent because we had played well enough to win both games and here we were with egg on our faces and not a point to show for our efforts. I was devastated, but not nearly as much as after the next match when we lost 3–1 to the Soviet Union in Frankfurt. That performance made me ashamed. I had asked them to play for pride and give a performance for their country but we capitulated.

I gave Woods a game, brought McMahon into midfield, fit-again Watson into defence and left in Hoddle who had played well against Holland and hadn't deserved to finish on the losing side. Watson, still not match fit, had to play because Wright had developed one of his mystery injuries, saying he was unfit but would play. I thought he was giving himself an excuse if he played badly and I told him so. I didn't want part of that and put Watson in to partner Adams.

It was a disaster as Hoddle, with only three minutes gone, tried to nutmeg Aleinikov, lost possession and the Soviet midfield player scored. Although Adams pulled us level when he headed home a Hoddle free kick, the Soviets scored twice against the shaky Woods through Mikhailichenko and Pasulko to send us home with our tails between our legs. Protasov tore us apart and our heads dropped. It was, without doubt, the worst performance in my six years and I was ashamed at the way we capitulated.

What the heck had gone wrong? What had happened to the best forward line in Europe? Lineker was flat and energyless – no surprise, since he was, as it transpired, suffering from the debilitating illness hepatitis. Waddle had not fully recovered from his hernia operation and both Beardsley and Barnes had gone flat after the effort they had put in for Liverpool in their long season. Not one of the forwards had played well.

As it was the media who had tipped us to win I thought maybe one or two of their jobs might be in jeopardy. Not likely, it was me they were after. They would neither forgive nor forget as a torrent of abuse rained down on me. Fortunately the FA were very strong and very supportive.

Two days later Lineker was in hospital. He had played with this illness in his body and no one knew it. Barnes and Beardsley were spent forces – but how do you spot that? And if I had left either of them out after the season they had enjoyed with Liverpool I would have been taken apart. They had both played out of their skins right until the end of the season.

I had entertained no thoughts of quitting after the Holland game; after all, why should I when the team hadn't played that badly in either game? This was different. Everyone was saying I should go, not solely the gutter press. I was left with my own doubts to contend with and my own sanity to worry about. Should I pack it in or should I give someone else the chance? In the space of ten days I had gone from being the manager with the best team to someone who should be sacked. If the FA had listened or been weak I would have gone.

I saw the Chairman, Bert Millichip, that summer before the Annual General Meeting and he was absolutely fantastic. It took 20 seconds for him to tell me he wanted me to stay on, saying, 'We can absorb the pressure – can you?'

'Yes,' I replied.

'Then carry on,' he said as he walked off. 'Get on with the job, Bobby, get us to the World Cup Finals again.'

He had obviously discussed it with Dick Wragg and the rest of the International Committee and they were all loyal and supportive.

I went off to Bermuda with Elsie for a holiday but I dragged the whole dreadful feeling of failure with me. The fact that Holland had beaten the Soviet Union in the Final did little or nothing to compensate for our defeats. With the tabloids switching to a personal attack on me, that was the worst summer of my life. I know I had done my best; other than playing myself there had been little more that I could do. But as manager you had to take the responsibility whether it was bad luck, injuries or plain old bad play. You have to accept that it is part of the job and not be afraid of it.

Every match from that point on was dynamite. I knew that a defeat or two would have the world down on my back and even certain drawn games and narrow victories increased the pressure to have me removed from my employment. I was expected to fail and, worse, many wanted me, and therefore the country, to fail. None of the pressure was coming from within the game, it was all from outside. Those inside, especially at Lancaster Gate, were very supportive and a great many people wrote to me, including managers from both England and Scotland. They knew that football is not about that sort of persecution.

I had to sit down and take stock. What was important was to qualify. I spoke at length to Don Howe and to Dave Sexton. Both were with me, both supported me but at the end of the day I had to make the decisions and make whatever changes needed to be made. I was going to keep what was good and leave out what was not international class. I had to look at quality youngsters like Parker, Walker, Pearce, Dorigo, Pallister, Gascoigne, Clough, Rocastle and Thomas. I had to consider the older players like Shilton at 38 years of age. He deserved another look but if he, Butcher or any of the other older ones I retained showed any weaknesses or frailties they would all have to go.

As for my best forward line in Europe, I reasoned that there were reasons why they had flopped and that Lineker, recovering slowly, Barnes, Waddle and Beardsley had not become bad players in the space of three matches. I had to look carefully at Glenn Hoddle and decide whether he was a luxury, whether we could afford to play him.

I had to get results straight away. If I started with a loss I would have gone. There was no margin for error and even the 1–0 win against the Danes did not stem the tide against me, neither did a goalless draw against Sweden at Wembley in our opening qualifying game. The performance was better than the result and had we won 2–0 it would have been fair. We got nothing for it. You would have thought we had lost 3–0 judging by the reaction of the papers. They wanted a public execution and as I faced them next morning at our usual debriefing session I thought to myself that if I were a new manager sitting there, both the result and the performance would have been considered encouraging.

The remarkable thing was the way players reacted. It was as though nothing had happened. The European Championships were last season and this was a new season. If you can't take defeat there is no room for you in the game. They build a protective shell around themselves.

Everyone had been screaming for me to pitch in new faces and I took the opportunity of doing that against Saudi Arabia. But when we could only draw 1–1 we became 'Desert Pratts', as the headlines changed from 'For God's Sake Go', to 'Go For The Love Of Allah'. Yet I was still helping the journalists by giving a press conference after midnight because we were flying home on Concorde while they were on their own.

I will never forget the reaction when we returned to Heathrow Airport. There were news reporters and camera crews everywhere asking when was I going to quit. I had to be protected by the police. I was almost knocked to the ground as they jostled me. These were the real hooligans. I was hurried off to a private room – and this after drawing a friendly where I had played Seaman, Sterland, Thomas, Pallister, Rocastle, Gascoigne, Smith and Marwood.

Team doctor John Crane was appalled and Don Howe said that if it were him he would pack it in. I avoided saying what I felt to the media and was thankfully hustled out of a side door while Chairman Bert Millichip stood up to the cameras and told them he had no intention of sacking me. He handled it well but it was me they were after. They treated me like Hitler because we had drawn with an experimental team in a place where Scotland, Brazil and Argentina had also drawn. I recall Scotland manager Andy Roxburgh telling me: 'Don't go. If you go and win you will get nothing and if you lose you will be decapitated. If you can do without a match don't play it. I warn you – you could lose there.'

But I needed a game and I was restricted by the government, the weather and mid-season breaks. I needed to blood some kids. There were far more reasons to play it than walk away from it, not least of all if we hadn't played it would have been more than four months without a match!

When I returned from Saudi I had an appointment at a Sports Aid Foundation Dinner. I was sorely tempted to pull out but in the end I am glad that I did not because I received a standing ovation when I appeared. It would seem that the public did not like what they were reading and were giving me their support. But, all the same, it was hardly a Happy Christmas ahead and the New Year was looking decidedly dodgy.

When we resumed our fixtures against Greece in Athens they were after me. Nigel Clarke from the *Daily Mirror* was interviewed by television and told them: 'We are here to fry Bobby Robson'. What do decent people think when they hear things like that? I have never seen so many journalists and TV crews for a friendly, all hoping we lost so that they would have their story of Bobby Robson going.

When we conceded a penalty in the opening minutes I turned to Don Howe and asked: 'Where's the frying pan – Clarke will be boiling the fat ready for me.' But we disappointed them all, particularly those in the *Daily Mirror* offices where the cameras had recorded the glee at England going a goal down. We battled back to win with goals from Robson and Barnes.

When we returned with this nice little victory under our belts the *Sun*'s chief football writer Alex Montgomery, who had been fighting my cause against all the odds, finally gave in and wrote that 'Robson Must Go' – and this after we had won!

Playing Albania in Tirana was another minefield and although the same two players scored we could have been in early trouble if it hadn't been for Peter Shilton who had come back to his very best. Robson had been sick all night with a bad stomach but he played magnificently as did David Rocastle.

The pressure eased just slightly, and by the time we played the Albanians at Wembley it had been deflected totally by the awful Hillsborough disaster. There was a genuine doubt whether the fixture would be played at all with Liverpool closed down as Merseyside mourned their many dead. The Liverpool players had not trained since the semi-final disaster but Beardsley and McMahon felt it was time for them to resume life, although Barnes was committed to a previously made promise to one of the bereaved families. He could not break it.

Peter Beardsley scored twice that night and played magnificently in a five-goal win. That was the first real sight of Gascoigne. I told him to stay on the right to keep our shape but as soon as he went on he raced over to the left, chasing the ball. He did clever things, helped make the fourth goal for Waddle and scored a great goal himself. He sent the crowd home with a smile on their faces and that is what football needed more than anything at that time.

We continued to stretch our unbeaten run as we drew 0–0, with Rojas in the Chile goal outstanding, and we beat the Scots 2–0, with Steve Bull scoring a spectacular debut goal, as we prepared for our vital home qualifier against the Poles on the unlikely date of 6 June. A year had passed with an eight-game undefeated run and the only real changes in the side were the return of Butcher and the introduction of Des Walker and Stuart Pearce. It was virtually the same side who had returned in disgrace. Lineker was superb, playing one of his best games for England as he scored in a 3–0 win with the other goals coming from Barnes and Webb. Both wingers, Barnes and Waddle, were outstanding.

We should have finished there but we had to honour a special Centenary game in Denmark. There were a lot of tired legs but we were determined not to sit out the summer on a bad result and after going a goal up we had to settle for a draw, finishing the season having played ten games, winning six of them. There was a sense of relief as well as achievement. The team was settled, confident, looking strong and solid and on course for Italy.

Sweden away in September sounded ominous with our past record in that early part of the season, especially without Bryan Robson, injured once more. But we were unbeaten in ten games and our confidence was high despite the summer break. Butcher, captain for the night, was the hero with his bloodstained bandage covering a 16-stitch gash in his head. The Swedish manager Olle Nordin had seen us thrash Poland and judging by his tactics, was clearly frightened, squeezing our wingers Barnes and Waddle with two full backs and two wide players. It meant that Sweden didn't offer much in attack until I sent on Gascoigne in place of poor Neil Webb, who snapped a tendon shooting for goal and put himself out for most of the rest of the season.

Gazza was all over the place and the Swedes were driving through the gap with substitutes Stromberg and Thern, and I had to hastily switch McMahon to plug the hole. Their best chance came when Walker superbly tackled Magnusson, who had been put clear, and then gave him back the ball as he tried to pass back to Shilton without looking at the scene behind him. It was a rare rush of blood from our best defender. He could have played it anywhere.

Once more our evergreen goalkeeper had saved us. In terms of qualifying, defeat then could have been serious. Within a minute we also had our best chance, falling to Waddle who drove the ball into the side-netting from six yards out. There were escapes at both ends but the result suited both of us, providing we didn't do anything silly in our last games.

Ours was in Poland and but for Shilton we could have lost and, as it turned out, we could have been pipped at the post for a place in Italy. The Poles changed their team dramatically from the game in June, becoming probably the most attacking team I have faced, with three at the back, four in midfield and three up – but two of the midfield were wide players and all seven attacked us with tremendous pace. Waddle and Rocastle spent most of the afternoon chasing back. Rocastle had his poorest match for us. I don't know whether it was the occasion or the responsibility which got to him but he was not the player I had admired so much.

But despite their possession and pace the Poles were restricted in the main to shots from outside the box, apart from a close range header from Celtic's Jacki Dziekanowski which Shilton blocked. The only time he was beaten was in the final minute when a long-range shot from Tarasiewicz rattled the bar from 30 yards. Tongue-in-cheek Shilton commented: 'I could have put it over the bar but I didn't want to give away a corner at that stage of the game.'

He could afford to laugh. Heading towards his 40th birthday he had just gone through an entire World Cup qualifying programme without conceding a goal. He had done me proud after my decision to back him. He was agile and fit, with status and presence. He was class, sheer class and as far as I was concerned he was my undisputed number one, heading for the record books in Italy and as keen and excited as ever.

We had all recovered our pride and had won our way to another final with what was largely the same team that lost three successive games in West Germany. I was pleased for the players, the Football Association and myself. I had returned their loyalty. It was a happy 'plane going home that night.

When qualification looked likely I had made a plea to the FA for the best they could get us. We didn't want an easy run in, we wanted to toughen up. The last thing we wanted was false guidance, another false dawn. If we were going to test our kids we didn't need to play Turkey and Finland, so what they gave me was Italy, Yugoslavia, Brazil, Czechoslovakia, Denmark and Uruguay before finishing with an acclimatising game against Tunisia in Africa. Five of those teams would be in Italy and two of them, Italy and Brazil, were among the favourites.

They were meaningful games and I was quite prepared to suffer defeats for the chance of pitting the likes of Gascoigne, Rocastle, Walker, Pearce, Parker, Platt and Bull against players and teams who would stretch them and tell me whether they could cope at the top level.

As we went into the game against the powerful World Cup hosts Italy, the sniping began again. We were predictable, boring, couldn't score goals and played the high ball into the box too much to ever break down the sweeper system. For three years we had been playing with Lineker and Beardsley up front, hardly the sort of strikers you pump high balls to! One of the critics was supposedly the Italian striker Vialli, who was widely quoted in the tabloids. He deliberately sought me out in the dressing rooms before the game with an interpreter in tow to tell me that he had said none of those things and had never spoken to the reporter.

It was too little, too late as far as Terry Butcher was concerned. He rolled up his sleeves and went out to tuck Vialli in his pocket from the start and kept him there until he was replaced by Baggio. I don't know how much that affected Vialli but he never recaptured his form and was eventually axed during the World Cup.

Had we won 2–0 that night no one would have complained. Waddle sparkled, giving a modern-day version of Stanley Matthews' wing play, but despite our quality we could not score a goal. It was our third goalless draw and as we left someone shouted out: 'Come on Bobby, give us a goal.' He didn't need to tell me, the same old nagging doubts were beginning to stir again.

Where would the next goal come from? The answer was provided by Bryan Robson who, after we had waited for over five hours for a goal, headed in Waddle's free kick after 38 seconds against Yugoslavia at Wembley on 13 December, significant because it was the fastest England goal ever scored at Wembley and paved the way to our 100th Wembley win. It was a good win, too, for Yugoslavia were no slouches. They had beaten the Scots 3–1 and topped the French in their qualifying group.

Waddle, who played at outside right against Italy, was on the other flank this time as I had a look at several players. Sir Stanley Matthews came in before the game and I told him to watch out for Waddle. Neither he nor I was disappointed. He was outstanding and I was beginning to think then that we had a World Cup winner in our midst, it was more than I could say of the Arsenal pair of Rocastle and Thomas. Their club form had dipped and I finished up subbing both of them that night, bringing on Platt and Hodge. It turned out to be a significant switch in the long term.

Skoro looked as though he might rob us of a deserved win when he scored a superb goal, but our 'Captain Marvel' Bryan Robson popped up again to score his second as Bull touched on Parker's centre. The crowd were enthusiastic, and we were still on a roll as we went into our winter break undefeated in 14 games. It felt great to be sitting on such a good result.

We needed it coming out of the draw in Rome with the Dutch and the Irish facing us again, as they had done in the European Championships. Who would have thought it!

We resumed three months later – what a joke that is in World Cup year – with another big one against Brazil. They were also on a long, undefeated run, having won in Holland and Italy before meeting us, and they brought all of their big guns with them, gaining the release of their Brazilian and Portuguese based players. I liked Italy but I felt going into this game that the team that won the World Cup would have to beat Brazil on the way. I wasn't far out, either.

It was a good high-class match, spiced up with a bit of controversy as luck went our way with an offside decision and a handball on the line by Stuart Pearce from a goal-bound shot by Muller. We scored through a Gary Lineker near-post header from a Peter Beardsley corner. It was so pleasing to win. People were now beginning to sit up and take notice. It was good for our credibility as the score flashed around the world. I was delighted, for I had now beaten them at home and away and in three matches had not lost to them. We also had the added satisfaction of an international quality performance by Chris Woods, who came off the bench cold after we lost the influential Shilton early in the game with a cut eye after a clash with Walker.

That night Platt clinched his place in the squad with an outstanding, unselfish display. He was playing in place of Robson and I decided that this would be the team, with Robson of course, to play in the opening game against the Irish.

Gascoigne came on for Beardsley that night but his chance was to come a month later in April when he turned in a virtuoso display to lead a 4–2 win against the adventurous Czechs. Robson gave him that chance with another brilliant display, coming off after an hour to a standing ovation. With no Waddle and no

Barnes, Steve Hodge and Trevor Steven took their chances well as did Bully with his two goals. Wright and Dorigo also left a good impression.

The Danes presented us with a different set of problems in May. The Czechs had played with freedom and we had punished them. The Danes had seen it and weren't going to make the same mistake. They stiffened their defence and played with a sweeper. They played typical Danish football. They didn't give the ball away and gave us a good game. I kept both Hodge and Gascoigne in and took the opportunity to look at fringe players again. Rocastle still didn't look at his best after a long injury and he was beginning to slip out of the reckoning. Hodge was making his bid and provided the cross for yet another Lineker goal. What would we do without him?

In between the games against Denmark and Uruguay I had to announce the squad to the players, the FA and the press. It's not nice having to tell a player he is not wanted and I had to tell four of them. By a strange quirk of fate, three were Arsenal players, Tony Adams, David Rocastle and Alan Smith. I was sad, particularly for Adams, but I put him on stand-by in case Wright's thigh injury did not clear up. I would have liked to take him but he could not play like Wright. Rocky was unlucky to have a dip in form at the wrong time but both he and his young Arsenal team-mate Michael Thomas would come again.

It was Bully's goals against Alan Smith's lack of goals which decided the extra striker. Steve Bull was my gamble – I was allowed one. Italy had a similar striker in Toto Schillaci, a player I had never heard of before the World Cup. Steve Bull could so easily have come off in the same way.

The other player to miss out was goalkeeper Dave Beasant but, as it turned out, he joined us anyway when David Seaman went home from Italy injured.

We went into our farewell game hoping to take that long, unbeaten run into the finals but it was not to be, as Uruguay handed us our first Wembley defeat for six years. But I wasn't displeased with the team performance. We played quite well and Gascoigne confirmed his place by reacting well to the South American opponents.

The only disappointment was, of all people, Peter Shilton,

who let in a soft, looping header and was beaten by a Perdomo free-kick when it looked as though we were going to win. Earlier in the match we had scored one of the great goals of the year or any year when Gazza played a fantastic ball 50 yards to Pearce on the overlap and his ball found John Barnes on the far post. The Liverpool player chested the ball down and as it dropped, volleyed it past Pereira. It was one of the best goals I have seen in my life.

The whole game was a good test of wits. Uruguay were threatening to outplay us until I pushed Bryan Robson up on Perdomo to stop him bringing the ball out, a tactic that changed the whole game. That's great education and the best part of football for me, when I can make a positive change to alter the course of a match. At least I thought I had altered it until Shilton got both hands to a 35-yard free-kick and still let it slip through. As far as I was concerned it was one of his worst mistakes for us. He is an honest man and he will feel he should have had it. In my opinion he changed his mind about whether he was going to catch it or push it out and ended up doing neither.

The defeat would have bothered me had we been well beaten or if we couldn't have coped with their technique but it wasn't one of those nights. The press were extremely fair the next morning. The criticism was realistic and both Thursday's and Friday's papers read well.

An omen of what was to come? Unfortunately not. I worked hard on my relationship with the media but, with a few exceptions, it was never fully returned. I hope Graham Taylor has better fortune.

5

Thanks a lot, Sir Alf

Of all the abuse, both personal and professional that I suffered in my eight years at Lancaster Gate, the most hurtful from both points of view was the succession of attacks from Sir Alf Ramsey.

Of all the people in football there are only three left alive who can begin to understand the complexities and complications of being manager of the England football team: Walter Winterbottom, Sir Alf and Ron Greenwood. Graham Taylor will join that select band in due time.

As a group we should expect the support of each other and, Sir Alf apart, we gave it and got it. Neither Walter, Ron, the late Don Revie nor the much-lamented Joe Mercer ever tried to take me apart. There was too much mutual respect. Only a former England manager can know how thin is the dividing line between success and failure.

But I feel Sir Alf, the only one of us to win the World Cup, betrayed that unwritten, unspoken rule by taking both myself and my players to task, undermining confidence within the camp and often at crucial times before we set off for a European or World Cup Finals.

I have never really understood why. Perhaps the motivation was for the financial rewards so often associated with newspaper stories of this kind. It could not have been through any personal dislike for, although we live only a few streets apart in Ipswich, where I have kept my house while in Holland, we had very little contact for two men with so much in common. We had both been successful managers at Ipswich Town who went straight from our little rural paradise to the hurly-burly of the England hot seat. We were both England internationals, me with 20 caps and Alf with 32.

When I was manager at Portman Road and Alf was sacked from the England position, I wrote to him telling him that he would always be welcome at our games and in our boardroom and sent directors' passes for the season to him and Lady Ramsey. He came once or twice but never looked me out and never thanked me. I didn't mind. I was just pleased to see a man who had done so much for the club and country that I loved. In fact I was surprised he was not there more often, particularly on our great European nights.

Despite Sir Alf writing in a tabloid newspaper that I had never got in touch with him to ask for his help and advice when I became England manager, the same could be said of him. He never once tried to reach me, either to congratulate me or to offer his assistance. It would have been valued and welcomed in those early days at Lancaster Gate.

I could understand that maybe he did not want anything to do with the people who had just fired him, but I was surprised and baffled that he cold-shouldered me, even more so when he suddenly became a newspaper commentator and began to take pot shots at me and the team.

There was one great opportunity for us to get together when we bumped into each other in the Chelsea boardroom. I greeted him and conversationally asked how he had travelled to Stamford Bridge.

'I came by train,' he answered.

'Oh,' I responded, 'I drove up and you are very welcome to come back with me.' In the light of his experience in Mexico, I thought that there was a great deal we could discuss before I took my team out.

But he stunned me when he replied: 'I came by train – I shall return by train.'

The man was known as a bit of a recluse at Ipswich, a man who never had too much to say. I felt a little awkward in his company on the few occasions we met because I felt that I had to drive the conversation along while he replied with a monosyllabic 'yes' and 'no' to everything. He always found it difficult to talk to the press too, and many feel that his signed articles were perhaps hypocritical after all he had said about the tabloids during his managerial career. My close friends were always amazed at the time I spent with the press and that I should be so forgiving with so many of them.

But why should Alf Ramsey be so different from Walter Winterbottom, Don Revie, Joe Mercer and Ron Greenwood, who didn't criticize other England managers? Was it because he was the only one of us to win the World Cup? Somewhere along the line did he put himself above us because of it? Did he believe that it gave him the right to have a go not only at me but the others as well?

Occasionally I would see him at official dinners when I would be invited as the current England manager and he as a past England manager. I was stunned when he wrote that the only time he saw me was when I was surrounded by the wrong sort of men in £1000 suits. Who did he mean? Most were guests who, like us, had been invited, most were comparative strangers and, in any case, what on earth was the relevance to football? It was damned unfair.

Just before we left for Mexico he came out with his choice of squad and team, who he would have taken, who he would have left behind.

Did he stop and consider for a minute what he might have done to the confidence of a World Cup–bound England footballer who he, the great Sir Alf Ramsey, said should be staying at home? It was destructive to the players and insulting to me. He was, in effect, saying that he knew far more than I did. I felt that by saying this he was putting undue pressure on the players and I did not expect it of a man of such stature. For someone who was so protective of his own players he was, I thought, thoughtless with mine.

I resisted the impulse to respond to his jibes because I was not going to become involved in an unseemly slanging match which could only have tarnished the image of the game and our profession. In fact, I much preferred to remember him for what he had done with Ipswich and England, unique in the game's history.

He was, I am told, very close to his players and, certainly, many of them took his side against me, notably two of his former skippers Kevin Keegan and Emlyn Hughes, along with those other 'successful' managers Malcolm Macdonald and Alan Ball.

I wonder if they would have done what they did if they had known the contempt in which they were held by some of their fellow professionals. Emlyn Hughes, in particular, lost many of their respects so completely that they branded him a traitor. Just as I expected support from Sir Alf so they expected it from an ex-England player who, they pointed out, hadn't been part of English sides who qualified for too many finals. Come to that, he wasn't much of a manager either.

Keegan's assaults saddened and then maddened me. I could understand them at first because I was the manager who brought his proud England career to a close and, without telling him first, left him out of the squad for my opening game against Denmark.

With hindsight I would do it differently now. I would rather not have fallen out with a player whom I not only respected but travelled to watch. When I returned to Portman Road after an England game at Wembley – I went to every one – I would hold him up as an example to all my players, telling them that here was living, breathing proof that you could still run and chase every ball even when you were very rich.

He had scarcely played that summer in the World Cup because of injury and I thought we would just see how we did without him, if only to start with. I even took the trouble to speak to all of the managers involved with him. But he went out of his way to make sure I never picked him again by his sustained criticism of me and my team selections. He's not the first international captain to be dropped and he won't be the last. We all have to suffer that fate, it is as much part of the game as it is for managers to be sacked.

But whenever the opportunity arose for him to have a go at me he did and, because he was a megastar, papers would listen and print whatever he told them.

Every year I fly out to Marbella with the Sports Aid Foundation for a charity golf match. Kevin, whose apartment then overlooked the course, was invited along but we scarcely saw each other and were never more than respectfully polite.

I still couldn't dislike him and I couldn't understand why he wanted to sustain the rather one-sided quarrel. I even wrote to him, via his manager Arthur Cox to be sure he received it, saying that we should bury the hatchet and stop supplying the papers with fodder. I offered not to mention it again if he would do the same. He never did respond.

Worse still, many felt he made himself something of a laughing-stock when, in April 1989, he put himself up as a candidate for the England job when I was to be 'given the boot', adding that he was the man to motivate the players, despite never having managed a boys' team in preparation, nor any other side for that matter, and living in tax exile largely out of touch with the English game. In my view that wasn't just an insult to me but to every manager who has or had aspirations to manage England.

It infuriated me. I felt that the game had made him safe and that he had left the country without giving the impression of wanting to put anything back. Those of us who could not afford to put our feet up went into management and coaching. We had to look for a job and when we got one we had to work hard with the threat of the sack hanging over us. We also worked with the kids, the youngsters who are the future of our game. Where was Kevin's contribution in that?

He played at the right time to cash in on his talent, and good luck to him, but why knock the very people who try to pass on to others what they have learned? It is they who keep the game flourishing, not those who retire completely from the game and then want to come back for the plum job.

Alan Ball was just a joke. I can only think that the lad was short of a few bob when the papers came knocking on his door. With a record like his in management I would have kept quiet, yet he had the audacity to tell me how I should be doing my work. Perhaps he couldn't live with what I had achieved at Ipswich. He was a good player, sure enough, but so was I and I didn't need to put my record as a player or a manger on the line.

At least he had an international record which was more than you could say for Steve Perryman who took me to task in his book on the strength of playing just one game under me for what was very much a B team. It was shortly before the World Cup in Spain and Ron Greenwood was taking the team to Finland and had asked me to take the residue to Iceland. Ron picked the squad and asked me to play Perryman because 'he deserved it for his long career with

Spurs'. In that short trip he decided he had seen enough of the England set-up to become judge and jury. He took it and us apart.

So did Terry Fenwick after a 20-match international career under me. He rewarded that loyalty by stating:

* I lacked inspiration and new ideas in training.
* That my right-hand man Don Howe had ideas on football which were boring.
* Poor coaching. No imagination.
* Trying to keep too many people happy.
* Producing England teams who couldn't win important matches.
* Being in the job for seven years and winning nothing.

It was printed days before we played Poland in a crucial World Cup qualifying game and he then turned round and said: 'I'm not being a traitor to my country. Nor is it meant to be anything personal against the England manager. I am simply trying to be honest and constructive about the England scene.'

You could have fooled me and it certainly cut no ice with the players, until recently his team mates, who were involved in that game. They were angry, very angry. So much so that they wanted to make a statement to divorce themselves entirely from the things that had been written. I told them that it was not worth replying as it only gave credence to the story. We let others take it up on our behalf.

The attack on Don Howe was particularly unwarranted. I couldn't agree in any shape or form with the cruel things said about this extremely talented coach who was not only very good but also well liked by all of the players he worked with. Far from being the dour, defence-minded coach portrayed to the public by the press, this Midlander is one of the funniest men I have ever met, marvellous company and steeped in football knowledge.

As for the training sessions we put on, we talked to the players and none could understand the complaints. In fact there were those who claimed that back at their own clubs they did little more than a couple of warm-up laps followed by a five-a-side.

So what was that all about? I always thought Fenwick was a good solid Geordie lad to whom I gave one hell of a chance, including a place in the World Cup Finals in Mexico.

Malcolm Macdonald was another who jumped on the bandwagon, accusing me of falling in love with Terry Butcher and Bryan Robson and not knowing when to leave them out. He claimed that Bryan Robson was embarrassed with the ball at his feet and that I only picked Butcher to lump the ball up the field. How anyone could attack these two fine players who literally gave blood for their country is beyond me. Again I can only imagine it was for sensationalism and for the money.

There were others from outside the game like Rugby League manager Alex Murphy. We had never met yet he not only questioned my ability but also told Chris Waddle how he should be playing and claimed that the players were playing for the wrong reasons. His qualification for knowing all about my job was that he knew how to handle professional sportsmen, but I wonder how he would have reacted if Tony Jacklin had told him where he was going wrong with his rugby players.

Criticism has never bothered me too much when it has come from the journalists because that is their job. But it digs deep when it comes from within the game itself, especially when you suspect that sometimes the motivation may be financial. I know this is true because of the number of times I have been offered cash to respond to some of these attacks.

The figures became larger towards the end, and funnily enough, the largest sums were offered by the very papers who had vilified me most over the past eight years. I am talking vast sums of money, more than I earned for a whole year managing England, just to sit down with one of their writers over dinner. I am human. It was so much that I paused and considered it. But not for long because there was always only one answer.

I'll talk to anyone about football for as long as they want but it wasn't often that anyone paid me for the privilege. For that sort of money they wanted more than just football.

It all escalated and got completely out of hand during my eight years as manager. I seemed to be the focal point of a circulation war with no one caring whether or not they were printing the truth or what they were doing to me and my family.

I was particularly concerned for my ageing mother and father. The press even got to my dad to interview him about his son Robert, and he was in his mid-80s then. They have had to put up with all sorts of hassle but thankfully we have been able to protect my mom from most of it. When I could see the way things were going I would tell dad not to let her see anything untoward and, if he had to read that sort of paper at all, to ignore what he read about me.

My three sons were adult and educated enough to see what was happening to their father. They were strong but from time to time they, too, were deeply hurt. I told them to forget about it. As for myself I didn't read the papers and I didn't listen to what people were saying. Why give myself a bad time? There was lots written about me that I never saw until we went through the cuttings for this book.

But not all the stories went by unnoticed. Some were so blatantly untrue that my solicitor drew my attention to them. Many were clear-cut cases of libel and my advisors wanted me to sue. But in many cases that would have suited the newspapers concerned down to the ground, giving them the chance to rake up all the muck once again and cheap at the price for them to gain further notoriety as the *Sun* did with Elton John, apologising with a full front page and even managing to turn that into a sales gimmick. The cost, the time, my background, everything is against the long build-up to a court case when you tell yourself they will have something new to occupy themselves the next day. You and the story that can scar your life become yesterday's fish and chip paper.

Elsie and I had only the *Guardian* delivered to our home and although their football writer David Lacey could be particularly scathing when he wanted to be, I never took offence and, more often than not, enjoyed it. Not for him and his paper the lies and half truths.

But Elsie is a bright lady and was well aware of what was being written even if she didn't read the papers herself. But throughout all of my ordeal, particularly those last two years, she was a loyal, steadfast supporter who backed me and got on with her own life. It is never easy being married to a footballer and even worse being married to a football manager.

Elsie had a lot to put up with right from the start.

We came from the same village in the North East. She was in nursing when we married, a State Registered Nurse from the

Sunderland Royal Infirmary and although she continued nursing when we were in London, she had to stop when we started our family, by which time we had moved to West Bromwich.

That's the problem with football. One minute you are settled and the next you are on the move, looking for new houses, taking the kids out of school, saying goodbye to another lot of friends. It was even worse for Elsie because we moved all the way to Canada and while we were there I had to leave her and the children in Vancouver, not knowing a soul, while I went off to Spain. It must have been very lonely with Christmas fast approaching.

Then there was my spell out of work after Canada, almost four months of not knowing what we would be doing with ourselves next.

Finally, there were those eight long years with England, away from home four nights a week on average as well as all the personal and professional abuse that was heaped upon me.

She leaned heavily on the church during those last couple of traumatic years. She found great solace there, never missing mass and being deeply involved in the church charity work.

Elsie also went to teacher training college as a mature student and when she passed out she taught infants for many years before switching to physically and mentally handicapped children.

Our own children are an absolute credit to my wife. They have grown up calm, relaxed and assured. I am very proud of them and with me being the absent father so often, am well aware of the major part that Elsie played in their development.

Through all of this period she never, ever became involved. She would not be interviewed and wouldn't even allow the journalists who wanted to talk to her or take her picture in the house. That, she said, was private and she was keeping it that way. She wouldn't even have her picture taken by a newspaper when we were leaving England for our latest adventure in Holland. The ones that have appeared have been snatched without her permission.

Throughout the entire period she has been warm and caring and that is why we have emerged together at the end of it all with her still by my side in Holland when many believed she would remain in our Ipswich house, just an hour's hop from the Netherlands.

In my view it is a shame that some people use the newspapers in order to further their own ambitions and feather their nests by selling their stories. Perhaps what they see is the money and not the hurt their lies can cause. They are prepared to degrade themselves, even though they look bad in the eyes of the public and even worse to their families.

That was one of the unexpected pleasures of Holland – no tabloid newspapers and no Sunday papers!

Peace at last!

6

Anatomy of a manager

Franz Beckenbauer is undoubtedly one of the most successful managers in the game, having taken West Germany to two successive World Cup Finals, culminating in triumph against holders Argentina in Rome. Not surprisingly his name was immediately linked with jobs around the globe, as he had already announced his departure from his national team duties long before the Finals. But, apart from a reported tickle from Aston Villa, he was not mentioned in England nor even considered as my possible replacement. I am not knocking the Football Association and, indeed, it would have taken Franz a good two years to settle into this vastly different environment. The demand is for instant success, and to understand the English game and the English temperament he would need all of that time.

The Football Association were fortunate to have so many good names to select from. Apart from their choice of Graham Taylor, there were other obvious candidates like Don Howe, Terry Venables, Howard Wilkinson, John Lyall, Howard Kendall and Brian Clough. But there may come a day when the options are not there. Would they have the courage to do what so many foreign countries do and appoint a non-national as coach and, more importantly, would it work? That has become a more realistic discussion with Villa's surprise signing of the Czecho-slovakian national coach Jozef Venglos as replacement to Graham Taylor, and his progress will be closely monitored at Lancaster Gate.

Maybe we are too hidebound; for while I support the nomina-tion of an Englishman to manage England it is only because he would be familiar with the language, the game as we play it, the players, training, temperament, tactics to suit. That does not mean that others do not fit the bill. World Cup winner Ossie Ardiles, for example, has long experience of playing in England, speaks the language and has all the qualifications, except that he has not managed for long enough and not yet at the very top level. But in the future? Who knows?

Even more relevant would be a Scot. I can see the diehards throwing up their hands in astonishment; but why not? It is not nearly as outrageous as it sounds: after all, Dr Andrew Stephen was a very popular and successful Chairman of the Football Association – and he was a Scot. Some of our best and most successful managers in England at the moment are Scots. Just look around. There is Kenny Dalglish, Alex Ferguson, George Graham and, up in Scotland, the worldly Graeme Souness, who has yet to manage in England but who played the vast majority of his career in the Football League and clearly likes English players, judging by the number of my internationals he has signed for Glasgow Rangers.

Jack Charlton, an Englishman, has had phenomenal success with the Republic of Ireland, while another Englishman, Mike Smith, did well with Wales and in the Middle East. It certainly wouldn't hinder a candidate in English business or industry to be Scottish, Welsh or Irish so why should it in football, especially if there is no obvious choice available among the Englishmen?

The fear that a Scot or a foreigner would not give everything for their adopted country would not apply. Jackie is an honorary Irishman and there was no team he would rather beat than England, the team he won a World Cup Winners' medal with! One of the most supportive managers at club level in my eight years with England was Alex Ferguson, although some of that probably comes about from working with Jock Stein and managing Scotland in Mexico and knowing the problems; but even so, he could so easily have taken the other line with the many problems he suffered in my tune-up to the World Cup Finals in Italy.

I certainly feel that managers like Dalglish, Souness and maybe Graham should at least have been considered for the job when it became available. Souness has kept in constant touch with the English game; Graham has spent all of his life in England; and

Dalglish has achieved more than most of the rest put together in his time at Liverpool.

But my guess is that they will all have to whistle for it. Taylor, a young man, has it now; and when it becomes available again my money will be riding on my first lieutenant and captain for eight years, Bryan Robson, even though he has yet to manage a team at any level! Obviously this time around would have been too early, and he has too much to give as a player but I would certainly have been more than happy to have pulled him in as my assistant to groom him for the job in the future. He is very like Franz Beckenbauer, with that wealth of playing experience at home and abroad in international football at its highest level. Franz stepped in without managerial experience, and look what he did for the Germans. Berti Vogts, Franz's replacement, is similar in background, and it will be interesting to see if he can maintain that frightening German tradition, particularly now that he has the East Germans to call upon as well in a united German team.

Robson has a deep knowledge of the game and has impressed me with his opinions on other players. He knows the international game backwards and has shown his qualities of leadership many times over. I certainly wouldn't have thrown him in at the deep end now, but who knows, in four or five years' time? It will depend which direction his life takes, but if he wants it – and I believe he does – there is clearly a place, or at least an opportunity, in football management for him. His one problem may be learning to deal with the press. Because of his bad experiences with the media he has more or less shut the door in their faces over the last couple of years. But unless things changed dramatically at Lancaster Gate he would have to alter his attitude if he were to manage England at some stage in the future.

The Football Association don't really want to handle the press; they want the manager to look after that. What can the Secretary or the Chairman say after a defeat, or when a squad is announced? It is not their role – it is part of the manager's job, and he cannot duck it. No one took more stick than me; but if I had said that I wouldn't hold a press conference before or after a match I would have been out of work the next day.

Robson, however, won't have it all his own way when the

time comes. There could be a challenge from Ossie Ardiles or former England international Steve Coppell, who has worked miracles in turning Crystal Palace around. He is intelligent, educated and, like Robson, knows the international game thoroughly. I just wish I had had his services as a player – that would have done for me.

Among others who have yet to go into management, I anticipate Ray Wilkins doing exceptionally well. He is, without question, one of the finest people I have ever met in the football family. Everyone looks up to him, respects him and admires him. He is good for the team and good for morale. He has all the basic qualities – as has another of my England captains, Terry Butcher. But until they try out the management game no one will know for sure.

No career in football management is plain sailing – and I can assure everyone interested that the England job is certainly not. You have to have a terrific desire to succeed, because the job will rip you apart if you don't have that. You have to take all the blows, deflect the criticism and still want to get on with it with enthusiasm. Whoever is offered the position will be taking part in a gamble, because until you have experienced what is involved you cannot fully appreciate what the job is about. There is no sure-fire anatomy of an international manager, and no guarantee that Graham Taylor will do any better than that other obvious choice, Don Revie. You can only speculate.

The basic attributes are easy to sort out: being in the game long enough to have gained experience; having played and managed with some success; knowing the big match scene; knowing how to handle the difficult or awkward player; built-in competitiveness; knowing the dressing-room and training-ground scenes and atmosphere; motivation; knowing how to cope with the media and how best to use the players available. A manager wouldn't be a candidate for the England job in the first place without those qualities. His judgement on the ability of players will have been tested in the transfer market; but it is not until he has selected a squad, picked a team and put his money where his mouth is that the real test begins.

People seem to think that managing England is just ten games a year – sometimes I have wished it was that simple. But I must confess that, at one time, I wondered what Ron Greenwood used to do to occupy his time between matches; and I can understand why a chairman like Doug Ellis, and other people, have wondered aloud whether the job can be done part-time in conjunction with another managerial or coaching role. Forget it. The task as England manager changes with the tides and time. It is not the same now as when I took it on and I doubt whether Ron Greenwood would recognise it – Sir Alf Ramsey certainly would not.

It was after the reign of Walter Winterbottom that the FA split the job of team manager and National Coach and although I understand that what happens at international level should be reflected below I am not sure that it is wise to try to combine the two tasks as I did under the FA's request.

I am 'coaching minded', and came through the Football Association's badge schemes along with people like Don Howe, Graham Taylor, Terry Venables, Dave Sexton, Ron Greenwood, Jimmy Hill and Howard Wilkinson, to mention just a few. I was aware of the responsibilities but maybe not the volume of work under the FA Coaching Education schemes.

I worked from the grass-roots right to the very top and while there were very visible problems in the professional game, it was not so widely noticed underneath the surface, where schools' football has been in dramatic decline over much of the country.

The introduction of the National School at Lilleshall for especially gifted playes was a big concept to grasp in my first few months. The first request from the FA was not to bring home the World Cup, or win the next three internationals, but to provide a blueprint for the 'pursuit of excellence' in football. They wanted to hit the jackpot right off and give a coaching platform for the future.

I could see the need and the urgency. When I was a lad a lot of time was spent playing cricket or football; but now there are 13 or 14 sports to choose from in some schools, while others have no facilities at all. Gone are the days when the geography master would close his atlas and take the kids for football at 4 p.m. Somewhere along the line football has suffered terribly in the teachers' in-fighting.

It meant that we not only had to look at the best of the

youngsters but also help the even younger ones start off. We had fun weeks all over the country, and the kids were disappointed because Bobby Robson wasn't at every one of them. There were hundreds of them and I went to as many as I could in the summer; but in the end we had to drop my name from it, as it was becoming counter-productive. But, even so, it was a great concept for football, the kids and even the parents. At £25 for the week it was the best baby-sitting rate in the entire country, subsidised by the Football Association.

In addition we set up around 1,400 coaching centres for boys and girls between the ages of 8 and 13. I went on a nationwide tour to set it up, having been involved in much of the early planning. A step up were the 131 Centres of Excellence all over the country, some set up at professional clubs on the doorsteps of the best kids aged between 11 and 14. The effect of that was that professional clubs could invite youngsters of potential from 11 instead of the previously agreed 14. Waiting until 14 was sheer madness: after all, would you deny a swimmer, a gymnast or a pianist top tuition from the best? But that was the stranglehold that the Schools' Football Association had on our game and our youngsters. The Germans, the Dutch and the Italians used to laugh when they heard of the obstacles we placed in front of ourselves. The Dutch, for example, run 20 teams from 8 years of age upwards but in our country the teaching has largely been left to schools and unqualified coaches.

That was the scene when I took over. No one fought it from within the Football Association, yet we were the ruling body. It made no sense at all. By the time the professionals got hold of the boys they already had bad habits ingrained into their game and we couldn't do a thing about it.

Even now the schools are still fighting it; they still don't really want to see our National School succeed, and they still won't recommend pupils. We asked the schools, but we received so few replies, and when we inquired we were told that the SFA had advised them not to respond. We had to rely on our own coaches and our own scouts, and they are loath to help in case they lose a good youngster to another club.

FA Coach Charles Hughes and I burned the midnight oil to set up the full-time school at Lilleshall in 1984 for boys of 14–16, looking after their education as well as their football. The big question we asked in those early days was whether we would get the best boys. We didn't. We got some, but not all. Maybe in future we will, because we are not only turning out good footballers but nice people with good manners, good attitudes, well educated and with good habits. Of course we had the odd bad egg, and there were one or two who had to be dismissed. But that was something we couldn't funk. We had to make examples of one or two who were caught watching the wrong sort of video or who transgressed the school's strict code of conduct. We didn't want just to produce good footballers: we wanted to send clubs good people. Dave Sexton and Mike Kelly were ideal on the football side, while housemaster Denis Saunders made sure the other side satisfied the educationalists.

We held trials from February to April, starting with hundreds of boys before whittling them down to 80, 50, 30 and then the final 16. I would be at all the final trials to assess. It is all set up now but, at the time, it was a massive task, and although Charles Hughes deflected a lot of it there was still a monumental amount of work, paperwork, to get through.

The ESFA never seemed to realise that we were not trying to take their team away from them. What we were saying was: 'Give us your boys and we will give you a better team.' But although we help finance the SFA they still call the shots, and they restrict the 5,000 boys at those 131 coaching centres to an hour's coaching once a week. That is what is holding us back. I know I am biased, but we have a marvellous programme that cannot give the kids enough coaching. We are not asking for the hours that are taken up with music tuition or chess practice or for other sports like swimming: twice a week for an hour a time would do. We wouldn't ask for longer, because their legs at that age would not respond to an hour and a half or two hours. They are all within an hour of home and it is a source of pride, or should be, to their schools when they are nominated.

At the tip of the iceberg there are the England teams, for the Football Association is the biggest football club in the country. We run Under-15, Under-16, Under-17, Under-18–19, Under-21, B and full international sides. Not even Manchester United or Liverpool run that many teams – and I was involved in every one of them. You can't run teams like that without players; and you want to pick the best there is, so scouting becomes another big task. I wouldn't go to watch Arsenal play Charlton just to check on the form of the likes of David Rocastle and Tony Adams, but also to look around at others from lesser teams. That is how I found our Under-18 full back Scott Minto from Charlton. Rocastle never went past him once all night, and the boy had the confidence and cheek to nutmeg my full England international. I was introduced to him afterwards, found out his qualifications and soon had him in the line-up. If you don't move quickly these days you lose the youngsters to Jack Charlton, or someone else who discovers they have claims in his international services. Drinking a pint of Guinness would seem to be enough to qualify for Jack's teams.

I suppose I watch a minimum of three games a week – more often four recently, with so many Sunday games, and they range from top of the First to the occasional Third Division match. Then there are the games abroad. You not only have to keep up with future opponents but also with tactics and trends at club as well as at international level. In addition there is the UEFA Technical Committee. I was nominated for that one to fill the vacancy left by Alan Wade. They meet four or five times a year for three or four days at a time, plus the travelling.

There are also the courses run by FIFA and UEFA and although it is extra work, the Chairman, Dr Jira of Czech-oslovakia, an ex-international and a lovely man, always tried to arrange them to coincide with a big game in Europe so that we could gather on Tuesday, go to the game on Wednesday night and home for Thursday. All very nice, but it is still work; and if it is to be done properly you have to put in the preparation as well as the attendance.

The part of the job that everyone notices, however, are the glamorous trips to Rome or Rio to watch Italy or Brazil – although even these are offset by the rougher rides to Albania, Romania, Poland and other not so attractive centres. Football has no boundaries. Unless your own team is playing, you are on your own and you have to know what you are doing.

I suppose on average I am away from home for four nights out of every seven, with spells where home is a distant dream even in summer – when there are tours, tournaments and coaching courses.

The daily post to the international manager is something to behold, from requests for a game against England to offers of being vice-president of this, presenting the prizes at that or making a speech at the other. I could be out morning, noon and night if I had accepted every one and, more often than not, they were commendable requests involving kids, hospitals, churches and charities. I admit that I found it hard to say 'No' and, as a consequence, spread myself too much. I hope that Graham Taylor does not fall into the same trap. As England manager you cannot ask for fees and, in any case, I would rather be at home. Jack Charlton and Tommy Docherty among others seem to do pretty well out of the circuit and who knows, now I am out of Lancaster Gate I may put in an invoice! That might shock a few people.

I also tried to answer all the personal letters – even those telling me how to pick my teams or how we should play; or amateur players and youngsters wanting to know how to get a bad ankle or a sore knee mended.

Then there are the interviews, millions of them, it seems, not just the English press, radio and television – all, apparently, growing in numbers by the day – but from every corner of the globe. They come from Hong Kong, Malta, Finland, Nigeria, all wanting to know what the England manager thinks. How can you refuse them, when they have come so far?

The telephone is every bit as bad. My secretary Michelle would list hundreds while I was out, and when I was in residence it was a struggle to make a call out when I might need to speak to Bryan Robson, Alex Ferguson or Brian Clough on some urgent matter.

Cloughie . . . there is a challenge in itself. How do you speak to Brian Clough? Who has got his home telephone number? I certainly haven't, and if he did ever go to the ground he was rarely available to speak to me. But he could always get me whenever he wanted me! Brian, being what he is, does it well but it wouldn't have worked for me in my position.

Ten times a year – you must be joking! Take the three weeks before Christmas, a time when the family man is making preparations for the big event, buying presents, going to parties, having fun. This was my diary the Christmas before the 1990 World Cup Final:

9 November   Speak at the Institute of Bankers in Ipswich — a long-standing, promised return engagement.

10 November   Drive to London. Fly to Venice in Italy. Chat to Des Lynam on the plane.

11 November   Italy v. Algeria in Vicenza.

12 November   Return to London. Assemble English squad for the Italy game. Watch Manchester United v. Forest on television, sweating on my players, particularly Bryan Robson.

13 November   Training with England Squad. International Committee meeting in afternoon.

14 November   Training with England. Drive to Brighton for England B v. Italy B.

15 November   England training in morning. England v. Italy at Wembley in evening. Midnight press conference at Heathrow.

16 November   Dawn call for flight to Cagliari via Rome.

17 November   Meeting in Cagliari. Tour Sardinia hotels after strong tip that we may be based there for first phase of World Cup.

18 November   Cagliari to Genoa to look at training centres and hotels.

19 November   Fly from Genoa to Cesena followed by three-and-a-half-hour drive to Bologna for training centres and hotels.

20 November   Fly from Bologna to Sicily for training centres and hotels.

21 November   Sicily.

22 November   Sicily to Bari.

23 November   Bari for training centres and hotels.

24 November   Bari to Rome for hotels and training centres.

25 November   Rome to London. Guest at Barbarians v. New Zealand Rugby at Twickenham.

26 November   Travel to Liverpool for Arsenal game.

27 November   BBC lunch to discuss World Cup rights and access to team hotel. John Bromley farewell dinner in evening.

28 November   Catch up on post and messages at office in London. Work late. Stay in London.

29 November   Continue office work, then Spurs v. Tranmere.

30 November   FLESA meeting in Birmingham. Ipswich in evening for speech at Mich D'Avray Testimonial dinner. Night in own bed!

1 December   Saints and Sinners Lunch at Savoy. Guildhall for Dinner and Concert with my wife Elsie.

2 December   Travel to Birmingham for Aston Villa v. Nottingham Forest.

3 December   London for Arsenal v. Manchester United, and Vaudeville Golf Society Dinner.

4 December   England squad announcement for press in London. Drive to Durham to see my mom and dad, only chance before Christmas.

5 December   Langley Park FC of the Skol Northern League to help the club in the village where I was born to raise cash for their floodlights.

6 December   Drive to Ipswich.

7 December   Drive to London for Concorde flight to Malaga for Sports Aid Foundation Charity golf event.

8 December   Return to London by Concorde.

9 December   Travel to Rome for the World Cup draw.

10 December   Rome to London for assembly of team before Yugoslavian game.

11 December   England training.

12 December   Training and England B v. Yugoslavia B at Millwall.

13 December   Training in morning. England v. Yugoslavia at Wembley in evening.

14 December   Office. London Transport Society Golf Dinner.

15 December   Office.

16 December   Charlton v. Crystal Palace. Drive home.

17 December   DAY OFF – SUNDAY LUNCH AT HOME AT LAST!

18 December   Drive to London for meetings in office.

19 December   Office in morning. Fly to Glasgow for Rangers v. Arsenal.

20 December   Dawn flight to Rotterdam for Holland v. Brazil.

21 December   Dawn flight to Sardinia for Italy v. Argentina.

22 December   Meetings in Cagliari to confirm hotels, etc.

23 December   Dawn flight to Liverpool via Bordeaux, France, for Liverpool . Manchester United and flight back to London. Drive to Ipswich.

24 December   Drive to London to see sons Paul and Mark.

25 December   In London with sons.

26 December   Drive to Wareham in Dorset to see third son Andrew.

Roll on the New Year!

It needs a special person to manage England. I am not sure that Brian Clough could do it and I am sure that Jack Charlton would run a mile now he knows what it involves. Both could, of course, handle the football side without too many problems; but as I have tried to show, it is so much more than that. Jack was able to walk out on press conferences in Italy, or not bother to see the media at all. He couldn't do that with England, and if I had had the sort of set-to with a cameraman that he had after the defeat by Italy in Rome I would have been hanged, drawn and quartered. Cloughie, as we all know, is hardly an ambassador or a conformist. He is apt to be swayed by whim – and his actions when he ran onto the pitch and cuffed a fan would have created mayhem in international football. Handling the media is a job on its own, and the spotlight is so intense that it is like being the Prime Minister of Football – with an election every month!

I used to think it would be lovely simply to be a technical man, a coach, as I am now at PSV. Bob Paisley, that wily old fox at Liverpool, would never have considered the England job. There is no low profile in this job, nowhere to hide. You cannot avoid the newspapers, the cameras, the non-stop exposure.

Certainly you have to be a football man; you wouldn't last a fortnight if you couldn't impart that knowledge and handle the best the country can produce in the biggest games. I'm thinking of games like the visit of Brazil to Wembley before the World Cup for a gate of £1,000,000, a full house of 80,000 and millions watching on television, all wanting a result and not caring that you are short of your top two midfield men Robson and Webb, and juggling with two untried internationals in Platt and Gascoigne instead. The responsibility is huge: you are acting for the country, carrying their hopes on your back, even though some may be spitting at you as you walk around the track, because you haven't picked one of their favourites.

Let's face it: there haven't been many who can speak from experience. I liked Walter Winterbottom, the first of the real England managers: he was an intelligent, kind man – even though he left me out for Bobby Moore in the World Cup Finals in Chile.

Whatever he did, before or since, Alf Ramsey, the international footballer who guided rural Cinderella club Ipswich to the League Championship, will always be remembered in football history as the man who won the World Cup for England. I envy him that.

At the time of his appointment no one would have doubted Don Revie's ability. He was the right choice at the time, an ex-international, successful, fought for all the big prizes; but in the end the pressure got to him, and he walked out abruptly.

Joe Mercer, or Uncle Joe, was called on to fill the gap – a great player who knew how to handle players. But he was never anything more than a caretaker, with only a handful of games in which to make his mark.

Ron Greenwood was knowledgeable and, more importantly, could impart that knowledge. He was honourable, intelligent and gave West Ham United stability and a fine team over the years. Sadly he became England manager too late in his career. Had he been appointed earlier he could have gone into the grass-roots and really done the business. In the end he was brought in to do a mopping-up job after failures to qualify in 1974 and 1978, and didn't lose a game in the Finals in Spain.

People forget that he took over an ailing team who had qualified for the World Cup only once in 12 years; and though he did well, he had injuries to key players like Coppell, Keegan, Brooking and Robson which left him with no real chance.

Then there was me ... and now there is Graham Taylor. What have we got in common? Not a lot. What is the formula? If the FA knew that, they would have Taylor's successor lined up already.

I immediately made it known to Graham Taylor that should he want anything at all from me I would be available. I shan't go to him, he must come to me; but if he does he will find me as ready, willing and able to help him as I was for any England manager in the past, from my playing days under Walter Winterbottom to releasing my skipper Mick Mills for Ron to play against Brazil, even though Ipswich had a game and we were fighting against relegation. That is what England means to me. That is why, long before I dreamed of becoming manager, I would go to Wembley to watch every single England game. It won't change now: I will be there whenever my duties permit.

Graham will find it a hard learning process, especially in those first couple of years when everything is so new, and so little of your past provides the answers to the problems which arise. That is why some while ago I put forward the proposal of an assistant, groomed to take over after serving a two-year apprenticeship, the way Berti Vogts has done under Franz Beckenbauer for West Germany. It doesn't guarantee success but at least it gives a fighting chance, because Berti knows what he will have to face. He will have learned by observation and not by the seat of his pants – the way I and others have had to with our system.

Graham is going into the job with the need to get results immediately. He will be judged not on whether or not he wins the World Cup in the USA in four years' time but whether he can qualify for the European Championships in Sweden two years earlier; and that's tougher than qualifying for the World Cup – I know. I lost only one qualifying game of any sort in eight years, and that cost us a place in the European Championship Finals in France.

A guiding hand would have been useful to me when I plunged straight into the trenches with my first game, a European Championship qualifying game away to the emerging Danes. I instantly caused an uproar by leaving out Kevin Keegan, the former England captain. I admit now that, with hindsight, I would have done it differently. What that decision did to me was to put me under immediate and intense pressure. It caused hatred towards me in my native Geordieland, where Kevin was a hero and seen as the Newcastle Messiah. It was not an easy decision. It was very emotive. He was such a star. I was a big fan of his and had used him as an example to my Ipswich players on many occasions. But I still maintain it was the right decision in terms of international football. He had served his time. He had chosen to play Second Division football and I couldn't see him surviving at the top level until the European Championship finals two years later, never mind the World Cup two years after that.

So I thought to myself: 'Let's be abrupt, let's see if there is anyone else around. While he is in the squad I will be tempted to play him and perhaps deny his successor the chance. If it doesn't work I can always bring him back.' But I did not realise how much it would hurt the man.

I had done my homework first, and had been advised by people close to England that he could be a disruptive influence at times, particularly in Spain when injuries sidelined him. It was not a decision off the top of my head, and I had spoken to a lot of people involved, including Ron Greenwood, Don Howe and Lawrie McMenemy; and as a new manager I felt I owed nothing to anyone. I could have avoided all that pressure and the aggravation by funking that decision and easing him out gracefully.

But in the end a manager has to manage, whatever the pressure, and if I hadn't been strong the critics would have accused me of being soft; and if he had failed they would have said, of course, that I should never have picked him in the first place. Which line do you take? Which option? I decided that as a new manager it was up to me. Kevin's complaint was that I didn't get in touch with him first – even though I wrote to him later, a fact he has never mentioned.

I have no doubt that Ron would have taken him to one side because Kevin was his captain, his man. I would have done the same if the day had come when I had to axe one of my old favourites like Shilton or Robson. In fact I had to do exactly that with Terry Butcher in Italy and have done it in the past with Trevor Francis and Paul Mariner. Had I had someone under my wing we could have discussed that at length, now that we know the repercussions. I had walked into a completely new media world from parochial Ipswich. I might well have handled it a bit differently, knowing what I know now.

Fortunately for Graham Taylor, Peter Shilton saved him from a similar problem by announcing his international retirement to coincide with mine, and Terry Butcher did likewise shortly before the start of the season. Graham will have thought long and hard about Bryan Robson especially after another injury delayed his entry into the 1991 season.

Graham is a solid sort of chap with a good background, and having a father who was a journalist will undoubtedly have helped him. Once he has picked his squads he will have to show that he can handle big players – players who are better than he was. I played in the World Cup in Sweden and was in the squad for Chile, but many members of my England squads were better players than I ever was, particularly the skipper Bryan Robson. But you still have to discipline, control, motivate and get the best out of them. They are largely strangers whom you may associate with for three days at a time 10 times a year – if they are fit and available every time. Under those circumstances you cannot hope to build the sort of relationship which forms at a club where you have daily contact and 60 games a year. To fit the jig-saw you have to mould these strangers from different clubs into a team within a system they can all understand and play in.

The new manager will have to be a diplomat, not just abroad but at home as well. He will need to get along with all the club managers, some of whom he will know won't be too keen on releasing their players every time. They are being awkward, not to hinder England but because they are looking after their own jobs and they feel they have to be selfish. They are not all like Alex Ferguson, who lost his big signing Neil Webb to play for England, and took it on the chin, bravely and uncomplainingly.

The worry about sending players back injured to their clubs is always present. As Ipswich manager I lost Kevin Beattie that way: he came back with a cartilage problem after playing against Luxembourg, and he was never the same great player again. The wear and tear left him arthritic. Managers tend to blame England for that sort of injury, even though it can happen anywhere, at any time.

One of the most difficult adjustments is to go from 60 games a season to ten. It means a change of emphasis, a change of thought, a change from everything you have done before. At home, even if you are playing a top team like Liverpool or Arsenal, you know exactly what they are going to throw at you; but go to Romania, Egypt or Czechoslovakia and you don't really know what is coming, no matter what data bank you have built up. It is very testing.

Whatever happens you have to keep your cool. That's the ambassadorial part of the occupation. You are under the microscope, under pressure, but as manager of England you can't run onto the pitch, no matter how much you might want to. You have to remain above everything, even after hand-ball goals and penalty shoot-outs which end World Cup dreams.

As a club manager you can always turn inwards to those who work with you, whereas in the international arena you are often on your own. In a visit to Cairo to watch Egypt I was invited to what I thought was an informal dinner. It turned out that the British Ambassador was there, and the local Minister for Sport, along with Cabinet colleagues and even the Egyptian Basketball manager. Worse still, I was expected to make a speech without any advance warning.

Then the British Ambassador invited me to a party for 16 top British surgeons who had been setting surgical exams for the local doctors. I could not turn it down; I didn't feel out of my depth mingling with these top surgeons, who all had so much in common with each other, but it was strange. I looked on it all as part of my education, as well as an obligation to my employers; but I can think of one or two top managers who might not have coped in those circumstances.

The Egyptian trip was one of the rare ones where I took my wife Elsie because I thought I would have plenty of free time in between the two matches I had gone to watch. She couldn't believe the demands for interviews. They were knocking on the hotel door, demanding I speak to them. I had to explain to her that I couldn't afford to create bad relations by refusing, and that I was batting for a lot of people back at home. It was a week of high diplomacy.

You certainly can't say the local team is hopeless. They wait for you to trip up, and then use it to motivate their players. I had to be particularly wary in this instance, as I had been misquoted before I even arrived in Cairo: they had the hump, and I had some bridge-building to do – not least because I could see even then that Egypt were going to cause us and others problems.

Graham Taylor will no doubt spot many other pitfalls and it

will be how he copes with them as much as how his teams perform which will determine his success and how long he survives. I managed eight years and in Italy I was far and away the longest-serving manager of the 24 teams. That should give a very good idea of the toll the job takes. And, without hesitation, I would say that the England job is as hard as, if not harder than, any of the others. Good luck, Graham — you will need it!

7

Gazza and my Dream Team

Peter Shilton
Mark Wright
Des Walker   Terry Butcher
Viv Anderson   Kenny Sansom
Paul Gascoigne   Bryan Robson   Chris Waddle
Trevor Francis   Gary Lineker
Substitutes:
Ray Clemence
Paul Parker
Ray Wilkins
John Barnes
Peter Beardsley

PAUL GASCOIGNE: RIGHT MIDFIELD

Paul Gascoigne emerged from the World Cup Finals in Italy not only as one of football's great characters but also as one of the few genuine stars of the competition. This happy-go-lucky Geordie, who began his World Cup adventure by forgetting his passport, captured the hearts not only of a nation but of the world with his cheeky skills, his remarkable energy, and his tears, not those of a clown but those of a footballing superstar.

A year before the finals I was only just convincing myself that he was going to make the squad as he struggled with his Mars Bar-induced weight problems and his volatile temperament. Six months later I had him pencilled in on the bench. Now, without a second's hesitation on my part, he takes his place in my Dream

Team selected from all of the players who have performed in my eight years as England manager.

On the evidence of what I have seen he can help England to win the World Cup in the United States in 1994. He can do for England what Maradona did for Argentina in Mexico back in 1986. He emerged from Italy as the best young player in the tournament, equal to the best of the rest, and had every player of every other country talking about him; certainly he was the name on everyone's lips when I arrived at PSV Eindhoven.

If he were available I would buy him at the drop of a hat, even if I had to mortgage the stand. How many are there like him around the world? I would take a chance on all the other things to have him in my side and talk of a £7 million valuation is not unrealistic when set beside some of the transfers in Italy in the summer, including Roberto Baggio's move from Fiorentina to Juventus for a similar fee. For me he went on beyond Baggio in the World Cup. He is a more complete, better player, always likely to win matches out of nothing.

We haven't produced many like him over the years, and it may turn out to be none like him, if he maintains his progress and goes all the way. He is precocious, cheeky, confident, tough, a winner. He is still a bit of a scatterbrain and probably always will be. He does not know the game deeply yet; he is still in the learning process, playing off the top of his head and doing what comes naturally. Sometimes I swear he doesn't know what it is he is doing but that is not a fault. It means he can try something and if it doesn't come off he can forget it and get on with his game. If it lets him down he dismisses it and as long as it doesn't occur too often in a game this adventurous spirit can be an asset.

When he played against Colombia at Wembley I knew I had to find a place for him in the squad. He had a year in which to get better, curb his temper and get himself into shape in order to be able to play in the heat of summer in pressure-cooker matches. I knew that I would have to handle this one with extreme care and bring him along gently if he was going to be anywhere near ready in time. He had already shown that he had a capacity to drop himself deep into trouble on and off the pitch, but sometimes you have to make allowances because he's different. Not everybody is the same but if you had two players of equal

standard you would take the disciplined one above the un-
disciplined one. There wasn't another around like Paul Gascoigne.
He was and still is a one off, unique.

By December I gave an interview when I predicted that he
could be England's version of Roberto Baggio who was, even
then, the rage of Italy and I said that if Gazza handled himself
properly he could be a star of the World Cup Finals.

But it was not until the late autumn that he had really begun
to make the full impact on me. I took some stick for dropping
him down to the newly resurrected B team against Italy in
Brighton and against Yugoslavia at Millwall. We played him in
the heart of a two-man midfield to see how he coped. We could
still see those blemishes of his but he was becoming more reliable
in football terms and responsible enough to be given a try in the
senior team engine room in the style of my partnership for
England with Johnny Haynes and Bryan Robson's with Ray
Wilkins. Prior to that he had made so many defensive errors and
had been so tactically naive in international terms that when
Dave Sexton took him on a B tour the previous year he played
out wide with the responsible midfield positions going to David
Platt and Terry Hurlock. Through those B matches we could see
that he was learning his trade and becoming more trustworthy
and the time had come to give him a try now that fitness, diet
and weight-loss were having an effect.

The competition at that time for the midfield places was fierce
with Steve Hodge having come back and Platt emerging but,
although I had been excited by the Villa man in March against
Brazil, I was more impressed when Gazza turned it on when he had
his chance against Czechoslovakia. Against all expectations Dr Jozef
Venglos' side came to Wembley to attack and it suited Gazza down
to the ground. It was almost like a testimonial with little tackling
and Gazza was electric, having a hand in every goal as we won 4–2.

It was a memorable night as he gave a magic pass from the left
half position to inside right for a most spectacular goal from
Steve Bull. He took on the entire defence to provide Bully with
his second and completed the night with a fantastic solo goal. He
looked tired and ready to come off when he burst out of the
pack, dummied the goalkeeper and finished with a ferocious
shot. It capped a fantastic match.

I needed to see him again and kept him in for a game against Denmark when he had to do far more chasing. Terry Venables had telephoned me to tell me that I would be pleased with his fitness and I was. At times he over-dribbled and sometimes he delayed delivery of his pass for too long, but on the whole he gave another good performance, lasting the pace, albeit with his tongue hanging out. I came away feeling he had shown a bit more intelligence.

I played him again against Uruguay and he came through the test once more. Although the result was disappointing he played well and more than held his own against tough opposition. It was a test of temperament as much as anything else. He was productive, used the ball well and the South Americans found him a real handful. He had now had three consistent games and showed he could play that important midfield role as long as he had a good player alongside him. With my plan to play both Waddle and Barnes it had to be someone I could rely on. The alternative was to play him and leave out one of the wingers and I didn't want to do that.

He can be as daft as a brush off the field and get away with it but you can't be stupid in danger areas on the pitch. Venables told me that the boy gets out there and forgets. He has so much confidence he tries anything. But in a World Cup you can't afford to lose the ball in your own box trying to nutmeg an opponent – nor in the English League, as Spurs found out to their cost during the season. With Spurs he had also tended to fade and I feared he might do that in our opening group.

What I couldn't do was wait. He was going to be a sensation in the 1994 World Cup but I hadn't got that sort of time. I wanted him to do it now in 1990, aged 22. To play him I had to be sure that he was fit to last the pace, could follow instruction and would control his temper. At club level he had been guilty of arguing with referees, and opponents could easily wind him up. With the FIFA crack-down it worried me that he would get himself sent off.

I had one more look at him against Tunisia and although he gave away a goal and over-reacted when we equalised, he worked well with Bryan Robson and I decided to start with him against the Irish because the positives were now outweighing the negatives. There is no question now that he is a big match player. The bigger the stage, the bigger the audience, the happier he is. He is so confident he believes he can handle anyone and do anything. The World Cup frightens some players but not him – he couldn't wait for games to start. He has the temperament, nothing scares him.

I have no doubt he can go all the way to the very top. Of course he has to avoid injury, be choosy in the company he keeps and select his future with great care. Can he keep his feet on the ground in the face of Gazzamania? Can he keep stable? He has the talent to take on the world and the biggest clubs will do their best to tempt him away from his mates, his local pubs and his comfortable surroundings.

What Italy offers him, by contrast, is an amazing amount of money, a fanatical environment and the greatest club football in the world at the present moment. If he was wooed away to Italian football he would love the soccer, he would be rich and he would be successful – but would he be happy? Without speaking the language and without a wife and family he would be lonely while life on the pitch would be different, too. Could he put up with it? Only time would tell.

But on the international front he can, if he looks after himself, be an England player for the next ten years and could win close to a hundred caps and score lots of goals to go with it. He would certainly start and star in my Dream Team.

PETER SHILTON: GOALKEEPER

Who else? One hundred and twenty-five caps, world records and still, for me, the best goalkeeper in the World Cup in Italy, even if he did give away that goal to Baggio in his last game for England!

But he might so easily have been missing from the squad altogether. I had to make a lot of decisions after what happened in the European Championships in West Germany, not least of all whether or not I should stay. The answer to that was an emphatic yes, stand up and fight. But where did I start? At the beginning, with the goalkeeper, 38-year-old Peter Shilton, one of the many the media wrote off after West Germany.

He would be 40 come Italy and there were signs of age. He wasn't coming for crosses the way he used to, all too often he was stuck on his line. He appeared to be having some difficulties with long-range shots. Should I keep him? Should I give Chris Woods his chance? But Woods hadn't looked too safe in the last match against the Soviet Union and while I wanted to be progressive, I was uncertain because they were both uncertain.

I doubted if Shilts would still be the number one choice but I decided to have another look at him in the friendly against Denmark. He deserved an early look after all he had done and if he had been nervy or shaky in that match I would have waved him bye-bye. It must have been at about the same time that Shilton made some of his own decisions, to keep in shape and to cut alcohol from his diet. It made him brighter and his reactions looked sharper. He saw the long-shots earlier and dealt with them a lot better.

I had to be sure and I had Mike Kelly follow him around the First Division as well as watching him myself. We both felt he looked good, in fact we reached the conclusion that he was getting better rather than worse.

I needed a few old heads to help on the kids and I decided to stay with him. From that moment he went upwards. He was brilliant in Albania and even better in Poland. He made two wonderful agility saves in Tirana and kept out a series of long-range shots in Katowice. In between he didn't let in a goal throughout the entire qualifying competition. His reactions were good, his sighting got better and the timing of his dives was in harmony with his reactions.

I talked to him and told him how pleased I was that he was back to his best. He wouldn't admit to it but I was sure that stopping the traditional drinking after matches had made a major difference. Drinking dulls the mind. Whether he acknowledges it or not I think it gave him that new lease of life and led him to the record books.

He finished the World Cup a legend. He couldn't go on for ever even though the way he finished he looked good for another couple of years to me. But by quitting he made it easy for new manager Graham Taylor. It was one less decision to make.

He has gone out at the very top, after a wonderful World Cup where many of the top goalkeepers struggled with a difficult ball. He was superb, made critical saves at critical moments and gave confidence to those in front of him. All England football fans owe Peter Shilton a debt of thanks. He will be a hard act to replace.

Chris Woods has been very patient and I hope he is given the opportunity after waiting so long. He was unlucky when he played against the Soviet Union because he had been suffering toothache and came into a side whose confidence had been shot to pieces by two defeats. He has been desperate to play but he has also held his hands up and admitted how good Peter is. He has been sensible; he didn't walk out the way Peter did when he was having the same problems. He kept his mouth shut and carried on working on his game and learning from the man he understudied as a kid at Nottingham Forest. He is a true international and had he belonged to any other country he would have a string of caps already. I admit I didn't like his performance against the Soviets but there were a lot of players in that side that I didn't like that day.

Since then he has proved himself. He showed in the goalless draw against Turkey that he has good hands. He didn't wobble and his temperament stood up again when he was suddenly thrust into the action against Brazil when Peter cut his eye in a clash with Des Walker. He adjusted to a situation suddenly presented to him with no warning and no time to warm up.

He has recovered well from a vertigo problem which threatened his career at Glasgow Rangers. He is calm and assured with a nice temperament. I always felt that I could put him in whenever necessary and come to that I would not have been afraid to play David Seaman or Dave Beasant either. The goalkeeping scene in England remains very good indeed.

VIV ANDERSON: RIGHT BACK

I was never lucky enough to have Viv Anderson at his best but he would fit in perfectly with the sweeper system we used successfully in Italy.

Tall, rangy and good in the air, he was the perfect player to put on the near or far post for corners, whether they were for or against you. No one could outrun those long legs and while he was not a robust tackler like Pearce his long spidery legs would reach out and steal the ball just when the forward thought himself clear. He was also a fine attacking player, good on the overlap, getting into attacking positions and always threatening goal from dead-ball kicks.

If he had a fault it was that he allowed opponents to bring the ball down and run at him. I never understood why he did that and why he didn't rattle them early the way Pearce does. But, even so, I would select him above the rest and there are a few good ones.

Liverpool's Phil Neal I rated. He was a Rolls-Royce of a player, a lovely passer of the ball and an excellent penalty-taker. He would have been ice-cool in a World Cup shoot-out! He never made a big hit with the Wembley public for some reason.

Gary Stevens also goes close because he is such a good athlete. Not as good a passer of the ball as Viv, he was steady in defence and attack and could go up the line as hard in the last 20 minutes as in the first 20.

DES WALKER: CENTRAL DEFENDER

One of the best markers the country has seen in many years and one of the best defenders in the world as he proved in Italy, even though in every game he played he was struggling from the effects of a challenge made on him off the pitch by John Aldridge in our first game in the Finals.

But you have to accept Des as he is. He won't go up for free-kicks. He won't bring the ball out from defence and when in possession he will look for his nearest team mate to get rid of the responsibility. No matter what Graham Taylor, myself or anyone else says to him he will never become a talker on the pitch or a runner with the ball.

Fortunately his defensive qualities far outweigh any other considerations for this Johnny-on-the-spot defender who seems able to seal up all of the cracks whether they are in the air or on the ground. It helps that he is lightning quick and possesses great anticipation.

Relaxed in Colorado Springs before the Mexican adventure

In deep conversation with Ray Wilkins, one of my favourite people, in Los Angeles

A quiet word with Glenn Hoddle after our narrow 2–1 defeat by eventual winners Argentina in Mexico City

Above: Bryan Robson is congratulated by Gary Lineker after putting England level against Holland in the European Championships. But we went on to lose 3–1

Right: Physio Fred Street and I walk off after the Holland game knowing our dream is over

Below: Tony Adams, so unlucky not to go to Italy, in a battle of the giants with Ireland's Niall Quinn in Stuttgart

Above: A crucial win after the European disaster and it shows as I leave the pitch with Danish manager Sepp Piontek

Left: The inscrutable Sphinx and the not so inscrutable Bobby Robson in Egypt

Below: Swamped by the Albanian press after England's first ever visit to this closed country

Gary Lineker opens our World Cup account for 1990 against the Irish after eight minutes

England's entire World Cup squad – including Dave Beasant our fourth goalkeeper

On you go Bully – I send on Wolves' prolific striker to shake up the Dutch

David Platt's opening goal against the brave Africans from Cameroon

Above: Record-breaking Peter Shilton is awarded a commemorative plaque by FA Chairman Bert Millichip before the Holland game

Right: The emotional Paul Gascoigne gives me a big cuddle after our breathtaking win over Cameroon

Left: Steve Bull in typical action against Belgium Frank van der Elst

Below: Des Walker became one of the World C stars despite a constant, nagging injury

Above: Rallying the troops before extra time against West Germany in Turin

Left: The party is over – we have lost the penalty shoot out to the Germans and tears are all we have left

Below: West German manager Franz Beckenbauer and I

Above: A familiar pose for yet another interview

Right: Gary Lineker was still hunting goals even in the play-off for third place against Italy

Below: Another day, another country. I start my new job in Holland with PSV Eindhoven

With ball and bodies flying around in the box you would ask: 'Who cleared that?'

Des.

'Who headed that out?'

Des.

If you needed a foot stuck out he was there: if you wanted a last-ditch tackle made Des would be on the spot; if a head was needed to flick the ball away from an onrushing forward Des was your man; a goal-line clearance and Des would fling his body in the way. An out-and-out defender who loves the job he does so well.

MARK WRIGHT: SWEEPER

Smooth, silky and very quick, with those long legs perhaps the quickest in the world at the back. His advantage to any Dream Team is his versatility. He is able to play libero, marker, left or right and, as he showed when he cut open his head against Cameroon, even in midfield!

He is pure quality on the ball. His control, dribbling skills, his distribution, long or short. He is a tall boy and uses his height so well. That was an amazing goal he scored against Egypt in Sardinia when he outjumped a very good goalkeeper at full stretch and was able to guide the ball down into the net.

But he is a complicated character and had he been more straightforward I, and England, would have had two extra years out of him. I feel that sometimes he uses small injuries as an excuse either for missing a match or as a pre-arranged excuse if things do not go so well.

Against Holland two years ago in the European Championships he vied with Bryan Robson as our best player but when it came to the 'dead' match against the Soviet Union he suddenly turned up with an injury saying he didn't think he was fit enough to play but would do so if I wanted him to. He did the same thing in Italy when a calf injury appeared from nowhere before the play-off game in Bari. This time I told him to play and maybe if I had done that against the Soviets he would have a lot more caps now.

Yet when he was suffering with a dreadful thigh injury when

we arrived in Italy he was keen to play, as he was when he cricked his neck before the tournament began and, even more startling, when he cut his eye so badly against Cameroon. His bravery is not in question for, after he had been ruled out by the doctor and the physiotherapist, he demanded to go back on with the cut eye completely covered and in real danger of bursting open like a ripe pumpkin. It was the same story before the semi-final against West Germany when you knew that nothing short of a locked cage would keep him from the game. He didn't even want to take a fitness test.

He is a complex character and in no way a coward or lacking in confidence. I am told at Derby that he has 21 fitness tests a season and passes all of them! Work out his complexities and you have an outstanding performer for the world stage and certainly a contender for anyone's Dream Team. I will pick him as my sweeper.

Wright eventually squeezed out Tony Adams from the 22 for Italy. The Arsenal captain was unlucky not to go having enjoyed his best-ever season for the Gunners and never having let down England in any of the games he had played. A thunderous character, brave as a lion with a devastating tackle, and a towering header of the ball. A natural leader, he is going to be a good captain who will inspire his own team and put the fear of God into the opposition.

But to go to the top or challenge for a place in my Dream Team he would have to improve his ability on the ball. I could not see how I could play him together with Walker because I would need one of them to pass the ball with some consistency. Tony brings the ball out more than Des and gets forward to score more than his quota of goals but what can pass as good in the First Division can be inadequate at international level.

What happened in Italy, I feel, totally vindicated my choice but it was a wrench to leave such a good, honest character out of the squad when he had contributed so much.

TERRY BUTCHER: CENTRAL DEFENDER

One of the very first names on my team sheet. What a character, what stature, what a patriot, what a player! I knew him better than most from my 13 years at Ipswich and it was wonderful to have him around at international level, someone I could trust and I knew would back me whatever the circumstances. I was never disappointed.

The players liked him as much as I did. He was a very strong personality in the dressing room, an example on the training field and a leader who knew no fear on the pitch even though he once came close to death through loss of blood after smashing his nose in a League game. How often did he finish a game with a head wound, the way he did in that outstanding performance against Sweden in Stockholm which helped us qualify for Italy?

You could ask him to do anything and he would never quibble. He was outstanding in Italy as I pushed him from pillar to post, dropping him, substituting him, playing him at right back, centre half and sweeper. He never moaned, never grumbled but got on with the job in hand, whatever it was.

He is a better passer of the ball than most realise. He has a fine left foot and there are few in the game better in the air than he is. There is none braver. He is always in where it matters most and where it hurts most and he has never shied away from the ball. In that respect he has been a huge help to Des Walker, for whenever Des had the ball he looked to give it to Terry.

Of course he has faults, who hasn't? He is a big fellow and slow on the turn. He is also very headstrong as his record proves. One of the problems is that he hates losing and I have even had to fine him for kicking down a dressing room door. People like that win you things. Ask Graeme Souness at Glasgow Rangers! He has a passion for the game and a fierce loyalty. In 40 years in football I have not come across anyone better and, but for the presence of Bryan Robson in the England side, he would have been captain many more times.

It was a good move for him, going to Scotland where he played for a good team and a good manager. He asked me before he went and I told him that it would not affect his selection for England, far from it, he was going to have the added experience of European football and he would be playing for one of the biggest clubs in the world. He didn't let anyone down in Italy and when I dropped him for the first time in my life he took it like the man he is. He also knew when to quit the international arena. I am convinced that when he finishes he will make an excellent manager.

KENNY SANSOM: LEFT BACK

A world-class full back who would get into any team of mine. He has to be good to oust a challenger of the quality of Stuart Pearce but he was special, skilful in possession, with a dextrous left foot that could cuddle and cosset the ball. He could get out of the tightest situation with a clever dribble, a shimmy or a dummy where other defenders would whack it and hope.

In spite of being small in stature he jumped exceptionally well and his timing in the tackle was exquisite. He always did superbly well for me and never better than in Brazil back in 1984 when we went to South America with a very young team following defeats by France and the Soviet Union. We looked set for a whacking with an inexperienced back four featuring Duxbury, Fenwick and Watson. Kenny was an example to all of them, never missing a tackle and shackling the talented Renato. John Barnes and Mark Hateley took the bulk of the glory for their great goals in that memorable 2–0 win but I shan't forget the performance of Kenny Sansom.

Unfortunately a lot will remember him for the error he made against the Republic of Ireland in the European Championships when he miscued a clearance. In fact I never actually dropped Kenny from the team; George Graham effectively did that by leaving him out of the Arsenal team in favour of Nigel Winterburn, one of his own purchases. It left Kenny out in the cold and I could scarcely pick him from the reserves. He had certainly not finished as far as I was concerned and, indeed, there was a time when he went to Newcastle when I was on the verge of bringing him back. I watched him and he was still playing well but he had put on a bit of weight and had lost a yard of pace.

He was a wonderful squad man, an excellent mimic and a fund of funny stories. He would take off Alan Ball, Sir Stan Matthews and various others but his best was the fall-about style of Norman Wisdom. That was the only time he looked to be in any danger of being injured – he was always fit and ready to play, was Kenny. If he was unfit I would have no qualms in bringing in Pearce, who has emerged as one of the outstanding left backs in European football, and close behind him is Tony Dorigo. Graham Taylor and England are fortunate to have two such quality players for the same position.

CHRIS WADDLE: LEFT MIDFIELD/LEFT WING

The injury to Steve Coppell cost myself and England dear. By the time I took over he was on the point of his premature retirement, and no longer the player who, had he been fit, would have walked into any select side and who would probably have still been around in Italy instead of being one of the best young managers in the game.

But, both as a player and as a manager, I have always liked a winger and I would always find room for one in my side, be it on the left or the right. That meant John Barnes and Trevor Steven in serious contention but, in the end, I went for the former Geordie sausage-maker Chris Waddle. More consistent than Barnes and able to play with equal effectiveness on either flank.

Strangely there was a time when he was not the most popular of players at Wembley. His and mine were invariably the two names which were booed when announced over the tannoy! It shows his class that he was able to win the crowd over and, in the season before the World Cup, became their favourite with a succession of outstanding performances, climaxing with a virtuoso display against Italy which left Maldini a broken man.

I always backed him because I knew that beneath those strangely unathletic, stooped shoulders was a remarkably fit and talented player, and I told him that as long as his club manager and his international manager were picking him that was all that mattered. At times he was genuinely world class – but maybe not quite often enough. His performances in Italy, particularly, lacked consistency.

Since moving to Marseille he likes to play inside in a free role, but often that is a road which leads nowhere and I felt he gave us better shape out wide which is where he had his best games for England. He has the ability, the skill and the pace to get beyond the full back and that spells trouble to any defending side. Playing a wide man gives the team shape, but to play a winger at international level he has to be good. Chris is.

It was a difficult choice between him and Barnes, it always was when they were both seen as rivals for the left-wing berth. A heads-or-tails job but, while John is perhaps more consistent with Liverpool, Chris has done it more often for England over the past three years. It is also a position in which I used Chris's former room-mate, Spurs colleague and singing partner, Glenn Hoddle and, indeed, he came to mind when I selected this team. The elegant Hoddle could do it down the left or right, he could go past people and he could have scored a lot more goals than he did. He scored only seven for England.

I have been criticised for not using Hoddle more than I did but I dispute that. I picked him more than any other manager, in fact more than 50 times and he would have had more caps but for the number of times when he was either unfit or unavailable. Hoddle himself much preferred the Gascoigne position, but to play Glenn in there you needed to design the team around him, with two behind him to let him run loose with no defensive responsibilities. Gazza is far more suited to that place with his better engine, steelier tackle and better heading ability.

As a technical player, Hoddle was unsurpassed in England, having every pass in the book and then a few more besides. But to bring that into effect you had to have people to win the ball and give it to him and you had to have others to do his running. Having said that, he gave his best performances for me in 1986 when I lost Robson and Wilkins. He came in with Peter Reid and did a sterling job, but he then had the help of Steve Hodge and Trevor Steven with no out-and-out wingers.

BRYAN ROBSON: MIDFIELD AND CAPTAIN

What can I add to the millions of words I have spoken and written about this outstanding but dreadfully unlucky player? Italy, I thought, was his great chance. A mid-season injury had left him with enough time to fully recover and go to the tournament fresh and ready. We both thought he was ready to shake off that injury jinx which had dogged him through two World Cups.

But it was not to be and, in fact, when he went off home for an operation he was carrying not one but three injuries. My heart bled for the man, and while Gazza shed tears publicly over his second booking in front of the world's television cameras, I cried privately for our inspirational and influential skipper; not for me but for him.

The only time he survived a tournament and showed the world his ability, he found those around him out of sorts and out of touch. That was two years earlier in West Germany. Now those around him were bubbling and fizzing and he was slipping off home again.

He is a truly amazing player; the bravest, most committed, strongest I ever had. He could do everything and did so for England. He has heart and industry, he could win the ball, pass it, score goals, play off other people brilliantly, read a situation before it developed, and could time his runs into opponents' penalty areas to absolute perfection. He was a wonderful inspiration and could lift sides on his own efforts – not by what he said, but by what he did. He missed 30 games under me and never saw out either of my World Cups. I often ponder what might have been had I been able to use a 100 per cent fit Robson all of the time.

Some said his bravery bordered on stupidity but without that courage he would have been just another good player. Malcolm Allison said he was his own worst enemy and that he should play with more common sense. I didn't agree with a lot that Malcolm said but I understand what he was getting at; Malcolm has been in the game for a long time but he failed to recognise that this bravery was the extra dimension that made Bryan Robson so special, so different to everyone else. He is from a separate mould. I was happy to take him the way he was, thanking God when I had him and suffering when he was not around.

It has not always been his fault. I blame Ron Atkinson and Manchester United for him not being fully fit in Mexico. Had they put the country before the club and let him have an operation early in the year he would have been fit and strong by the summer. I begged Ron but he said the club's need was as great as ours and I had to respect that. Had he undergone surgery on his dislocated shoulder he would have been out of the Manchester United side for two months and Ron felt that without him they would win nothing. As it was, they kept him, won nothing, and we were denied a fit Robson for the World Cup in Mexico.

In Italy he finally succumbed to Achilles' tendon trouble, a bruised heel and a damaged big toe. The players liked having him around but once he knew that his World Cup was over he got depressed and the best thing for him and his club was to return home for yet more surgery. I owed that to United manager Alex Ferguson, a Scot who has given England huge support since moving south of the border. If all managers had been like him the path would have been a lot smoother for me.

We did remarkably well without Bryan but obviously we missed him. He is three players in one, a defender, midfield player and a phenomenal goalscorer. He was dominant in set-plays at both ends.

Maybe I am biased but I could see no failings. Off the field maybe, but never on it. I would be proud to have him as skipper of my Dream Team – fit, of course.

GARY LINEKER: STRIKER

When I first picked Gary Lineker for England a good many critics asked 'Who?' Gary was with Leicester City then and had spent as much time out on the wing as he had through the middle. But I could sense that in this slightly-built, electric-heeled goalscorer we had a real find.

He came in after we had performed awfully against Wales as a substitute against the Scots and, although he didn't make an immediate impact, he has since established himself as one of the world's best, topping the scoring in the Mexico World Cup with six and standing third in the all-time England scoring lists behind only Bobby Charlton and Jimmy Greaves. I see no reason why, if Gary stays fit, he shouldn't play on for England and challenge Greaves' 44 goals and Charlton's 49-goal record. He is a marvellous finisher, rounding off everything everyone else tries to do. He has done exceptionally well for me and we would have been poorer without him.

Gary is not a complete player by any stretch of the imagination. He has the odd quiet game and sometimes a movement breaks down when it reaches him in general play. Now and then his passes go astray and he doesn't always hold the ball up. But against all of that he loves to score goals. He will hunt and he is brave. He will get in amongst the biggest dirtiest defenders in a bid to score a goal. I have seen him hammered to the floor time after time and he still gets up and gets on with the game. He never whinges and never tries to get anyone sent off. That all paid off for him against Cameroon when, with the minutes ticking away, he was twice sent crashing to the ground when it looked as though he would go clear, and twice he got up, brushed himself down and scored from the spot. That is really cool finishing amid the sort of tension there was that night with the prize of a place in the World Cup semi-finals at stake.

Sometimes I get irritated with him when an injury keeps him away from training for longer than I think it should or when he is flicking the ball away instead of holding it and waiting for support. But most of the time I like him very much. In terms of movement off the ball, timing his runs, making team-mates play the ball into space so that defenders have to turn, he is the best there is. He will go for anything in the box, never thinking about the challenge only the ball. He is up there with Greaves, Law, Best, Rush, Francis who all possessed electric pace which gave them that extra yard. He wouldn't have got half the goals without it.

By and large he scores mainly with his right foot from inside the box, adjusting his body to get into position, but he has shown that at the very top level he can score goals with his head and with his left foot; it was a left-foot shot which put us level with West Germany in the semi-final.

Gary didn't like to train the day before a match, when he would conserve his energy, or the day after, when his body would seize up from the hammering it had taken. When you played twice a week that didn't leave much scope for training! But he was always around for shooting practice – except on match day. His type of training was all sharp, quality work and, to be fair to him, he always looked sharp and in good nick and never needed a sweat suit to shed extra pounds.

Off the field he is a dream. He is polite, courteous and helpful. If there was any public relations work to be done for the kids, an interview with the press, or a badge to present to some young player, he would be there with a smile. He has a wonderful reputation and continually enhances it by being available and affable. And why not? The game is tough enough and there are enough bad guys about without him joining them. He has shown the youngsters in the game that you can still be a top player and a top money-earner without slagging people off. He is a good advert for professional football.

TREVOR FRANCIS: STRIKER

Trevor Francis was on the way out when I came in but I had still seen enough of him to want him in this team, ahead of Tony Woodcock, Peter Beardsley, Peter Withe, Clive Allen, Mark Hateley, Paul Mariner and John Barnes, to partner Gary Lineker up front.

He possessed blistering pace, an eye for goal and a stunning shot, often without any sort of backlift. You didn't realise how hard his shot was until you were out there on the training pitch with him. He had a shot like the kick of a mule, he was a really clean striker of the ball. He could head it, too, particularly if the goal was in range.

Can you imagine Lineker and Francis at their best playing together? They would have been a handful for any defenders in the world. I am sure Trevor would have been the perfect foil for Lineker – not only making goals, but scoring them as well.

He was a true thoroughbred and, like any class player, he always suffered from knocks and bruises after a game. He would join the squad late from Italy, where he was playing his club football, and the joke among the backroom staff was guessing what the injury would be this time. Certainly Fred Street would spend a lot of time working with him. But once pronounced fit, he was a major problem for any defence to cope with. I liked him because he could play anywhere across the front line. He could go wide on the right and get great balls into the box, and when he was out on the left he would cut in and have a pot at goal. Play him anywhere up there and he was comfortable. You could play balls over the top for him to chase or play them to feet for him to turn and take the defence on. He was not afraid to run at a defender, particularly in the box. That's why he gets my vote – he would score more goals than Peter Beardsley.

I must say, however, that I was very cross when he bad-mouthed me in the newspapers for leaving him out of the squad for Mexico, and taking Beardsley in preference. I had given Trevor every chance to recover from a fractured cheekbone but eventually felt that a fully fit Beardsley could give the team more. Events proved me correct and I suspect that for a player with an obvious career in football management, who is usually a very pleasant young man besides, that article is now a source of embarrassment. I don't hold grudges. I remember him for the way he played football and that is why I would pick him.

RAY CLEMENCE: SUBSTITUTE GOALKEEPER

Ray Clemence was an experienced, mature goalkeeper of real international standing. When I took over I was not going to alternate between the top two 'keepers as Ron Greenwood had done before me and I went for Shilton, a decision I have never had cause to regret. At one stage there was nothing to choose between Ray and Peter, the country was lucky in the extreme to have them both.

Clem was a tall, commanding figure with long arms. It made him good on corners and crosses and his agility allowed him to make vital saves to help Liverpool and Spurs to so many trophies.

PAUL PARKER: SUBSTITUTE DEFENDER

It shows the rapid strides Paul Parker has made after only coming into the team during the World Cup that he can take his place on my substitutes' bench as part of the squad comprising the best 16 players of my eight years in charge. He deserves it not least of all for his versatility. Remember I played him at right back and, everyone told me, he was not a right back. I even agreed with Ray Hartford, his old Fulham manager, when he told me that Paul was not even a full back.

What he is though is a very good defender – so quick and an excellent clean tackler. He sticks with people so well and, even though small, is a fine jumper. Very much like Walker, there is nothing he likes more than being given a job against a front player. He thrives on it.

Against Holland he expected to be playing right back but because of their tactics we moved him into such an advanced position that he was more of a cross between right-side midfield and a right winger. He adapted to it but probably had his best game against Belgium when he started wretchedly and grew in stature until he was one of our best players at the end of the two-hour slog.

If Graham thinks like me, Paul Parker will figure prominently in the England team's future. Paul will be able to play anywhere for him, including centre half and sweeper.

RAY WILKINS: SUBSTITUTE MIDFIELD

Ray is one of the best people I have ever had the privilege of working with – a really good professional, dedicated and with the ability to impart his knowledge and deep understanding of the game to others.

He was a player everyone liked, whether it was in the hotel, at the training ground or in a match. But he was never afraid to speak his mind when he disagreed; on the other hand he was also able to lighten the tensest of atmospheres with his ready, bubbling humour.

He was still an outstanding player when the World Cup came along, and when I was struck with a glut of injuries and loss of form I seriously considered bringing him back into the squad. He would have come without complaint even though I had left him in the wilderness for so long. My only reservation about his game was that he would sometimes play too square and, at other times, go too deep to pick up the ball from the back four. He didn't score enough goals either for such a capable player. He used to let Robson have his head, happy to back him up and be his insurance.

If I had to pick anyone out of the current crop of players to be a successful manager in the future it would be Ray Wilkins. It would be unthinkable to lose him to the game. The game needs people like him.

JOHN BARNES: SUBSTITUTE

John is the great enigma of international football and the biggest mystery of my career. Why couldn't John Barnes play for England the way he played for Liverpool? I have to admit that I do not know. I am as baffled now as I was at any time I talked to him throughout his international career with me.

If he was a 'chicken winger' I could understand it, but we are talking about a brave man, certainly no coward. He is built like a cruiserweight boxer, can't be shifted off the ball. and wins headers when the boots are flying.

Twice made Footballer of the Year by the very people who slaughtered him for his lack of consistency in Italy, he is so talented; lovely on the ball with Brazilian-style movement, possessing great first touch, capable of putting in super crosses and taking every variety of shot – bending the ball or curling it. No one enjoyed watching him playing for Liverpool more than me.

If you were to talk about him and remind me of him at his best, I would have him in instead of Waddle in a minute, that's what he does to you. How can you leave out a man of this immense talent? That was the dilemma which continually faced me. Some blamed me, others blamed his West Indian background, while a psychiatrist pointed the finger at his strict upbringing. It was all so daft. The real answer can only be given by John Barnes himself, for the answers to all such questions must lie within, and it is up to John Barnes to sort it out if he wants to be remembered as the great player he is.

I did everything I could for him because, in the end, if I could get him playing it would be to my benefit and the country's. I talked to him, I encouraged him, I picked him every time I could, played him wide, played him at centre forward. There would be the odd flash, the odd exceptional game, but he couldn't reach out for that extra 15 per cent which turns a good performance into an international or world-class performance. It was a shame because he is such a lovely player; there is no one better to watch when he is truly on song.

As for the suggestion that it was because he felt more West Indian than English and was too laid back because of his Jamaican background, I couldn't disagree more. I found him passionate about representing England. As for motivation, he was desperate to do well in Italy, not solely for his country, but also for himself, as it was no secret that, eventually, he wanted to try his luck in the Italian First Division. This was his great chance on the world's biggest stage but instead of coming back talking about him, everyone came back with the names of Gascoigne, Platt, Walker and Wright on their lips.

I don't know whether Graham Taylor can find the magic ingredient. If anyone can it is him, as he knows John from their days together at Watford, but I don't think Graham could give him any more than I did. I honestly saw him as someone with that extra ability who could actually help us win the World Cup. A shame, there is no doubt about him as a player or as a person but as a truly great international footballer the question mark remains.

PETER BEARDSLEY: SUBSTITUTE

Peter has always been one of my favourites; sharp, quick-witted and very busy – a real team player who worked non-stop for the benefit of those around him.

He came to the fore shortly before the Mexico World Cup and earned his place, knitting together the front scene and the winger. His only fault is that he still doesn't score the goals he should. It isn't as if he is a bad finisher, he is one of the best and he would go into the box on a dribble, but only rarely as the second striker to get the ball. He was always outside the box. We talked about it at length without ever fully resolving it.

But he was great to train with and I am sure he was great to play with. I know that Lineker loved having him alongside. He has a good football brain and talks the game well.

Despite his achievements and his status within the game he remains humble and it is not beneath him to carry the bucket or the skip whether he is in or out of the team, and he is always one of the first to offer himself if any volunteers are called for. It is because of people like Peter Beardsley that I will miss the England job so much.

8

All roads almost led to Rome

SARDINIA/TUNIS
Friday, 1 June

Rest and recuperation were over as the staff and the players said their last farewells to the wives and girlfriends who had joined us in our peaceful beach-side hotel, the Is Morus, for that first week in Sardinia, far from the bustle of the Port of Cagliari, the scene of the battles to come. We had moved our clothes and other bits and pieces a few miles up the road to the even more isolated Is Molas Golf Hotel the night before and left only what we needed for the short trip across to Africa and our warm-up game against Tunisia in Tunis. The ladies were leaving after us on their flight back to Luton Airport and England and they were at the guarded gates of the hotel to wave a last goodbye with the promise they would rejoin us not if but when we reached the semi-finals. There were plenty of half-smiles but no tears. There was the usual warm goodbye from my wife Elsie, wishing me all the good luck in the world and knowing what it meant to me. How supportive she was after all she had been put through again in the past few days. She was off home to Ipswich and the house we planned to keep on while we made a new life in Holland, and then on to the North East to see her sister and mother who were both ill. It had been good to have her by my side instead of worrying about her being besieged at home by reporters looking for more juicy titbits and the exclusive interview.

I felt it was back to business. Tunisia was just 55 minutes away, the right part of the world, with the right temperature of around 82 degrees. The change of scenery would do everyone good, breaking up the month in Sardinia and putting everyone in the mood against a side similar in style to our opening-phase opponents Egypt. That was an important factor, as was the fact that it would sharpen the minds after a week with rather more relaxation and sunbathing than training, well deserved after their long hard season, I might add.

It was a risk, I knew that. We wouldn't be as sharp as we might but we were not going to read too much into it as we wanted to keep things ticking over until the tournament began in earnest. But at the same time we realised that the press would take it seriously, particularly if we slipped up in any way at all.

Our arrival in Africa was uneventful, with the usual interviews and a great deal of local interest in our goalkeeper Peter Shilton. The British ambassador, a nice man, greeted us and joined us for a bit of lunch before we went off to look at the bumpy, hard pitch we were to play on the next day.

The team, with Barnes playing through the middle and the deserving Gascoigne in midfield, was the one I had strongly in mind for the opening game against the Irish and I was confident and relaxed when I went to bed after the traditional lamb kebabs, thinking that we could cast aside the defeat by Uruguay in our last match by getting back to our winning ways with, I thought, a couple of goals to spare.

TUNIS/SARDINIA
Saturday, 2 June

The sun, stronger than it was in Cagliari, shone out of a clear blue sky and after breakfast I was able to lie by the hotel swimming pool with Doctor Crane, going over my notes before the team meeting. I felt I didn't need to motivate them other than to say that they were playing for their World Cup places; they must have known that this was the team I had in mind to open the tournament and it was up to them to convince me that I was thinking along the right lines.

However, we did not make the most auspicious of starts when, just an hour before the kick-off, we found ourselves stranded at the roadside in our coach outside the stadium in the middle of a furious row between our escort and other uniformed men. We had, it seems, taken the wrong road to the stadium. The press members in the coach following behind must have wondered what had happened when they suddenly passed our bus going away from the ground! We sat waiting while the obstinate local police refused to give an inch until a senior official intervened and we were allowed to carry on.

We might have been better off if they had refused to let us in. The game was disappointing, to say the least. We started off well enough. Peter Shilton was a spectator as we forced a couple of well-positioned free-kicks which we wasted horribly while Bryan Robson, of all people, completely mistimed his jump from Gascoigne's free-kick. Had we scored then I believe we would have gone on and scored two or three more.

Instead it was Tunisia, to the delight of their fans, who took the lead after 26 minutes with what I can only call a freak goal as Gazza, on the bumpy pitch, sliced a pass and, from fully 40 yards, Abdelhamid Hergel, all on his own, volleyed the ball over the top of the surprised and helpless Peter Shilton. I could hardly believe it. The only comfort was that it could have happened only on a pitch like this.

It was not too clever. It was a hot, sticky day and the last thing I wanted was for us to be chasing a result. I told them not to panic at half-time, that we were far and away the better team and we were making chances. If we kept playing, the goals would come – I hoped! The quicker the better as far as I was concerned.

But it still didn't go well. Although Barnes and Lineker held the ball up well through the middle, Chris Waddle looked jaded and he and Gary Stevens were not playing well down the right while Steve Hodge was suffering from sunstroke on the left. We were not getting behind their back four at all. We were also experiencing some problems in our defence where Terry Butcher was having problems coping with the pace of their lone attacker. That was giving me food for thought and when he was booked, cutting his head in the same incident, I took the opportunity to bring him off. I didn't see what he had done but I was annoyed after my instructions to cool it. He would be angry and frustrated, but that was his problem. I had other things to do. I put Butcher out of my mind for that moment, thinking I would have words later. Silly prat.

Mark Wright, whom I intended to use against Holland, came on and I also took off the dizzy Hodge, brought on Beardsley and moved Barnes back to the left wing. I also sent on David Platt for Waddle and, with time running out, Steve Bull replaced Gary Lineker. We were facing an embarrassing defeat when Gazza sent Barnes away down the left and a typical cross gave Bully the chance to score yet again. I must say I fancy this boy every time he gets the ball in front of goal – nowhere else, just in that crucial area. I don't plan to start a game with him but he is going to be a more than useful weapon to have coming off the bench when opponents' legs are tiring, a real handful for anyone.

One thing that annoyed me as we celebrated our face-saving 89th-minute equaliser was Gazza making an exhibition of himself celebrating in front of the Tunisian bench. It was hardly Brazil we had scored against in a five-goal thriller, and he was being his usual immature self. He has a lot of talent but he still hasn't grown up; he lets his emotions run away with him. He is still not a seasoned international but I was not displeased with his overall performance. He had worked as hard as anyone on the pitch. He needed a rollocking over his behaviour, however, and I jumped up to pull him away and tell him to get on with the game.

Not that there was much more than seconds left. It was a relief. The result wasn't that important – the top teams were losing to amateurs and all sorts of teams, as so often happens in these last few days before the big ones come along. But some of the things I had seen disturbed me and what had been a straight-forward build-up to the Irish game had changed somewhat. Barnes had looked fluent when he switched to the left and little Peter Beardsley had shown he was well on the way back to fitness after his long spell out with injury, thus offering me my old, experienced front unit of Waddle, Beardsley, Lineker and Barnes.

There was only time to give Terry Butcher a rapid bollocking in front of everyone before we were off to Sardinia, but judging from the questioning of the media we were in for another major roasting in the papers on Sunday and Monday, although nothing compared with what it would have been but for Bully's last-minute equaliser.

On our way back to our new hotel I was able to give the game and my line-up more thought. Gazza had certainly done enough to keep his place even if I reverted to my old line-up, which I had changed, ironically, partly to accommodate the Spurs player and allow him to show me what he could do. I liked his motor and his work-rate in the heat. But I felt let down over the system we had been developing. However, I wasn't going to worry. I would let others do that for me. At least they wouldn't be calling for my head this time as I was going anyway. On the 'plane I could sense that they were ready to pounce; for the sake of selling their papers, for the sake of a headline they will not be backing us. Why do they do it? We are all trying our best to do our jobs and pick up our money on Friday. It's a rotten industry they are in.

Tunisia 1 (Abdelhamid Hergel 26) *England* 1 (Bull 89).
HT: 1–0. Att: 20,000.
Ref: Medjiba (Tunisia).
England: Shilton; Stevens, Butcher (Wright), Walker, Pearce; Waddle (Platt), Gascoigne, Robson, Hodge (Beardsley); Lineker (Bull), Barnes.
Tunisia: Ztouni, Ben Yahia, Hich-ri, Ben Neji, M'Hadbi, Khemiri (Farah), Mahjoubi, Sellimi, Hergal (Dermesh), Tarak, Roussi.

SARDINIA
Sunday, 3 June

Another bad Sunday morning. Most of my problems seem to stem from the media these days and I find myself waiting in dread to see what falsehoods they have been through this time. Not the sports pages – I can take that – but the constant assault and assassination of my personal character. Why don't they just leave me alone? It's not even as if any of it's true. It is rubbish.

An early swim, breakfast and off to Pula for training. I took the team who had played the previous day in light training, a tone-down day to get rid of the lactic acid. We used the ball a lot and it was amusing and enjoyable. Don's working those who didn't play hard. I know that Sunday is the normal day off after a Saturday game, although some psychologists say the players should train on Sunday and rest on Monday. Football is full of theories, habits and superstitions. But does anyone really know? If you won, you did it right. If you lost, you did it wrong. That's the bottom line.

There is no doubt that a win, after the defeat against Uruguay at Wembley, would have been a good confidence booster, but we kept playing and on the whole the team defended well. They kept going until the final whistle, which was why we got a draw out of it.

I used the Butcher incident to stress the need for good behaviour on and off the pitch, pointing out that as an England captain I didn't expect that sort of problem from him and that I certainly didn't expect to see him throw an England shirt on the ground. I asked for his version and he was full of remorse, saying that it had all come from frustration at the way the game was going and the fact that he wasn't playing that well. He said that he had run at the defender because he was holding him at every corner, throw-in and free-kick. I have seen that frustration explode in Butcher before at Ipswich and I warned him that these days television picks up everything, every action.

For the rest, I told them to forget the result in Tunis. All that should concern them was working for the opening match; everything was geared towards the Irish. Again I pointed out that we owed a lot of people for what had happened two years earlier. Tunisia would be forgotten once the World Cup started – incidental, one of those results. I believed that, so it was easy to say it convincingly.

We used the rest of the day to familiarise ourselves with our new headquarters, and some of the lads were quick to take advantage of the adjacent golf course while others made use of the swimming pool.

SARDINIA
Monday, 4 June

I had been told by the press that Terry Butcher had head-butted the defender but neither I nor any of the other players had seen it happen, nor what had caused the cut above Terry's right ear — hardly the place to get a cut with the old Glasgow Kiss! Everyone's attention had been on the free-kick when it happened and it was the linesman who drew the referee's attention to the incident, leading to the booking.

But that morning back home in England the BBC had isolated the frame on film on breakfast television and shown that it was, indeed, head against head. The BBC had dragged the FA into it, asking what action was going to be taken, and, of course, the press had leapt on it.

The FA back home in London had done the right thing. They had said it was my problem and up to me what action I took. There was no directive from Lancaster Gate. As far as I was concerned the referee had handled it and it would be in his report. He didn't see the need to mention it to me at all. I had taken Terry off not because of any head-butt — I didn't even know — but because I needed to give Mark Wright a run as I was planning to play him as a sweeper in the game against Holland. He needed a run while Terry was definitely a little below his best.

But here I was suddenly under pressure from the press asking me what disciplinary action I was going to take. The *Star*, for whom Terry wrote a column, wanted me to send him home. I ask you! You don't shoot yourself in the foot days before a World Cup starts and send home one of three centre backs for something you didn't even see. Barcelona defender Ronald Koeman had stopped an Austrian a couple of days earlier with a rugby tackle. I didn't hear the Dutch screaming for him to be axed from the squad. They might even have congratulated him for saving a certain goal. If we had adopted the same approach against Maradona in Mexico we might have won the World Cup four years earlier — but it is simply not our style.

I just wanted to kill the whole thing as quickly as I could. I had already torn him off a strip and as far as I was concerned the matter was ended, apart from using it to point out to all of the squad what could happen. Maybe it will turn out to be a blessing in disguise. We will probably win the Fair Play Trophy as well as the World Cup. What would they all say then, I wonder?

John Brewer, the physiologist, had arrived at the hotel and set about testing the squad to see how the acclimatisation was going. They had all been tested in England and the results, heartbeat and pulse rate, would be compared. Barnes, Waddle, Robson, Gascoigne, Lineker and Woods were the first in the queue.

Elsie telephoned from home to tell me that there was an illness in the family. My brother Keith had suffered a heart attack, quite a bad one. We had kept it from Mom, telling her that he was in hospital because he was suffering a little high blood pressure, because we were worried what the news might do to her. It was all a bit of a blow. Keith was lucky to survive the ambulance trip, Elsie told me, and he was in intensive care. He was told he needed absolute quiet – fat chance with me for a brother!

But work had to go on and I had a meeting scheduled with FIFA area representative Heinz Maroski. He was another who wanted to talk to me about player behaviour. Didn't anyone look at our disciplinary record? He asked about the arrangements in Sardinia, which were all fine with me. He stayed on for dinner, talking for most of the time. He also gave us a very long form to fill in about our preparations, plans and all the rest. It was a drawn-out affair and I wondered when we were supposed to look after the football.

SARDINIA
Tuesday, 5 June

Sometimes I seem to go from one interview to another. After my usual early-morning dip I had a long session with Desmond Lynam who had flown in specially. It wasn't too much of a problem as we trained on the hotel grounds that morning, giving fitness tests to Steve Hodge, Stuart Pearce and Des Walker before leaving for a hastily arranged game against a Sardinia Select XI. We needed a run-out, but the team we had arranged to play were still heavily involved in their domestic programme with promotion and relegation still in contention.

This suited us better. It was only 75 minutes' drive instead of three hours. Before the game against Uruguay I was asked for permission to perform an anti-hooligan stunt that involved scoring an own goal from the kick-off. I had responded something along the lines of 'at Wembley – you must be joking.' If we had to do it at all this was a much better opportunity and I explained it to the players while a note was passed out to the media. The only problem was that the crowd couldn't hear the announcement and wondered what on earth was going on when we played the ball back from the kick-off for Steve McMahon to score past David Seaman.

Before the game we threw lollipops to the kids and distributed a few other gifts to the locals who had come in their droves. There were no problems. The security was faultless, as it always was, quite fantastic with cars and helicopters – every bit as heavy as it had been in Mexico but much less obtrusive. They did it really well; I even had one of the armed guards delegated to me personally. I was never told officially, but whenever I looked around he was there, I was never out of his sight, yet I didn't even know his name. It was lovely, very reassuring.

They were there again as we scored 10 goals without reply. Webb and Beardsley scored three apiece with Bull (2), Platt and McMahon adding the others.

The most crucial performance from my point of view was that of Peter Beardsley who looked fresh and sharp. He hunted creatively in the first half and after a few words at half-time was very penetrative in the second. He had obviously shone, because all of the questions at the after-match press conference were about him.

Their judgement was correct. I had decided that Peter was going to start against the Irish despite his seven-week lay-off. Steve Hodge, having played so well before we left England, did nothing to change the direction my mind was taking. Bully was useful again and Platt was OK.

The one blot on the landscape was a neck injury to Mark Wright. I didn't plan to play him against the Irish but I felt that after his thigh injury he needed a 90-minute run-out. He didn't get it. I had to pull him out and switch around the defence. I thought to myself: here we go again. He gets these injuries. He had got one in a warm-up game in West Germany two years earlier, and two years before that he broke his leg and missed out on Mexico.

I badly wanted him for the Holland game. What made it

worse was that Paul Parker, back-up for the sweeper role I was going to use Wright in, was nursing a bad ankle, leaving me with only two central defenders.

We were back at the hotel by eight and after dinner we sat around and chatted, desperately wanting the competition to start.

SARDINIA
Wednesday, 6 June

I was now being accompanied on my usual early swim by the Birmingham City director Jack Wiseman. After breakfast I had a technical meeting with Don Howe and Mike Kelly and told them the team that I wanted to play against the Irish. Their reaction was fine. They never interfered unless I specifically asked. If in doubt I would ask what they thought, but in the end would follow my own ideas. It's my job. I'm the manager. It will be me who carries the can if it goes wrong. Not that I think it will.

I was going to play Shilton, of course; Stevens, Walker, Butcher, Pearce across the back; Waddle, Gascoigne, Robson and Barnes in the middle, with Lineker and Beardsley up front. With the exception of Gascoigne, it was largely the team which had carried us through the past two years with only one defeat.

We also arranged the training schedule for the next six days, and talked about the need to work on the back four, free-kicks, freeing the wingers because of the double cover, using Beardsley to let loose Barnes and Lineker to free Waddle in order to by-pass Ray Houghton and Kevin Sheedy. We knew that the Irish were going to hustle and harry us, squeeze us and make life difficult. We were going to have to fight for the scrapings. We talked about how to stop the long ball into our back four: Robson and Gascoigne to drop off and sandwich their front two. All those things we had to start working on if we were going to curb a team with a very good record behind them.

It led to a lively morning's training in Pula with sharp work, good finishing in the box and pressure work on Pearce and Walker in the middle of a hail and rain storm. No wonder the islanders liked us. They had enjoyed little or no rain for two years until we arrived.

John Brewer tested Steven, Stevens, Butcher, Dorigo, Beardsley and Platt while the physio team looked after Peter Shilton, Mark Wright, Paul Parker and Chris Woods who had strained his back. I was sure Shilts was going to be fine but it was uncomfortable all the same to be down to one fit goalkeeper and two fit central defenders.

After lunch we opened the hotel to television crews and reporters from around the world. One of them was my old Fulham team-mate Graham Leggat who was working for Canadian television. The Italian press flooded in to talk to our players. The seniors Robson, Walker, Butcher, Barnes and Pearce were tremendous, making themselves available for two hours.

We also watched the Derby, courtesy of ITV, direct from England and at tea-time I at last managed to squeeze in nine holes of golf with Jack Wiseman. The players were also allowed nine holes to practise for a tournament arranged by Wilsons the next day. While we were playing we came across Gazza driving one of the golf carts like a dodgem – no shirt, shorts rolled right up to the top of his thighs. Jack chased after him and told him to make himself respectable and to behave properly on a golf course. At the next hole Gazza came over and apologised and the incident was forgotten with smiles all round. He is a very likeable chap is young Paul; all the lads like having him around and he has fitted in really well. He is full of humour, full of fun – but sometimes he doesn't know when to stop. He has a nice personality but he still has to learn that life isn't a continual round of pleasure and fun. I was pleased that he had apologised. That went a long way and showed that, at least, he was maturing and taking notice of the senior players around him.

They were also taking notice of him. Earlier that day, with our walking wounded hobbling around the hotel, he had suddenly emerged from his room crying out for our physiotherapist Fred Street. Everyone turned to look and see what was the matter, and there he was bandaged up like a mummy, left arm in a splint, one eye covered, head, calf, thigh, arm, ribs all swathed in what turned out to be toilet paper. Everyone was in stitches as he lurched towards the pool, eventually tumbling in head first and emerging covered in soggy toilet paper. But his mood is good, his form promising and he could, if things go for him, make an impact on this World Cup.

SARDINIA
Thursday, 7 June

What a beautiful day! This was the sort of weather we had expected all the time – bright, clear blue skies and already warm at eight o'clock in the morning. It was a good job I was up early, for the 'phone was soon jangling. This time it was Steve Wicks, the former Chelsea player now working for the team's agents First Artist Management, wanting *Bryan* Robson. How often had that happened over the past eight years, and how often had Bryan been woken prematurely by someone chasing me? Still, it wouldn't be for much longer – there is no Robson at PSV other than me!

John Brewer was busy again with his tests, this time putting Webb, Seaman, Bull and McMahon through their paces. In training I concentrated on work with my proposed team, partly showing my hand but without telling them. One of the problems with 22 players on a long trip is that every one of them believes they deserve to be selected and expect to be. It would be nice to let them know early, but there are going to be 11 who feel let down and they can affect everyone. It is something I have had to wrestle with for eight years and there is no easy answer. I have tried every way.

We worked at and talked about the things we would do against the Irish with the press and television cameras peering through the gaps in the gates around the ground. The Irish TV crew had arrived and they couldn't believe how many press-men were waiting to see England, compared with their own camp. They asked me how I coped. Somewhat surprised, I countered: 'Isn't Jack having the same problems?'

'No,' they laughed. 'Just the usual press and six or seven extras.'

To round off the session we let in a lot of local children, some of them handicapped, giving them souvenirs, photos and the usual autographs.

The afternoon was spent at the golf tournament with Wilsons. That was a great day with some fine golf played. I did well enough with 21 points, but that wasn't good enough to get a prize. That went to Steve McMahon, a good player, who won in a play-off over the short water hole. He also won the putting prize but the driving prize went to non-golfer John Barnes. No one could believe it as he crashed the ball a staggering 315 yards after just an hour's practice. Everyone was so amazed that they measured it out and a plaque was going to be made to mark the event. The Wilsons pro was hitting the ball only 260–270 yards. Most upset was Tony Dorigo who struck a massive 300-yard drive and still couldn't claim the prize.

Barnes is just a natural sportsman and his effort made the day notable. Everyone was relaxed and I thought nine holes were just about right. So close to the game, a two-day event would have been too tiring. We finished it off with a glass of wine or beer and I set off for my latest round of interviews, met John Brewer to discuss the physiological results and then attended a security meeting. Graham Kelly arrived but there was little time to chat, just a quick hello.

SARDINIA
Friday, 8 June

At last the waiting was over. Not for us, unfortunately, but the World Cup was actually going to begin that day with the holders Argentina facing the outsiders Cameroon in Milan. Nevertheless, much of the talk in the hotel as we enjoyed a rare day off was over the sensational news from England that Swindon had been relegated, instead of promoted, because of illegal payments.

I was much more concerned with what was going on in Italy, and while it was a relief that it was all getting under way it was also somewhat poignant as it crossed my mind that, whatever happened, this was my last World Cup. There is nothing quite like it. There is so much effort to qualify that you have to come out here to try to win it, vie with the very best. It is worth every nightmare, every hassle, every problem just to be here and to be involved in the crucial Finals. The problems are all part of it. This is what I gave up the quiet life with Ipswich for – the pinnacle, the apex – and it comes to only a few people.

Not a day had gone by in the past four years when I hadn't thought or wondered what lay in store this time. I thought we had the talent to go all the way but I had learned that you get to the last eight and after that who knows, because from then on everyone thinks they can win it and all of them are capable.

There were no regrets. No one had been left behind who should have been here. England were represented by the best 22 players available at that time. I was convinced I had the right squad, with playing depth. There were no serious injury doubts and I felt I had finally got rid of that, having suffered my share of bad luck in that department in the past. We deserved a change of luck this time.

I had plenty of time to ruminate as I had a swim, took some sun, had a snooze, read a little and had a golf lesson with the local professional. The players were able to knock a few balls around, but no proper golf, just a quiet day (if that is possible with Gazza around).

It wasn't a completely free day for me. There was a noon press conference at the golf club, well away from the players. One of the Italian journalists asked why the English were so critical of their team. I told him that he had asked the wrong person and to ask the press. There was no response forthcoming.

The opening ceremony was at 5 p.m. and the game with Cameroon kicked off an hour later. We all watched it together and you could feel the atmosphere become charged as we witnessed one of the great World Cup upsets in history as the African outsiders, with two men sent off, beat Diego Maradona and reigning champions Argentina. Cameroon were fit, strong and fast on the break and hadn't come to Italy to make up the numbers. Even when they had two sent off they were not afraid to attack. Most would have held on to the lead given them by the salmon-like leap of Omam Biyik and the poor dive of Pumpido, but not them – they flew into the attack.

French referee Michel Vautrot was guilty of over-reaction for the first sending-off but dead right for the second. We don't tackle like that and don't expect other people to. What a way it was to start a World Cup. Cameroon had handled Maradona better than we had done four years earlier in Mexico. He hardly had a kick. It was all a salutary lesson that no one could be taken lightly in this tournament.

After dinner I had a security meeting with my own staff. I

didn't mistrust players but I wanted them to stay on the compound and let us know whenever they were going out. The news vultures had gathered and were looking for a story to justify their presence. I wanted to make sure no one did anything daft that we might regret. I stressed that I needed to know every movement. I did not want to take any chances.

John Brewer talked to the players about the tests and explained what they were about. He was encouraged by their response, even more so when a few sought him out privately to ask for more information. It is encouraging when you get this sort of reaction. I suspect that eight years ago Emlyn Hughes and his crowd would probably not have been interested; they would have been more concerned with getting on with their game of cards. The results were encouraging, better than before the Brazil game. Acclimatisation had gone well. No one had put on a pound, not even Gazza, who was very good with his diet.

The light entertainment that night was the second half of the game between Northern Ireland and the Republic. I had bought the video with me especially for that moment. Pass me the aspirins — I got a headache just watching those balls pumped into the area.

I also broke the team news to the players that night. I could see Neil Webb was disappointed after all the work he had put in to get fit for the World Cup, having been a regular before that. Steve Hodge, too, had looked like making it before we came out. I understood, but there was no room for sentiment. They were the best 22 but they couldn't all play. I asked them to keep the team to themselves.

The disappointment, I must stress, was all down to football, nothing else. It is often suggested that the modern player is overpaid and greedy, but in all my time with England they accepted what was offered without murmur. I am sure they would have played for nothing if asked.

But all would benefit financially. The senior players have always been very generous in that respect, insisting that the bonuses should be spread evenly through the entire squad. Because of their attitude I felt obligated to get them the best deal possible, and this time the FA were slow coming forward and not at all generous at first. I had to go back and say: for Pete's sake let's get it clearly defined and right before we get out there so that no one is in any doubt. I got what I wanted for them but it still did not compare with some of the fabulous bonuses reported for other teams, particularly the Italians who were talking about a quarter of a million pounds each if they won the Cup. The mind boggles.

SARDINIA
Saturday, 9 June

I slept in even though I was aware that I had made the news pages again next day. Phone calls from home told me that reporters had tried to see my brother in hospital, and they had even been to see my mom who didn't know until then that Keith had suffered his heart attack. I had told no one. But there it was splashed across the front page. I was staggered. Was it really that important? I felt that it was an intrusion into family affairs which had nothing to do with football. I suppose I should be used to it, but I am not. I have learned to look after myself but the family shouldn't be involved in that way.

I sat by the golf course and watched Birmingham City in the shape of Jack Wiseman and Mike Kelly take on West Bromwich Albion through Don Howe and Bert Millichip. I envied them. I was stuck with yet another press conference, this time for the Sunday newspapers, where we talked about Cameroon, relating the analysis to Egypt whom I knew to be a good side, and we also discussed the problems such strict refereeing might throw up.

I had lunch with Graham Kelly and couldn't resist asking how the negotiations were going to secure Graham Taylor as my replacement. I had read that Doug Ellis was doing daft things about compensation and suggested that once the talks were finished the FA might like to invite Graham Taylor out to join us. I wouldn't have minded him being around for two or three days to observe what was going on, but not to get involved – this was my World Cup and I was jealous about it. Kelly seemed delighted but added that Villa were asking for a great deal of money for a manager they took for nothing from Watford. The FA were in no hurry. They weren't going to panic over any delay. They were prepared to wait it out. Sensible. Mr Ellis couldn't be seen to be denying England a manager.

I followed this with a technical meeting with Don Howe and Mike Kelly and then, booted and suited, we went into Cagliari for a civic reception with the Lord Mayor — all very dignified, all very proper. We also picked up our accreditation at the press centre, a two-hour job, and finished with our allotted 50 minutes on the pitch.

The lights were good, the pitch not bad, although the penalty spots were a bit low. We got our penalty-taker Gary Lineker to try them out and he had problems. Maybe we were being a bit ambitious, having been awarded only two penalties in my eight years in charge. Still, who knows how our luck will break?

We used our time well with a 9 v. 9 game. Crossing for the 'keepers to get used to the lights, shooting and set plays to get used to the weight of the light ball.

The tournament was now well under way with Italy beating Austria, Colombia beating the Emirates and, surprise, surprise, Romania toppling the Soviet Union.

SARDINIA
Sunday, 10 June

My daily dip had become something of a ritual and I had time to indulge before doing a live TV AM interview with Geoff Clarke from the hotel about my hopes and fears, and a promised chat with author Peter Davies.

The Irish influence took over our training. We knew what Jack's side would try to do. They would attempt to wear us down, try to steamroller us. We hurled in long throws, free-kicks, things we would have to combat in the actual game, and then tried to get the ball down to play our own brand of football. If you don't win the first ball, make sure you win the second ball, getting to it before any build-up. No matter how much you want to play you can't stop them kicking the ball when they have it, and this is what is going to come at you thick and fast. All you can do is compete, build your confidence and resort to different techniques yourself. I was confident we could do it. Peter Beardsley was the key. He could make us tick and bring our ball-players into the action.

Fitness was going to be important and our tests showed just how fit we were. I told them the match was going to be played at a frantic pace but we would not sag because of our conditioning, and this might be the period when we won the game.

We also discussed at length the strict refereeing and its implications, coupled with the stern instructions from me, the Minister of Sport and the Football Association. Refereeing was clearly going to be a factor of the tournament. FIFA President Joao Havelange had put the wind up the officials and whatever over-reaction there was from them, FIFA were going to have to back them.

There was no excuse. We had it all there in black and white in our instructions and we had discussed it at length in the World Cup Workshop in Zurich before the competition – not just the usual things but tucking shirts in shorts, pads in, stockings up, standing 10 metres from the ball. These were all things that could cause a caution and once you had your name taken you were forced to play within yourself. After Butcher's stupid situation in Tunis I had to spell it out and ask them if they were clear. It was going to be trial by TV and we were not going to get away with anything, particularly with our supporters and their reputation.

Why not clean up the game? Let the footballers play football. I am all for that. Of all the things I hate most the worst is the use of the elbow to the opponent's head. It is dangerous, horrible. It breaks jaws and splits eyebrows. That is what I call violent play, as dangerous as the over-the-top tackle. Send them off. That is the only way to stop it. If one of mine resorts to that sort of tactic he will be off anyway.

You could tell the game was getting close. There was a bustle about the place. All sorts of people were arriving from home: Peter Swales, Gordon Taylor, Denis Howell, Colin Moynihan's contingent, my brother Tom and son Mark should have been among them but our travel representative Brian Scott, who had gone to meet them, rang me from Cagliari airport to tell me that not only had they not arrived but their flight was not even in the airport computer as existing. I was in a flap and even rang Elsie to make sure they had the details right. The flight eventually arrived although no one at the airport seemed to know anything about it. Very strange.

The United States were brought down to size with a 5–1 pounding by the Czechs in the afternoon, and in the evening West Germany were outstanding in their 4–1 win over the talented Yugoslavs, while Brazil looked good in their 2–1 win over Sweden.

But it was the Germans who caught the attention. Don Howe and Mike Kelly agreed. Lothar Matthaus looked in a different world to the rest and Beckenbauer's team instantly became our favourites and the team to avoid – a strong reason not to finish third behind Holland and Ireland in our group.

SARDINIA
Monday, 11 June

The first call of the day was Elsie to wish me well and ask if Mark had arrived safely.

Training that morning was voluntary but 16 wanted to go and they trained hard and well. We try to honour the wishes of players who have their own routines on match day. Gary Lineker doesn't like training on match day and neither does his room-mate Peter Shilton, while both John Barnes and Chris Waddle preferred not to this time and I personally pulled Mark Wright to one side and told him to keep away. I didn't want to risk him, and I told him why. However we played against the Irish, whatever the result, he was in against the Dutch. Bryan Robson had a fitness test on his injured heel, doing a few sprints under the eagle eye of Fred Street, but there was never a doubt in my mind about him playing.

The morning had sped past and we all went off after lunch for a snooze with no obvious feelings of nerves among the players. The place was deserted, the silence punctuated only by the distant, muted noise of Steve Bull, unable to sleep as usual, watching one of his adventure videos.

In the afternoon we watched another shock result as Scotland lost to Costa Rica. There was no gloating from me. I felt sorry for them. It was our football on show and at risk and Scotland losing knocked the British game. I felt sorry for manager Andy Roxburgh, too. I knew what he would suffer and I could be in the same boat five hours later. But it has to be said – they didn't play well.

Before we set off I did a live interview for *Saint and Greavsie*. They tried to get me to confirm the team, asking whether I was going to play Bully. I told them I would play the team who could handle the match. I hoped I was right.

We set off in ample time – too much so, in fact. Despite our being 40 miles or so from the ground the road to Cagliari had been closed to all but official traffic and we sped through, arriving two hours before the kick-off. Far too early, leaving a lot of time to kill. The Irish had been misled, too, and it was all a bit nervy.

I was a little apprehensive but I felt that we could beat them. We had waited a long time for this chance, everyone was fit and the team, extraordinarily similar to the one which had lost 1–0 to Eire two years earlier in the European Championship, was extremely motivated. There were no apparent nerves in the dressing room. Everything looked normal. The question nagging me was whether Peter Beardsley would have his old sharpness back. He had looked good in training and in our warm-up games, but this was different.

Where was the hot, balmy night we had all planned for? When we got out on to the pitch the temperature plummeted, lightning flashed against black clouds in the background and a gale blew. It was more like home in November than Italy in the summer. We made a good start against the wind. Just what we wanted. Chris Waddle played a deceptive, long, curling ball into their area and Gary Lineker took his chance superbly, forcing the ball over the line. Coming after only eight minutes that should have settled any nerves that were around and it clearly rocked Jack and his boys. I felt then that we could build on that and if we were still in front at the break we could go on and win it well with the powerful wind at our backs.

It was not a pretty sight as we were forced to battle against the elements and the anticipated Irish tactics, but it looked increasingly as though we could cope as we defended well with Shilton, making his record-equalling 119th appearance, using his box to great effect, handling around the extreme edges. He was brave, too. They aimed their long throws straight at him and sent Cascarino and Aldridge charging in. Any cowardice or indecision on his part would have been fatal. His only problem lay in his kicking which, against the wind, was allowing the Irish to come straight back at us again.

We were not getting the ball down on to the ground the way I had hoped and when we did we were panicking and knocking it off first time. Under those circumstances you expect the defenders to do it, but not the quality forwards we had on display. I expected more and hoped to get more in the second half, especially from Waddle and Barnes.

Half-time stretched to the usual 15 minutes and during that time the threatened storm swept in, bringing down the temperature even further and killing the wind. The stadium flags went limp and our advantage disappeared. The standard didn't improve a lot and we didn't create much in the second half, while the Irish created even less. We quelled their aerial onslaught and we were never outrun in midfield. I was confident they wouldn't score against us and I wasn't worried how the match looked as long as we won it. We could play the pretty stuff later, once we had got off to a good start.

We should have wrapped it up when Chris Waddle was clearly upended by Kevin Moran for as clear a penalty as you could ever wish to see. I couldn't believe it when the West German referee Aron Schmidhuber waved play on, saying Chris had dived. Our luck with penalties hadn't changed after all, even though slow-motion television replays later that night confirmed, frame by frame, that there was not the slightest doubt.

Had we gone two up then it would have been all over and the result would have dominated rather than the quality of what I have to admit was an awful game to watch, all blood and guts and very little football. But while the rest of the world might have been shocked, I always knew it was going to be like this and I was getting pleasure out of winning and watching the clock tick away as Jack became more and more irate in the dug-out on the other side of the half-way line, with no one creative enough to open us out.

He could obviously see this himself for he brought off Aldridge, who left his mark with a wicked late tackle *off* the pitch on Des Walker, and instead of bringing on Niall Quinn he added to his midfield with McLoughlin of Swindon. That left Butcher on Cascarino, Walker spare and McLoughlin where he likes it best, in midfield free to run from deep positions. I decided to stiffen it up by bringing on Steve McMahon, who had been so impressive in the build-up to the competition, and took off Beardsley who had simply not done the job we hoped. But if everyone did their job now for the last 20 minutes, we would win 1–0. I would be a wizard if it came off and a fool if I failed.

Macca is a good defender and can shore things up. Those were his instructions – shadow their number 21 and make sure you tighten the game. Sadly he made a personal error within minutes of arriving on the scene. At Liverpool he would have whacked the ball away but I was telling him to get the ball down and play it. It's sod's law. He tried to get the ball out to Waddle, miscontrolled it and it fell to the one fellow, Kevin Sheedy, who could take advantage from that position with a cross shot. How often have we seen him do that for Everton? It doesn't matter that McLoughlin was standing in an offside position nor that the ball dipped late under Shilton's arms. It was a goal and a precious point had been snatched from our grasp 16 minutes from time.

I swallowed my disappointment and shook a delighted Jack Charlton's hand. He had seen his team get out of prison and he said that we could both go through now. I didn't see him again that night.

The dressing room was very flat. Macca had gone. He was sick. Not only had he given the ball away, he had also got himself booked. We were all disappointed not to get the two points. I would have liked to say a few words to my players but there was no time. FIFA had laid down strict rules about talking to the press and I was hustled away.

We had to wait for Gazza to provide the urine sample for a dope test and by the time we got back to our hotel it was the early hours of the morning. I wasn't going to give lectures at that time so I just reminded the players that the Irish would be jumping for joy because they had a point – the same as us. They were convinced they were on their way; so should we be. Two more points from the remaining two games and we would qualify. It was crucial that we ended the night on a positive note and not on how poorly we had played.

England 1 (Lineker 8) *Rep. of Ireland* 1 (Sheedy 73)
HT: 1–0. Att: 35,238.
Ref: Schmidhuber (West Germany).
England: Shilton; Stevens, Butcher, Walker, Pearce; Waddle, Gascoigne, Robson, Barnes; Beardsley (McMahon), Lineker (Bull).
Rep. of Ireland: Bonner; Morris, McCarthy, McGrath, Moran, Staunton; Houghton, Sheedy, Townsend; Aldridge (McLoughlin), Cascarino.

SARDINIA/SICILY
Tuesday, 12 June

It was 2.15 a.m. by the time we finally arrived back at our hotel – too late to talk. I was due for an early start later that morning at a press conference in the luxuriously appointed Forte Village down the road where most of our press contingent were staying. They had their own magnificent press centre where I had arranged to meet them. Before we left I watched the Waddle 'penalty' again along with Don Howe on a video given to us by the BBC and was more convinced than ever.

It cut no ice with the world's press who had gathered to interrogate me, especially the English pressmen who were sharpening their talons as I walked in. It was clearly going to be a difficult morning, a David Miller type morning. The *Times* correspondent wanted to talk about the shape of football, not really about the match just gone nor the one coming up. I was taken by surprise by the tone of the questioning.

I couldn't understand why it was all so heavy after one match. After all, we hadn't even lost it. These were the sort of questions I could have expected after losing three games and going out like we had in West Germany. This time they were being too pessimistic, all too hasty. We had been involved only in the opening skirmish, not the war, and we were a whole lot better off than some of the other teams, like the Scots, Argentina and the Soviet Union, who had lost to supposedly vastly inferior teams.

I had heard it all before, as recently in fact as after the goalless draw in Poland that saw us through to the Finals. It was the old war cry and Gianluca Vialli, the Italian striker, had been quoted in at least one English newspaper saying that England were old-fashioned, stereotyped and easy to read, Vialli actually apologised to me before we played Italy at Wembley days later, claiming that he had said none of that. If he had he must have wished he hadn't by the end of the evening after a brilliant English display when Chris Waddle turned Maldini inside out.

I tried to tell them that they were being too hasty and not to get despondent because of one match. I don't play the long-ball game; I never have and none of my teams has. The game just happened that way. If we had not shown the spirit and the will to fight we might not have had that point.

The tenor of the questioning left me stunned. Miller asked: 'Should you go round telling managers to get some conformity?' Imagine me trying to tell Kenny Dalglish, George Graham or Brian Clough how they should play! How pathetic. Every manager will play how he wants, with the players he has available – even Jack Charlton! I still think I managed to be coherent in my responses but I would have liked to walk away. Maybe I should have done exactly that. But I was honouring an agreement that I would meet the press the day after the game to talk about the Irish match. Here I was defending our football. I was under attack. I survived it and came through, having put over my own point of view. Those guys have hours to think up their questions. I have five seconds to form an answer. You can look a complete numbskull. You can emerge with distinction or come out a buffoon. It means being a man of the world in football terms.

A small group of us left for Cagliari airport straight after the conference to catch a private jet to the Sicilian capital of Palermo to watch the other two teams in our group, European Champions Holland and outsiders Egypt. I had seen a lot of both and I told Ron Atkinson, who was doing television work for the game, that Egypt were not mugs and had half a dozen top-class players but I didn't really think they could handle Holland. They did, deservedly drawing 1–1, and with a little luck they could have won.

While our game was ugly, not at all good to watch, this was excellent. The question I had to ask myself was whether the

Egyptians had played above themselves or were Holland 10 degrees under. In truth it was probably a little of both.

As the Dutch were our next opponents they were occupying much of my attention. They had been in my thoughts for a long time, ever since the draw in Rome, and after conceding five goals in two games against them I had long since decided to deploy a sweeper for the first time in my international managing career – but I couldn't finalise the line-up until I was sure of the fitness of Parker and Wright.

Oddly, I thought very little about PSV even though some of my new players were out there performing. England dominated. They were all that mattered at that time, as I tried to explain to the persistent Dutch journalists who wanted to talk to me. I was simply not ready.

When substitute Wim Kieft scored after 58 minutes I thought that was it. I didn't think Egypt had the talent or the character to come back, despite the outstanding way they had played. They did. They equalised through a penalty from Abdel–Ghani eight minutes from the end and could have gone on and won it.

But Holland had finished quite strongly, with Kieft on for the disappointing Vanenburg while Witschge had taken over from Erwin Koeman. I thought that they would start with that team against us and began my planning accordingly. I had gone to see them play in order to pick my team, and it confirmed that van Basten needed to slip Walker only once and he would score. The presence of Wright would tighten it all up. It was a worthwhile trip but I was worried that we might feel the Dutch backlash, that they would get their form back against us as they had two years earlier. We were going to have to provoke them, fight them with an even bigger passion.

I also made up my mind to play young Paul Parker because, with Wright alongside, he could get up the line better than Gary Stevens. All this was going through my brain as we flew back to Sardinia, arriving back at 3.20 a.m. totally whacked; I decided to have a lie-in – until 8.30!

SARDINIA
Wednesday, 13 June

Elsie telephoned as the alarm went off, asking if I was OK and coping. I was a little baffled. Was there something else in the papers? There was. Elsie told me that both poor Macca and I had suffered a terrible mauling. The *Sun* had even suggested on their front page that we should all be sent home. If every country had taken that attitude there wouldn't have been a competition left. It was all so reckless, so impatient. I just hoped that we were going to make them eat their words. I asked Elsie what she was doing reading the papers, but she had only seen the headlines on breakfast television. We both had a good laugh. I must be getting used to the pounding.

I was back with the players and it was no use pussyfooting. It had been a solid performance through the team to the forwards. Then it broke down: no football, no passing moves. Peter Beardsley wasn't able to hold the ball up as we had hoped he would, while Gary Lineker had no sort of service. Wingers Chris Waddle and John Barnes worked as hard as anyone but were never able to get going. We defended too much. We were also timid. Some even looked a little nervous and Stuart Pearce admitted that he was.

'Why?' I asked.

'Because it was the World Cup,' he answered.

'That's why I have given you 20 games so that you wouldn't be nervous when we came to the World Cup,' I said.

Some complained that the pitch was too tight, others said it was too slippery. Footballers always seem to find excuses. I suppose I did when I played.

Having cleared the air, we trained well. Spirits were lifted. It helped us get out of our misery. We got our heads up, and even the press conference went better. We went back to the hotel for lunch with the plan to return to Is Morus on the beach for a little sun and relaxation, followed by dinner and a promised concert by the colourful and extrovert concert violinist and rabid Aston Villa supporter Nigel Kennedy. But before we left Peter Shilton came up and asked, quite seriously, if we could delay our departure on the two- or three-mile trip for 15 minutes. I didn't mind, but I was intrigued and asked why. Peter replied: 'I have a horse running at three and I have been waiting for nine months for it to go. I want to get a bet on.' Peter didn't recommend that we follow him. Good job. It finished third. I hoped that wasn't an omen for where we would finish in our group!

The afternoon presented a lovely change of scenery and we all relaxed – all, that is, except Bryan Robson, whom we kept away because of his niggling injury problems, and Paul Parker, who had not been sleeping well. They were to join us for dinner.

I was looking forward to listening to Nigel Kennedy and his pop star girlfriend Brix play their instruments, but the whole evening and almost the whole World Cup was wrecked by a telephone call. It was an Italian-speaking English liaison officer named Jane Nottage who told me that the *Sun* was going to run a story next Monday saying that several of our players had misbehaved and taken to bed one of the Italia '90 hostesses who had until recently worked at our hotel.

'What,' I said, '*seven* of our players?'

'No,' said Jane. 'Several. I think three.'

'Who? Where? When?' I demanded, adding, 'I don't believe you.'

'It's hurting me to tell you,' she answered. 'It seems to be right. I felt I had to tell you and warn you.'

'All I can do is investigate,' I said. 'I will ring you back.'

John Jackson from the *Daily Mirror* was next to ring, asking to speak to Glen Kirton and repeating the story. I had thought about it and decided I didn't believe it. The players were not that stupid, knowing the consequences of any slip with so many newshounds around. The superb day and evening had been wrecked. I scarcely heard the special act that Nigel and Brix had put together for our delighted players.

We had planned to eat early so that we could return to watch Argentina play the Soviet Union, but as the boys settled down I switched off the television and told them exactly what had been said and asked for some very honest and forthright answers. It was no use anyone saying 'no' if it was 'yes', because it would come out eventually. I told them: 'If any of you answer "yes" we will do our best to protect you – if it is "no" we will know what to do. This whole thing is too big for anyone to tell a lie.'

I watched their faces as I talked to them and the look of surprise, horror and finally anger convinced me that they were blameless despite the fact that Jane had told me that £20,000 had been paid to the hostess to name the players involved. They were seething but the atmosphere was lightened when one, who shall remain nameless in case his wife gets the wrong idea, asked in a plaintive voice: 'If there was a gang bang why wasn't I invited? That isn't fair, boss.'

Bryan Robson asked if names had been named, adding that if they printed any of it there would be a lot of money to be made in court. But waiting for a court case is a long process and the publicity would wreck the players' and probably the team's World Cup. What we had to do was stop it before it was printed. The initial shock had turned to relief, so sure was I that nothing had happened, and as the story was not going to be carried until Monday we had plenty of time to slap in an injunction and kill it off.

SARDINIA
Thursday, 14 June

The pleasure of the morning swim and breakfast with Don Howe, Jack Wiseman and Mike Kelly was abruptly ended when Glen Kirton telephoned from the airport to tell me that the *Daily Mirror* had run the story on its front page. I was seething and immediately called the players together to make doubly certain we were on solid ground. They confirmed in the strongest fashion that no one was involved. Most didn't even know the hostess, a pleasant but unremarkable girl. I knew that the cork had come out of the bottle and that now the others would follow it up.

The players were so sick that they came to me and said that they didn't want to be on the same field as the press. It was a private session anyway and I agreed that they could be on the coach and on their way back to the hotel before the media were let in.

I gave them the first inkling that they would be playing with a sweeper against the Dutch in training that morning. It shocked them. It had never been discussed. The closest I had got was to tell them earlier that however we played against the Irish it was a squad game and changes were certain at some time or another. With so much on their minds they took it in well, playing and then talking about it. It seemed as if it was something they were keen to get their teeth into.

The players made their silent protest and left me to handle the hundreds of pressmen who streamed in when we opened the gates. It was a lot of hassle and needless worry when I needed a clear head just two days away from a crucial game against Holland, one of the tournament favourites. The denials were coming in thick and fast, with some of the journalists turning on the ones who had helped fabricate the story. The poor girl had denied everything and had refused the *Sun*'s offer. She was suffering terrible humiliation in that part of the world, where morals are still of the old-fashioned variety.

At least I was able to talk football with the genuine writers who wanted nothing to do with a story which had started with one of their own kind in a hotel bar as a joke. Some joke. Shilton was the main topic of conversation with the football writers as he was about to break Pat Jennings' record with his 120th international appearance, despite the fact that some South Korean midfield player had claimed more.

But the hostess story would not go away. We had a team discussion that night but it was constantly interrupted by worried wives of players ringing up to ask what was going on. Who could blame them? Seaman, Robson and Barnes were all called away one after another. The press had been bothering their wives at home for their reactions. In order to get their full and undivided concentration, I had to block all calls.

In the middle of all these goings-on David Seaman, who had hurt his thumb in training, had the X-rays which showed a fracture. That was him out and we were immediately on to FIFA asking for permission to replace him with Dave Beasant. Poor Seaman. He was shattered, but Beasant rang back ready, willing and able to fly out at a moment's notice. How lucky we were to have four such talented goalkeepers on call.

We weren't the only ones. Argentina had lost Pumpido the night before with a broken leg, but their hopes had been kept alive by a somewhat fortunate win against the Soviet Union.

It was hard to concentrate on what was going on elsewhere, but Spain and Uruguay had shared the first goalless draw in Udine, Italy had squeezed a 1–0 win over the USA, Cameroon had followed up their win against Argentina by beating the fancied Romanians, and Yugoslavia had beaten Colombia 1–0.

SARDINIA
Friday, 15 June

I had mentally rubber-stamped the decisions I had taken earlier. All I needed now was to be sure all of those I wanted to play were fully fit. There was Parker with his dodgy ankle; Butcher with his sore knee; Robson with his bad toe (can he get his foot in his boot – the nail lifted against the Irish, it bled and was ragged and sore, with Fred saying after the game that it needed 10 days' rest?); Lineker also with a bad toe; Wright with a cricked neck.

We worked hard on our new system, mainly tactical rather than physical – where players should be in relation to the expected Dutch front three of Kieft, Gullit and van Basten. I tried to keep the whole thing secret because I had never before played a sweeper in eight years and I assumed it would take Dutch manager Leo Beenhakker by surprise. The only way he would know would be if we leaked it or if one of those cameras poking through the gaps in the fence picked it up.

There was a massive press conference after the session, the biggest yet; Dutch, Italian, English – they came from everywhere. Among the players Shilton was the man they all wanted to talk to about his historic record which would beat Pat Jennings' 119 caps.

I tried to steer them clear of discussions on hostesses and concentrated on the Holland game. The *Mirror* had attacked me in a leader column for supporting my players, but then, I knew they (or someone else) would because I didn't stand back or duck the issue. I took the responsibility on behalf of the players and I got attacked again. They said that I was a bad, inadequate manager. This after two jobs in 21 years! I was being attacked simply because I told the world that their story was untrue. But you cannot beat them. They always have next day's paper to come back at you. I told Glen Kirton it would happen and, unfortunately, I was right again. I came out of the whole affair paying for it.

One thing was for sure – when they heard my team line-up I would pay for it again if it all went wrong. I couldn't guarantee anything. I had set up my tactics but a trip, a penalty, another

personal error could mean a 0–1 defeat and I would be to blame, just as I had been at fault in West Germany even though few questioned the line-up before we began.

I asked Don and Mike what they thought. They said they were glad it was me and not them. They were totally supportive, saying, 'We are right beside you. You have our backing.' But I was confident. I thought Butcher, Walker, Wright, Parker and Pearce would defend Shilton's goal. Robson looked a little better and with Gazza's growing maturity I couldn't see us losing. Another draw would do, leaving us to beat Egypt to make sure of our place in the second phase.

The team knew the line-up and they seemed pleased. We had a long team meeting that afternoon. We looked at Holland v. Egypt to study set plays, and our own poor free-kicks and corners from the Tunisia game. We also looked at the Dutch defensive strategy.

FIFA told us that we could replace Seaman after seeing his X-ray plates. Beasant could come. Seaman wanted to stay but we had to be firm and tell him he could come back out for the semi-final and final. Touch wood. I told him personally and he was disappointed; he had wanted to stay with us. A superb player for the squad.

In the evening West Germany looked as good as ever as they destroyed the Emirates 5–1, while the Czechs beat the disappointing Austrians. It was beginning to sort itself out.

SARDINIA
Saturday, 16 June

I was into a routine. A swim with Jack Wiseman before breakfast and a welcome phone call from Elsie to wish me luck at the start of the day. Another interview with Des Lynam on my hopes and fears. He also tried to prise the team from me. I kept quiet, but somehow it had already leaked back home through some devious means.

I was worried about Butcher. I made him train to convince me that his knee was better. There was still a lingering doubt over Parker and I wasn't going to gamble with two of them, not after my past experiences. It would have been suicide with the new line-up as well.

I still fancied us but I was under no illusions. The Dutch were great in 1988 and were still very good with some of the world's outstanding players, and if we beat them it would be a magnificant performance. I was taking the biggest gamble of my international career. The fact that I was going to leave anyway, whatever happened, may have helped in some way but I don't think it influenced the main decision because I had made up my mind so far in advance for this one. Still, maybe I was a little more relaxed than I would have been and that can only help.

I did a live interview with Jimmy Greaves at half-time in the Brazil–Costa Rica game, which the Brazilians eventually won without looking at all convincing. I had a quiet afternoon after that – reading, sitting in the sun, snoozing. It was very peaceful. Not a sound. All the players were in bed and it was like a graveyard. Oops! That's the wrong word to use. It's a funny old time just before a big match – I suppose a bit like the troops just before a big battle, except we were not putting our lives on the line. But it is a marvellous moment and I am going to miss it in many ways.

We weren't going to make the same mistake that we had made the previous time. We left at 6.45 on the dot, arriving with a minute to spare before the 7.30 deadline. Perfect. I turned to Don and said: 'Like clockwork – if the rest of the night goes like that we will be on our way.' I spoke too soon.

In the corridor I bumped into my three PSV players Gerald Vanenburg, Erwin Koeman and Hans van Breukelen. I smiled and said: 'See you all soon.'

'Yes, Mr Robson,' they replied in unison.

'I am looking forward to it,' I said.

'So are we,' they answered.

It was my first contact with my new life.

My inner calm collapsed within a minute of the kick-off. I had guessed their team wrong. If I had fooled Beenhakker, he had certainly put one over on me. Hans Gillhaus lined up at outside left with Witschge at left midfield. I knew we had a problem. It was important to keep that cover through the middle and I wasn't going to change it. It meant playing left-sided Terry

Butcher at right back for the first time in his long career. He had done it for me at left back at Ipswich, but no one had ever asked him to play right back. I suppose there is always a first time for everything, but I admit that had I known their team beforehand, Gary Stevens would have played instead of Terry. I turned to Don and said: 'We could be in trouble here.'

Butcher, written out of the team by most of the press, coped magnificently. Gillhaus, in his first international, gave him no problems. The Dutch player's natural move was into the middle, towards Wright, leaving Parker to pick up Witschge in front of Butcher – and he did a very commendable job indeed.

It was a superb match, a complete contrast to the opening game. We created the better chances and, with any sort of luck, would have won. They also played much better than they had in their first match but although they put us under some fierce pressure, forcing 13 corners to our three, we restricted them mainly to long-range efforts which Peter handled with the minimum of fuss. They admitted later that they thought they were lucky, and the way we defended, in the air and on the ground, clearly deflated them.

But there were still problems to solve. At half-time Fred Street came to see me and Doc Crane to tell us that he did not think Bryan Robson would last the game. He had had an injection in his toe but his Achilles' tendon trouble had flared up once more. It shook me.

I waited until everyone had left the dressing room then pulled back David Platt and told him the situation and that I was going to use him rather than McMahon. I told him that he could do a better job on Gullit, who was looking much more like his old self than he had in the first game, even though it was a complete change of role. I told young Platt: 'You've got the legs, the discipline and the aerial ability. Don't let him dictate to you. Get your own game going as well. Gazza can't do it all the time on his own in midfield and if it is our ball and possession is secure, take Gullit into their box.'

I was hugely impressed with the way he accepted the news, and he was obviously looking forward to it. He was even more animated when he went on 20 minutes later. Both his response and his attitude were excellent. He looked the part and was never out of his depth in as big a match as you could get, marking one of the world's great players.

At the back Wright read everything and looked truly majestic, bringing the ball out from his central position and looking like a midfield player. Our full backs were bombing on and Gazza was looking more mature with every passing game.

Our only real problem was when van Aerle broke down the right, making it two against one. To curb this I shifted Chrissie Waddle out there and although he did a job on the flying Dutchman, he simply stood in the hole. He thought he was doing a great job for the team, but I wanted more from him from a creative point of view. He still looked 'leggy' to me, while John Barnes, playing where he wanted through the middle, was disappointing by his own standards. I was hoping for so much more from these two outstanding players.

Barnes had enjoyed another fantastic season for Liverpool but his demeanour and tempo were altogether too laid back. We were screaming for him to go on, run, fight, because we know what he can do. Four years earlier we had left him out in Mexico after starting with him, and he had been lethargic in West Germany.

What's the answer? I fully believed that John could be our match-winner in Italy. Maybe it is because the game at international level is played on a different plane, at a different mental pace. Maybe it is that he cannot raise that tempo within himself. I don't know. It is baffling because he is such a high quality technical player.

I put Steve Bull on for Waddle on the hour and he almost scored with his first header. I put him on to chase and for a bit of spirit, to shake up those Dutch defenders.

We were the better team and deserved to win. But I wasn't too bothered with the goalless result. We had two points and even a draw with Egypt would see us through. What's more, it was a classical sort of game with the ball on the ground, played in a good spirit and at a high pace. It was typical of the sort of football we had served up at Wembley and totally divorced from the Eire match. I thought we would get a good press. We deserved it.

What we wanted now was to beat Egypt and win the group, because that was going to be the most comfortable route.

At home with the dog in Ipswich

Looking grim – feeling worse after our European disaster in West Germany

Spot the real me – that's Spitting Image on the right . . . or is it?

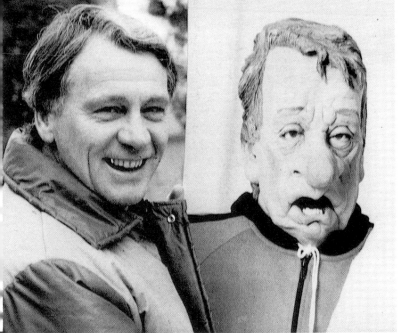

Sharing the bench with my backroom team

Not even the rain can dampen the spirits of live wires Paul Gascoigne and Gary Lineker

We know it's Holland to play but who's going to be their manager? Thys Libregts was in Rome but Leo Beenhakker took them to Italy

The delightful Is Molas Hotel in Sardinia

Bryan Robson knew no fear but succumbed again to his injury jinx. Here he holds off Ireland's Chris Morris

Chris Waddle and Paul Gascoigne team up to take on the Irish

Paul Gascoigne holds off Hans Gillhaus of Holland

The hotel had laid on champagne for our late-night return. I thought the boys had earned a glass. So did the Minister for Sport. He was pleased. No trouble on the pitch and less than anticipated in the city. Tonight I would sleep well.

England 0 *Holland* 0.
Att: 35,267.
Ref: Zoran Petrovic (Yugoslavia).
England: Shilton; Parker, Butcher, Wright, Walker, Pearce; Robson (Platt), Gascoigne; Waddle (Bull); Barnes, Lineker.
Holland: van Breukelen; Koeman, van Aerle, Rijkaard, van Tiggelen; van't Schip (Kieft), Gullit, Wouters, Witschge; van Basten, Gillhaus.

SARDINIA
Sunday, 17 June

Father's Day. Rang my Dad, spoke to Mom and talked to my brother Keith who is still groggy from his heart attack. Dad (Philip), who is 86, was happy after our performance last night. He is a big England fan and a regular visitor to Wembley for games. Keith also watched the game on television. Was that wise?

Hurried through morning swim and breakfast to be down the drive at the Is Molas Golf Club for my press conference with the English and Italian journalists. They had appreciated the game, too, although there were a number of smart questions about playing a sweeper for the first time in such a big match. Imagine what they would have said about it if we'd lost! I talked about the injury situation, the concern over Robson and Lineker, and the afternoon game between Egypt and the Irish. We would certainly know how the group was shaping after that.

The golf was good, too. We had a match against the members, all very relaxing. What a difference getting a result makes to everyone and everything! There was a Dutch group at the golf club and they insisted that I join them for a drink. I finished up presenting their medals and making a speech. The things I let myself in for. Still, it was all good fun and good public relations. I talked to the Minister and he, too, was in good humour. He mentioned that the team had behaved impeccably. I replied: 'They always do!'

I couldn't help a chuckle as I watched Jack's team struggle to a goalless draw with Egypt in a tedious game, not that I didn't want them to win. He was hoping to win and clinch his place in the second phase, but although they dominated they couldn't create chances. Egypt defended well, particularly Hany Ramzy, a fine sweeper of great quality. But this wasn't the Egypt who had performed to well against Holland. They could clearly sense the chance of qualifying and had gone into their shell, looking for the draw they eventually got. They managed only four shots in 90 minutes and Jack was critical of their tactics. I thought that was more than a little hypocritical. It was significant that everyone was saying how good our game was to watch and what a contrast to our first game, while, for the second time, everyone was having a go at the Irish game. I said nothing and let others make up their own minds.

But the result made it interesting, for all four teams were exactly level, and if we drew with Egypt by the same score that Eire drew with Holland we would all have to draw lots to see who went where and which team would go home. What a short straw that would be. But I was counting on beating Egypt and relished the prospect of topping the group so that we could stay put for a couple of days extra before heading off for Bologna. The players knew that was the target, and if we couldn't get a result against Egypt we would deserve whatever fate befell us.

Belgium beat Uruguay that night even though one of my PSV players, the veteran full back Eric Gerets, was sent off, albeit somewhat unfairly. It was interesting because we could well face Belgium in the next round, depending on other results. They were a very good team – even with ten men.

SARDINIA
Monday, 18 June

The levity of the previous day vanished. Not only was David Seaman going home, so was our popular doctor. Seaman was a bit down. He would dearly have liked to stay, but there was no point. Doctor Crane was going home for a family funeral. Before he left David Seaman came back to see me. His depression had been replaced by anger. Mike Langley from the *People* had telephoned and asked him to confirm that he had fractured his thumb separating two fighting players. David was annoyed. I simply told him not to worry about it. Where the hell did they dig them up from? We were all there when David injured his hand in a training incident with Paul Parker. This one was so daft it wasn't even worth worrying about.

We made training an open day, letting in our supporters who arranged raffles with shirts, tracksuits and other gifts we had passed on to them. We, in turn, were presented with copies of the New Testament by the Catholic church who had been so good to our supporters over the past week or so in Cagliari. It was prudent to accept the kind gifts, and at least now the players could look up John 3:16 to find out what those posters at every ground were on about.

The English and Italian press wanted to know about the injuries to Robson and Lineker. In truth I was concerned about both, Robson with that Achilles' tendon trouble and Lineker with his toe which we had been forced to drill twice to drain the blood. Gary was doing no training between matches and eventually it was going to take its toll.

The afternoon was free and I was invited on to the boat of David Dein, the Arsenal vice-chairman. It was a warm, lovely day in the harbour but there was a force-seven gale blowing outside and we didn't go out, just lazed on the boat. David and his wife Barbara were marvellous hosts and good conversationalists. It also got me out of the Lord Mayor of Pula's beanfeast. I needed that break away.

When I returned everyone was back from the Mayor's do – very quickly in fact, opting out of what I am told was a very good meal and some rather novel entertainment. The former Liverpool player Craig Johnston was at the hotel and I spoke to him about the Unesco project he was working on. He had provided the lads with a video camera to do some candid shots. I needed to watch out for that!

I had a meeting with Don and Mike and told them that I was not going to play the sweeper system against Egypt even though everyone was expecting me to. They weren't going to play with more than one up and I needed the extra man forward to try to win it and clinch the group.

I had made my mind up also that Terry Butcher would be the one to go. It was a hard decision but there was no way I could leave Wright out after the way he had played. I also decided that I was going to start with Wolves striker Steve Bull. I hadn't originally brought him out to start matches, rather to bring on as a shock weapon, but he had forced himself into contention. He looked fresh and busy in training and his finishing was a joy. If it didn't come off I could always change it, but I thought he might present the Egyptians with a different sort of problem. There had been a massive campaign for me to play him, but you can't react to things like that. I picked him because I thought he was right for that match. Beacon Radio even sent me a tape recording from Bully's supporters. Did they really believe I had the time to listen and take notice? But I like Bully. He may not be the best in the world outside the box but he is a hell of a nice lad and some goal-scorer.

The first phase was now coming to its conclusion. Cameroon crashed to the Soviet Union 4–0 but they stayed top as Romania and Argentina drew.

SARDINIA
Tuesday, 19 June

My old mate Mike Shapow woke me early with a call from Los Angeles to say well done, and that he was on his way to cheer us in the Final. 'Wait and see what happens in the next game,' I urged, but assured him we would win, it was just a question of where we would be next.

At breakfast I saw Gary Stevens, one of the few still coming down to breakfast. Most skip it or have something light in their rooms. Looking at Gary I thought: 'Poor beggar. He's out of the side and has done nothing wrong.' In fact he was one of the better players against the Irish. Then he saw the team play well without him. He didn't ask to see me because he didn't want to create waves. He is very fit, very athletic and can get up and down the line. So can Paul Parker, but he is a better defender than Gary and a touch quicker. It is tough to drop players who have never let you down – first Stevens and Peter Beardsley and now Butcher.

Peter asked to see me and expressed his disappointment that I hadn't told him personally that he was to be left out. I remember reading that Kenny Dalglish had dropped him and he found out from the newspapers. I don't know whether it was true but it can happen. I should have told him and didn't. Things come at you fast and furious in the World Cup. You try to think of everything but there is no way you can explain every decision to everyone. A manager picks 22 and they are all at his disposal to use as he thinks fit. I can do what I want and I don't have to give a reason because it is going to be me who carries the can at the end of the day. He took it fine. He always does. Peter is not only a good footballer but also a very nice person. He departed saying that I had his full support and that he was fit and would fight his way back into the team.

From Beardsley I went to Robbo. I had spoken to Fred Street after the Holland game about the skipper. He had looked at the Achilles' tendon carefully and there was no swelling but it was incredibly tender to the touch for such a tough warrior. I believed we had a long-term injury on our hands. Worse, I could see that we were looking at another World Cup without our captain. My heart bled for him. He was so unlucky. I believe he thought the same; he was so depressed, and he already knew the feeling from bitter experience.

I beckoned him to me. I was going to tell him to be optimistic, to give it five days' complete rest and see how it felt. But he beat me to the punch and said: 'I'm glad you called me over – I want to tell you something. You remember the faith healer Olga Stringfellow? I have invited her over.' I was flabbergasted and said nothing as Robbo went on: 'I know I should have seen you first but I am desperate. It's my last chance, my final resort. I rang her last night and told her to come straight over. I hope you don't mind. I believe in her and if I don't play now I won't play in another World Cup. Give me this chance.'

How could I say no? He should have spoken to me first, of course. He should also have consulted the medical staff. But his decision was made on the spur of the moment and out of sheer desperation. He followed this up by saying that no one knew, nor was there any reason to tell anyone.

Wrong. Doc Crane was still away in England but Fred Street had to be told immediately. I promised to try to keep it secret as far as I could but said that I had about as much chance as a one-legged man in a bum-kicking competition.

It was a hot day and we restricted training to an hour. Apart from Robson, Lineker was still not training, nor was Hodge with his hamstring trouble, and that morning Steve McMahon had reported with a neck injury, making three midfield players injured. I kept my mouth shut about Olga at the press conference and no one asked. But for how long?

I punished the players later on. I made them watch Egypt v. Eire. Ugh! The ball couldn't have been in play for more than 50 minutes. After the team talk I told them that we would be playing without a sweeper. I don't think they liked it. Tough. I was the manager. Player power? I don't think so.

I managed to get in nine holes of golf with my son Mark before watching Italy look very expressive against the Czechs with goals from Baggio and Schillaci. There were four games that day as the Groups A and D were wound up, with West Germany having their worst game so far with a 1–1 draw with Colombia, Austria beating the USA 2–1 and Yugoslavia grabbing second place in Group D thanks to an easy 4–1 win over the Emirates.

But the best part of the day came that night at dinner. When we arrived Terry Butcher and Chris Woods were already there, caps on inside out and turned round, tee-shirts back to front, shorts reversed and shoes on the wrong feet. Not only that, they began with coffee, went onto sweet, then main course, followed by pasta and finished with soup. The lads thought it was hilarious but what really impressed me was that Terry knew he was out of the team at this stage, even though I hadn't officially announced it. That is his character. That is his spirit. And don't forget that he was the one who earned the point that took us to Italy with that immense performance in Sweden when he cut his head open. People forget. They can be disloyal. No wonder the lads get upset.

SARDINIA
Wednesday, 20 June

It was the first time in my life I had dropped Terry Butcher, and that spanned a lot of years. I told him first, before anyone else. I owed him that. I said I was going to change the team and that I was going to leave him out. He had more than a good idea but it hurt him all the same, and it hurt me, too. But I knew I was right to do it and you cannot let sentiment rule. Wright has elegance and pace and can bring the ball out. He and Walker can cope on their own and that will give us a better chance up front. He listened to my explanation and agreed. He took it like a man, saying: 'That's all right, gaffer. I am fortunate to have the caps I've got.'

'How many is that?' I asked.

'Seventy-four,' he replied.

'I'll get you up to seventy-five,' I promised.

He laughed. He could have taken the line that I was leaving him out after a fine performance when he had been forced to play out of position. He didn't. He accepted it like the captain he is.

Before that I had gone through the latest Olga episode. A worried Fred Street came in to see me, saying that this was a hot potato and he couldn't see how we could keep it under wraps with the woman already out here. It was on my mind, too – another front-page story.

The FA chairman, Bert Millichip, had arrived the day before and I woke him up to put him in the picture, I didn't want him finding out through a phone call or a story in a tabloid. He appreciated the thought. It was outrageous but it had worked with people like Ian Wright and Robson himself, and if it came off we would be laughing. Bert agreed as long as it was divorced from the FA. He said he would tell only Graham Kelly to keep it to a minimum. But, even before ten o'clock, Graham Kelly was on the line saying to me: 'Guess what's in the *Sun*.' Not only had they known about it, they even had someone on the plane with her!

What a good thing I had told the senior officials. It made me late for the bus to training, something I hated when the players did it. I always told them that if it was a train they were catching and they were four minutes late they would miss it. You can imagine the hammering I took. Everyone was making train noises as I pulled Bryan out (as much for cosmetic effect as anything else) to tell him the latest development. He couldn't believe it.

I told the players before training what the team would be – Bull and McMahon in, Robson and Butcher out – adding that they were the only ones who knew and to see how long we could keep it to ourselves this time. It was clear they had anticipated staying with the sweeper system. I told them to trust me. I stressed that if we won we would head the group; draw and we could be anywhere, even going home.

Bull was in and Butcher was out. There was no Peter Beardsley. He was not himself and he was not scoring. If we got our crosses in, Bully might just get them in a 4–2–4 line-up. I am sure the players wanted to keep the sweeper system – but I didn't ask them. It wasn't up for discussion, never has been. That's for the birds.

Olga was the fascination at the press conference, especially to the foreigners who hadn't heard of the *Sun*'s front-page exclusive. It was not really the sort of thing I wanted to talk about on the eve of a very big game.

Neither did I want to discuss the day-off antics of Paul Gascoigne. He had, like me, been out on a private yacht, had a couple of beers in the hot sun and, in typical style, clowned about. The only problem was that he did it in the very busy Forte Village which was heaving with journalists and supporters who had come in for the game. Give the lad full credit. He held up his hands and said he had been out enjoying himself. Good for him.

I changed hurriedly and was picked up by the local NATO base commander Group Captain Stone who took me out to where the 9th Squadron were based, along with Germans, Italians, Dutch and Americans, for a thrill–of–a–lifetime ride in a Tornado. It had all been cleared with the Ministry of Defence. I had to wear all the gear: the special pressurised suit, helmet, oxygen mask. I went through the ops room to be briefed about the procedure for ejection. It was all very impressive, very professional. I was told firmly: 'Don't touch anything yellow and black and don't touch the joystick.'

Two aircraft took off. I was in one and Group Commander Stone in the other. We were in the air for 50 minutes, round the south of the island, over the golf course where we waggled the wings at the players from low down. We were going at 400 m.p.h. but it felt like a smooth 60. It was fantastic, very exhilarating as we went up to Mach 1, 800 m.p.h., burning fuel, low over the sea, no more than 20 feet from each other. We didn't do it for long; these two babies cost a cool £27 million apiece. Back down to a gentle 400 m.p.h. felt like floating. It was like sitting in my Jag on the motorway. I felt as though I could reach out and touch the mountains. It was all so peaceful, quiet and serene. It certainly took my mind away from tomorrow's make-or-break game. I would probably have fretted if I had stayed back at the hotel.

I learned that it had not been easy to arrange and had taken a bit of pleading, but it gave me one of the best thrills of my entire life. The ground crew, including a Geordie lad who strapped me in, told me that was the nearest they ever came to the Tornado and I was, indeed, very privileged.

I got back to the hotel in time for dinner and couldn't understand why Butcher, Stevens and Waddle were all dressed up. Because we had taken over the hotel lock, stock and barrel, meals were a casual affair, but these three were in FA suits, white shirt, ties, sunglasses and slicked-back hair. They had dressed for dinner and were sitting there when everyone else arrived. Fred Street was convinced they were up to something. But they said nothing and just kept on eating as though there was nothing out of the ordinary.

They were visible only from the waist up because of the tablecloth, and when they stood up all they had on underneath were the smallest of jockstraps. Without a word they took off their jackets, shirts and ties, and showed their backsides and walked out. We were convulsed with laughter and it was all in order as the only other people apart from our group were the waiters, who could scarcely stand up for laughing. Bert Millichip, Graham Kelly, the committee, everyone found it funny; it was wonderful for team spirit.

In the evening we watched Brazil and Scotland. Brazil maintained their 100 per cent record to match Italy but their 1–0

147

win reflected how close the game was. At half-time I left the players' room and came across John Barnes walking in the hotel gardens looking very glum. He was upset over a huge spread in the *Daily Mirror*, which he had had faxed out to him, saying what a difficult childhood he had had in Jamaica. There was more from some psychiatrist bringing in me, Graham Taylor, all sorts of people. They had done a very thorough job.

It had all stemmed from a Channel 4 television programme he had done some years before which, I understand, hadn't even made the screens. In it he talked about his normal, healthy childhood where, if he was naughty, he got spanked. This had turned into a beating. We talked about it and I told him if it was not correct just to get it out of his mind, forget about it. 'Don't let it get to you.' I told him the best reply was to go out against the Egyptians and play the way we all knew he could. 'Concentrate on getting your game right.' I didn't consider leaving him out at that stage but it had clearly got to him and I would have to keep an eye on the situation.

I saw the rest of the Scotland game and I thought them unlucky. For me they had done enough to get a draw. They had played for that draw, knowing that if they got it they would qualify. They must have been gutted. Naturally we didn't want them to do as well as us, but we didn't want to see them go out now. We thought they had played well and there was a lot of sympathy for them. Taffarel denied Mo Johnston with a great late save and Muller's 81st-minute goal was enough. The Jocks were on their way home.

So were Sweden, the team who had topped our qualifying group, losing to little Costa Rica after being a goal up. You can take nothing for granted in a World Cup. We didn't want Egypt adding to the shocks.

That meant playing 11 fit players, and I wasn't at all sure that Gary Lineker was fit. I asked the doc if he could be given the jab at 6 p.m., so that he could put his foot in a boot and kick the ball to give me some idea of whether he could play. I knew that Gary would rather leave it because it was going to hurt, and he told me: 'I think I am going to be all right.'

I was in a corner. The doctor didn't want to inject him three times in a day. But I still wanted some sort of guarantee. Doc Crane looked at me and said: 'Play him and take a chance – or leave him out.' I had already done that with Robbo. Still, if we lost we would probably be going home anyway. He would play. I would keep my fingers crossed.

I had a word with Barnes and at least he seemed to have recovered his spirits.

Back in Mexico 14 years ago I had been staggered to take a good-wish call from an old-age pensioner living in Newcastle. Mrs Porter, a Cockney by birth but a Geordie by nature, used her precious money to ring and wish me and her favourite player Peter Beardsley well before every game. I had spoken to her a couple of times since but now she was back in all her glory, saying: 'I couldn't let it go. I am going to bring you luck.'

I hoped she would.

SARDINIA
Thursday, 21 June

My diary told me that this was the longest day. I hoped that was meant literally and not metaphorically. It began the way most of my days began with a quick swim followed by a live TV AM interview, this time with Lawrie McMenemy linking with Mike Morris in the London studio.

I was anxious to get away to check on Gary Lineker and Bryan Robson. Lineker's damaged big toe was blue and angry and it again needed an injection. The doctor suggested we do it there and then to appraise the benefit and to try to fit the foot into the boot while it was numb. He also wanted to cut the bed to remove some more of the blood and reduce the pain. Lineker wasn't keen – who can blame him – but he agreed. I could do without all this with my star striker. Why couldn't I have fit players like everyone else? At least, that was how it seemed to me.

Olga had arrived at 8.30 and had gone to see Bryan Robson in the medical room. Just like Bryan, I was praying for a miracle, but I had planned all along without him. I had written him out of this game, the next and maybe the entire tournament.

Later it might have surprised ITV viewers to see me having lunch with my 'foes' from the press on the day of the game. Ironic, maybe a little hypocritical, but these were the football writers I had been travelling with for the past eight years. Some I liked, some I admired, some I respected; one is a close friend. Nevertheless, there were one or two with whom I wouldn't have accepted an individual invitation to lunch without a very good reason. But this was a group who had chipped in together to present me with a magnificent antique map of the island and a wonderful lunch in the Forte Village, and there was no way I was going to insult them by asking to see a guest list first. It was time to be gracious, and it all went very well. I must admit I gave it some thought before I attended. But I have never been one to bear grudges – say your piece and get on with life. On the way back to my hotel a great many people had stopped me to wish me and England well. It was appreciated.

We won 1–0, while Holland and the Republic of Ireland drew yet again and had to be split by the drawing of lots at the Hilton Hotel in Rome. Lucky Jack took second place while the Dutch were pitched in against the powerful West Germans. We didn't care. We had won our game; we had won our group. We had what we wanted even if it meant playing the talented Belgians in Bologna in the next round. Rather them at this stage than the Germans.

We timed our journey to perfection, arriving bang on the dot of 7.30. Egypt arrived a quarter of an hour late and were fined. A bad start for them. This time there were no selection surprises but Egypt played the way we expected, making it tough, just as it had been for the two teams before us. It was very tense with so much at stake and we were never complacent.

The Egyptians were well organised, had a nice system and half a dozen very neat players. But they were overly cautious and didn't threaten us until after Mark Wright had scored the only goal of the game in the 58th minute.

What a goal it was, too. Des Walker had been fouled near the touchline bringing the ball out. Gazza wanted to take the free-kick but found Des in the way of his run-up. He sensibly asked Swiss referee Roethlisberger if he could move the ball, was given permission and floated the ball to the back post where Wright jumped higher than anyone I have ever seen. His first goal for England, and what a cracker – and how important.

The Egyptians were distraught at losing. They had built up

their hopes and dreams in their two previous matches and totally believed in themselves. When that final whistle blew they simply could not believe they were out. Goalkeeper Shoubeir, whom I had rated as outstanding long before these Finals, was beside himself. He collapsed to the ground in tears and then went into hysterics. He was so bad they had to call in a doctor. He screamed and was clearly in a very bad way. He couldn't control himself and I feared he was heading for a breakdown. Defeat was too much for him, and you could see how much this game had meant to them all.

We heard the Irish result as we left the Egyptians weeping on the pitch and knew then we had taken the group and that we could stay on at our hotel and rest up before our next game instead of rushing off to Genoa to play Romania on Monday or to Milan to face the Germans the day before. The other two could draw lots for that.

But my pleasure was a little tempered with disappointment again in John Barnes and Chris Waddle, two players I had hoped would be stars of the World Cup. Lineker was obviously struggling with his poorly toe, and Bull, without service, was not as involved as he or I would have liked. Chris was still looking a little weary and had still not rediscovered the awesome form he had shown before the French season dragged on into the summer.

But the real problem was John Barnes. Again he looked lethargic and I was more than a bit worried about him. Hassan, his marker, was a tough cookie but no more difficult than the full backs he had murdered in England that season. John was always on the fringe instead of at the heart of things. He created so little. I wondered, in retrospect, how much that psychiatrist's report had had to do with his form this time.

We got through with a good defence and good set plays. I sent on Beardsley for Bull and Platt for Waddle. Both looked good in their short spells on the park.

We hadn't played brilliantly but we had scored, held on and won. Holland had gone in front against Egypt and had drawn. We were on route one, on the highway with all late kick-offs, a good rest before our next game and avoiding the big guns until the semi-finals. It was up to us.

Back at the hotel we had champagne and a meal. Even though it was into the early hours I held a brief assembly to talk about the next two days and what I expected of them. Tomorrow would be a day off. I told them to use it sensibly. I said: 'Stick tight to the hotel. We have too much to play for to wreck it now. I want to know if you go out and I want to know where you're going. Keep your discipline. Enjoy it – but above all be professional.'

I finally turned in at 3 a.m. I was exhausted but happy. It had been the longest day, but not a bad one!

England 1 (Wright 58) *Egypt* 0.
HT. 0–0: Att: 34,959.
Ref: K. Roethlisberger (Switzerland).
England: Shilton; Parker, Walker, Wright, Pearce; Gascoigne, McMahon; Waddle (Platt), Bull (Beardsley), Lineker, Barnes.
Egypt: Shoubeir; I. Hassan, Yassein, H. Ramzy, Youssef, Yaken; A. Ramzy, Abdel-Ghani, Abdel-Hamid; H. Hassan, Ahmed El Kass.

SARDINIA
Friday, 22 June

Up at 7.30 – four and a half hours' sleep. Not enough. But I wanted to see my brother Tom and son Mark off as they were returning home. I am going to be tired later on. Had an early meeting with Bert Millichip and Graham Kelly concerning an invitation from the local Organising Committee to attend a farewell function at the Is Morus in the evening. I needed to keep the players away from that sort of thing at this stage of the competition.

Saw Bryan Robson at breakfast. He was seeing Olga Stringfellow at 8.30 in one last attempt at a miracle, as she was due to fly home. He was pessimistic. Only he knew, and he told me today: 'It feels as though it is going to snap every time I try to increase the pressure.' I told him that it was a warning, his body telling him no.

From one senior player to another. This time it was Peter

Shilton who was waiting to talk to me in private. He had decided to quit international football once our interest in the World Cup had ended and wanted to tell me now that we had qualified. He was going to carry on at club level but felt now that he had broken the record it was time to retire while he was still at the top. His timing was perfect, and I told him so. Had I stayed on I would certainly have been looking hard at his future. The last two years he had been fantastic, but he was 40 and I couldn't see him being involved in the next World Cup – and that is what it's all about.

It crossed my mind that he had solved a very delicate problem for the incoming manager. The decision had been made for him by Shilton. Peter's only problem was the timing of the announcement to the public, and I advised him to wait until we were either out or won it. He agreed. We wouldn't say anything to anyone.

After breakfast I began the media run, starting with David Davies and the BBC and ending with the daily and the Sunday papers, finishing two hours later.

Another afternoon on David Dein's boat beckoned. I left with Doc Crane for a late lunch and an afternoon of water sports. We cruised under the hot sun for a couple of hours. I water-skied, rode a ski-bike and was pulled at speed while perched in a huge inflatable inner tube. The Deins were, again, outstanding hosts.

The people of Sardinia and, in particular, the local Organising Committee, had also been outstanding hosts. Nothing had been too much trouble and while they were fair to everyone in our group, they had definitely taken a shine to us, particularly the President, Andrea Arrica, his son Stefano, who was attached to us as a liaison officer, and the well-connected Secretary Roberto Pappalardo. They did extremely well for us and were so glad we had qualified.

SARDINIA
Saturday, 23 June

For the first time since we arrived on the island I had a day clear of the press. At least, I thought I had! I hadn't let anyone down for I had seen the Sunday newspaper men on their own after the daily and Italian press conferences.

It was another blazing hot day, but training went well. The boys were clearly uplifted by winning the group and qualifying for the second round. But there was no Bryan Robson around and Lineker was still struggling with his bad toe. Steve Hodge, who had been slowly recovering from a hamstring injury, hurt his groin and had to come off. He was very sheepish about it. Compensating for one injury, he has created another. He is in trouble. It has not been a good World Cup for the Nottingham Forest player so far, and it does not look like getting better.

Neither does Robson. I had a meeting after lunch with the skipper, Fred Street, the doc and our travel man Brian Scott. Bryan was honest. He knew that the Achilles' tendon was bad and was not getting any better. We decided that in view of what he was saying we should send him for examination by his own orthopaedic surgeon and that we would fly him home that day if possible. There was a direct flight to Manchester at 3.30 but it was just too tight – a pity, because we could have had him back before anyone realised. We wanted to get him home with as little fuss as possible. After all, he was England's captain in a World Cup and this was very big news. We booked him on an early flight next morning under an assumed name.

Barnes, Butcher, Walker, Steven and Stevens had made the trip into Cagliari for some shopping and while they were there they took the trouble to visit a couple of injured supporters who had survived a fatal crash the day before. The kids could hardly believe it. It was a good public relations job and typical of the players' attitude. Pity the newspapers aren't as good at finding out this sort of story and printing it as they are the other sort.

Don Howe, Mike Kelly and I managed to get in nine holes of golf that afternoon with some of the locally based RAF guys, and I returned to a string of messages from journalists. Somehow the Sunday papers had got hold of the Robson story. I hadn't even told my chairman yet – in fact, I hadn't even mentioned it to Don while we played golf. That was my first task: tell Mr Millichip, before I did anything else. I then sought out Robson and the doc to tell them. No one had the slightest idea how it had got out so quickly. Bang went Bryan's easy trip home, and I told him: 'You are England captain – you handle it.'

That night the mother of the boy who had been killed on the way to the game was invited by Graham Kelly to the hotel for dinner. I had a few words with her and so did Peter Beardsley, John Barnes and Steve McMahon when they discovered that she and her son were Liverpool fans. They were brilliant, sitting and talking to her, using the experience they had picked up counselling the grieving after the Hillsborough tragedy. She was surprisingly calm. The storm was still to come, I feared.

I telephoned Dave Sexton after dinner for a long chat about Belgium. Both he and John Lyall had watched them and we arranged to meet in Bologna on the Monday. I had been able to watch the last stages of Czechoslovakia's 4–1 win over brave Costa Rica as Skuhravy grabbed a hat-trick.

Far more interesting from an English point of view were the latest heroics from veteran substitute Roger Milla as his two goals sank Colombia and put the Africans through to the last 8 – significant, because if we won our game we would meet Cameroon in the quarter-finals. Now there was a fascinating prospect.

SARDINIA/BOLOGNA
Sunday, 24 June

Up at the crack of dawn to take Bryan Robson to the airport for his flight home via Milan. We were congratulating ourselves on how well we had done to keep him under wraps. The local officials had organised a back-door entrance and a private room in which Bryan, Glen Kirton and I could wait. There were no press, no TV, no photographers. The flight was called and Bryan was ushered through ahead of everyone with an old lady and a small child. We waved him off and turned away, thinking how clever we had been, when we bumped into Alex Montgomery from the *Sun*, Harry Harris of the *Mirror*, Bob Driscoll from the *Star* and Rob Shepherd of *Today*. They were off to see Holland play West Germany and were on the same flight with goodness knows who else – wouldn't Bryan be pleased!

We stayed on at the airport to await the rest of the squad for our own departure to Bologna. A press conference had been called by the local press chief at the airport. John Jackson, the veteran *Mirror* news reporter who has been on so many of these trips, didn't waste words. His was the first question. 'Is this the end of the Two Robsons?' he asked bluntly. No sympathy, no expression of bad luck. This was a hard newsman doing his job. It may sound cruel but this, to him, was no more than a football injury and not in the same league as some of the genuine tragedies he has covered.

Knowing Bryan, this may have been the end of his World Cup – he wasn't going to be back – but come the following season he would be scrapping for his England place. He told me he had no intention of joining his mate Shilton on the retirement list. But as far as Bryan Robson and Bobby Robson were concerned, it was the end. He would no longer be my decision. His next international selection would be decided by Graham Taylor.

It wasn't the end of me, either. We were still in the competition and quite fancied ourselves for a place in the last four. No, there was a bit more of Robson senior to come yet.

We settled into our new headquarters. It had been a hot, sticky day and the players were given permission to relax, sunbathe and swim. I kept a fatherly eye on them and suddenly realised how quiet it was. Where was Gazza? I asked and was greeted with a few strange looks until someone pointed to the nearby courts and said: 'He's playing tennis, boss.' Sure enough, there was Gazza chasing about the court and, it must be said, playing very well against some American fellow he had met and chatted to on his travels. 'Oy!' I shouted down to him. 'What do you think you are doing? Get up here at once.' I tried to explain that he may have had energy to spare then but it was energy to save. We were going to need every last drop.

I tried to tell him how easy it was to sustain an injury, pointing out that Kerry Dixon had done that self-same thing in Mexico City four years earlier and had ruled himself out of contention with a cut eye. This lad was young, he didn't think ahead. You had to think for him. He needed all the guidance he could get. Once you told him, that was fine; he took it on board. I didn't want to be a killjoy, but he would need that energy on Tuesday when we played Belgium.

'What if you pull a muscle?' I asked. 'What would the folks back home think about me letting you play tennis? Go and have a good swim.' Gazza accepted it. He is hyperactive, and if he can only channel all that energy into football, what an asset it will be.

That evening one of the favourites, Brazil, went out, losing to the champions Argentina. Everyone was sorry about Brazil. They were much the better team and lost to the one bit of magic we have seen from Diego Maradona. The competition may have lost something with the exit of the Brazilians but as professionals we should derive some satisfaction from the fact that one of the favourites has gone. Wouldn't every team left in the FA Cup raise a cheer if Liverpool went out – whatever their absence did to the competition in aesthetic terms?

Thinking of Liverpool, I invited John Barnes to my room for a chat about his personal performance. I spoke to him about himself. He had been lacklustre in all three games and I was worried about my potential match-winner. I had played him out wide and I had played him where he wanted, through the middle, and it had still not happened. I felt he could give far more to the team.

I told him I wanted to encourage him. I asked him what he was not doing for England that he did for Liverpool, or was it something we were not doing for him? In other words: 'How can we bring out the best in you?' There was not a better player in the tournament. I could understand it if he was a 'chicken-winger', as we used to call them, but the last thing he could be called is a coward. He never flinches and he is a strong character.

'Why can't you be dominant?' I asked. 'It's muck and nettles from now on, no second chance, and we need you to fight and be enthusiastic.'

He claimed he was not drained as he had been two years earlier at the European Championships and that he had not lost confidence. I could vouch personally that there was nothing wrong with him physically because he was magnificent in training. That is why we kept picking him; you couldn't leave him out. His quality on the ball was second to none. I explained to

157

him that if I didn't think so much of him he wouldn't be in my room talking. I would just have axed him.

'I want you in the team, I want you on song,' I said. 'What I don't want is you standing off. Is the game too big for you? Are you worried?'

If he was worried, and clearly he was, I would try to help him, so I added: 'I have not picked the team yet but I'm picking you and I'm picking Chrissie because I need you both if we are to win the World Cup, especially now we have lost Robson. Everyone needs to give a little bit more and you are one of the seniors, one of the mainstays.'

We trained that night and liked what we saw. The pitch was beautiful and the lights were excellent. I worked with Walker, Barnes and Lineker, who were all injured, myself. I didn't want anything competitive for them at this stage. The others looked lively, with Trevor Steven catching my eye. It was one of those nights when they all looked fresh and fit.

We missed most of the Holland–West Germany match because of training but I watched on tape as another of the favourites crashed out. Two of most people's last four gone. It was a good day for us without kicking a ball in anger. We knew all about Belgium and Cameroon, and we could now go a long way if everyone pulled together – maybe all the way. That's just what I had told John Barnes.

BOLOGNA
Monday, 25 June

Slept late. Fred Street woke me up to tell me that John Lyall and Dave Sexton had already arrived from Verona and we spent a couple of hours going over the Belgians. It was good information – the sort I had come to expect from these two experts.

It was more than I could say for our press relations. They had now sunk to their lowest ebb without me knowing what was going on. The aptly named Nando Macchiavelli, the local press chief who had thrown everyone into confusion by changing the venue and time of the press conference the previous day, was at it again. We were scheduled to meet in the nearby press centre, only to be banned because it was being used by FIFA. Instead he switched it to our training ground but provided no facilities other than a table and three chairs.

The result would have been chaos anyway but he made it even worse by letting in only the Italian press, leaving the English and the rest fuming on the street outside where they had been for a couple of hours. While I was talking to the Italian press the players, bored with waiting, got on the bus to return to the hotel and were just setting off when the rest of the media were let in. All hell broke loose as they crowded round my little table and tried to get to the players.

Paul Parker got off the bus to talk to Michael Hart from the *London Evening Standard*, only to be dragged back in by his team-mates who wanted to get away. Gazza threw a paper cup partially filled with water and suddenly we had a major incident on our hands, with TV cameras from all over the world happy to get something on film. It was the day before a major game. The football press didn't want all the hassle and neither did we, but the culprit escaped without blame.

We had trained well once more, working with the sweeper system which I had decided to use. I told the players: 'That's the style – but not necessarily the team.' I had not been happy with one or two of the performances and I wanted a couple of them to sweat on it. It never hurts, and there is a big sense of relief when they see their name on the list, even if they are so-called stars who think their selection is automatic. I know. It happened to me. I am from the same stock.

The International Committee had arrived in Bologna but, as usual, there was not a scrap of interference from any of them.

In the afternoon I had private sessions with Waddle and Webb. I wanted to keep Webb going. Bryan Robson had gone home but I had decided to play Steve McMahon again and I knew Webby would be disappointed. Poor lad; it was Catch 22. He had only trained and was not match-fit. I could see he was losing that little bit of sparkle and bubble and I needed to tell him to keep his head up, let him know that he was not forgotten. I had to pick the best 11 for the game, not for me nor for him but for the nation. I told him that he had done brilliantly to have beaten the surgeons' predictions by getting to Italy at all, and to wait for the sort of breaks which had come the way of others.

Chrissie Waddle was a different matter. Like John he is intelligent and a good talker on the game. In Marseille he had been given a free role and played out of his skin, just as he had for us in the autumn. But he hadn't achieved a lot for us in Italy so far. I knew he wanted to play in that same free role, but I have seen people play there before and wander all over the place without getting anywhere.

I was straight with Chrissie. I told him I was taking Barnes out of the wing position and that meant I wanted to keep Chris wide. But first of all I needed to know how he felt. Was he fit? We had scored two goals in three games and needed to create more. I thought he could do that for me from the wing where he had so recently thrilled the Wembley crowd, tearing Maldini to pieces against Italy. The poor Italian hadn't known whether to stick or twist that night.

'That's your best game,' I told him. 'Not coming back and picking the ball up off Butcher, hitting speculative 50-yard passes towards Lineker. You have got to mix it and get into those forward positions where you look so dangerous.'

At his best Chris Waddle is true world class and that is exactly how I needed him against Belgium if we were going to win.

The Irish put a little more pressure on us by beating the Romanians in the first penalty shoot-out of the tournament. They did well. It was a hot day and a 5 p.m. kick-off. The Romanians missed the suspended Lacatus and without him they could not break down the resolute Irish so well marshalled by McCarthy and McGrath. In the end it came down to penalties and Pat Bonner was the Irish hero as he saved from Timofte, while David O'Leary, not recognised as an expert, finished it off with some style.

Italy beat Uruguay, with goals from new hero Schillaci and Serena. They won with a bit to spare. Their challenge was growing.

It was my 35th wedding anniversary and I rang Elsie from the quiet of my room.

BOLOGNA
Tuesday, 26 June

You get the strangest calls. This time it was from Australia, Adelaide to be precise, and a complete stranger who wanted to help me and England. Apparently he had a friend who worked for Belgian television and he'd told him that their goalkeeper Michel Preud'homme was weak at the near post and on corners, and crosses. He thought I should know. Amazing, isn't it? And what's more, it coincided with reports I had had of this extrovert's performance against Spain in the previous round. Then there was dear old Mrs Porter spending her pension on another call to Italy to wish us well. These are the real people, the real supporters.

Physiotherapist Norman Medhurst, who works for Torquay, then asked if I would help out a local reporter from Devon who wanted a 'scoop'. He didn't want much, for his first question was: 'Can I have the team?' He didn't get that, but I did give him his interview. I also spoke to a journalist friend about the disastrous press conference the day before and asked what was the best way out for all of us if, or rather when, we got through the next round.

It was another very hot day and only a handful trained, with Don Howe and Mike Kelly taking no more than five or six who wanted a loosener, and they were soon back for the 11.30 team talk I had called to watch the edited highlights of Belgium v. Uruguay, provided by Vince Craven. I told them we were back to three central defenders and went through the set plays for and against, using Wright as the sweeper with Walker on the quick De Grijse and Butcher on Jan Ceulemans. Butcher may not be the most mobile, but I needed him in both boxes and for his spirit.

I had McMahon marked down to track the talented Enzo Scifo and paired Gazza with Franky van der Elst with instructions to disengage and get Waddle and Barnes going. 'Play well,' I told them. 'Do your jobs and we can win it.'

Everyone went to bed but I was so hot that I wandered down to the pool with my American friend Mike Shapow and Mike Kelly. As I was pulling myself out of the water I slipped and crashed down on my ribs on the sharp edge of the pool, sliding into the water. I had cracked a rib and I was in agony. The doc gave me pain-killers and I had to hide it. I just hoped it would be our first and last injury of the day.

Before we left for the ground I had to satisfy myself that John Barnes had fully recovered. He passed his fitness test comfortably.

Dave Sexton and John Lyall were right about everything they had said and written about Belgium, except the goalkeeper. He was superb. He took everything. I wonder what my friend Down Under thought of his performance.

It was a great match, a dramatic match but played in a wonderful spirit and, as the Americans say, it went right to the wire.

Paul Parker started nervously and finished as one of the best players on the pitch. I suppose you could say exactly the same about us. Certainly the Belgians began better, with Shilton making a couple of important saves while Ceulemans took advantage of Parker's error to hit an upright. We came back well, with Barnes putting a good chance straight into the 'keeper's hands before scoring what looked to be a perfectly good goal, flagged offside by the Austrian Helmuth Kohl.

John was convinced it was a good goal and when he told me at half-time Lineker overheard and also claimed his 'goal' had been a good one. Television totally substantiated Barnes' claim, while those level with Lineker said that he was too quick for both the defenders and the linesman.

The Belgians were giving us just as much trouble, with Scifo proving to be quite a handful for McMahon. He would be for anyone, with that pace. Scifo also rattled the woodwork and from the rebound we swept straight upfield and should have scored as Lineker broke clear only for the ball to slide away from him. It was that sort of game; even, high quality, ebbing and flowing, and I felt sure that one goal was going to be enough to break the deadlock.

I sent on Platt for the now tiring McMahon with about 20 minutes remaining. The Liverpool player had had his hands so full of Scifo that he had been unable to support his front two. Even Gazza was tiring and it struck me that now he knew why you don't play tennis before a game of this importance and quality!

We had our problems and they grew as the thriller progressed without any sign of a break. Barnes, playing better, indicated that his groin was giving him problems, while Lineker's toe was hurting now that the effects of the injection were wearing off. But to compensate, Waddle was world class this night, running at defenders, getting the ball into the box, doing everything I had asked.

We needed a goal. I pulled Platty over before I sent him on. I told him he was fresh while others were tired, that he had a great engine and should try to break off Scifo to see if he could get up between our two strikers and cash in on Scifo's cheating. It was a purely tactical move but I was forced into another by taking off the limping Barnes three minutes later and replacing him with the eager Bull. Bully should have scored with his first touch as Lineker sought him out only for it to hit Bully's shoulder from eight yards out. It was the sort of chance he eats in training every day.

Platt was enjoying himself and almost scored with a great volley, and we had a certain dash about us. But this was a game of many twists and turns and suddenly Walker felt his injuries catching up with him. His leg and ankle began to hurt as he tired, as they had in every match following that nasty tackle by Aldridge in Cagliari. The Belgians had sent on the former Spurs striker Nico Claesen and he was using his electric pace to exploit Walker's problems. Then Butcher went into a challenge which everyone on the bench thought had broken his leg.

We had used up all our substitutes, and extra-time beckoned. It was going to take all our spirit, but I knew we wouldn't die because we possessed such good characters. Gazza added to our problems when he was booked for a foul on Scifo, diving in when he didn't need to. I just hoped he wouldn't regret this caution later on in the tournament – if we survived. It put him on a knife edge not just for this match but for any which followed. It's the bits and pieces which make the complete player and Robson certainly wouldn't have whacked his man in that position. Experience teaches.

This was now a battle of survival and as we switched around for extra-time, I told them they all had to give that something extra to compensate for our two injured players, especially late arrivals Platt and Bull. 'Wright,' I said, 'you've done well but now you have to give us more. You may all be tired, but look at

163

them. They are worse. It's down to character. Are you going to fight? Who wants to win most? Don't give it away. If it has to go to penalties, then so be it. We just need one break. Keep doing it.'

We ran ourselves out in search of victory in extra-time, particularly Gazza. One of the most tiring things in football is running with the ball. By the end he was walking with the ball he was so shattered. It may have looked as though we were playing for the draw. We weren't. We were shattered physically and mentally but still not that far gone to give it away.

Somehow Gazza raised the energy for one last run, only to be up-ended by the equally tired Eric Gerets. Gascoigne stood on the ball and looked as though he was just going to knock it off, keep possession, keep it safe. Don and I were up on our feet screaming for him to get it into the box where Butcher and Wright had joined Platt and Bull.

We need not have worried. Even though he couldn't possibly have heard us he followed our instructions to the letter, curling a magnificent ball out of Preud'homme's reach, on an angle over the top of the defenders. Platt read it to perfection, timing his run, taking it over his shoulder and hooking it home on the volley. It was a great goal. A spectacular strike and, at that stage, the goal of the tournament. The scenes of jubilation were incredible. Even I did a jig.

I pulled myself together and started shouting to Butcher and others to get themselves together. I remembered Brazil equalising against us within 17 seconds. I need not have worried. There was hardly time to restart, never mind equalise. We were through to the quarter-finals to face Cameroon. I was up off the bench to thank Guy Thys. But he beat me to it. A thoroughly decent man whose team played well and could have won as we had. I hope I could have taken it the same way.

The scenes in the dressing room were fantastic. We were all exhilarated because we had all settled for a penalty shoot-out. The bus ride back to the hotel was an experience in itself. The ritual after a victory like that in England is to celebrate late into the night, having a drink. I hate it. It is one of the reasons why I let the England players go straight home after a Wembley international. Don Howe agrees. He always says: 'You punish your body in play and then punish it again in drink. Why do it twice in one day?'

By the time we returned to the hotel and had our meal it was into the early hours. We had to travel to Naples in a few hours and we were in the quarter-finals of the World Cup. I don't know what they thought about me. In fact, I didn't care. I went round and told them to go to bed. 'John Barnes, you couldn't finish the match – to bed. Chris Waddle . . . Paul Gascoigne – to bed.' David Platt had long since gone. He is one who doesn't need telling.

I told them all I would buy the drinks at the end, whenever that was. One glass of wine or beer was what they were allowed by the doc. That was enough.

Also through to the last eight were Yugoslavia, who had also won in extra-time, beating Spain 2–1.

England 1 (Platt 119) *Belgium* 0.
HT: 0–0: Att: 34,500.
Ref: Mikkelsen.
England: Shilton; Parker, Butcher, Wright, Walker, Pearce, Waddle, Gascoigne, McMahon (Platt 71), Barnes (Bull 74), Lineker.
Belgium: Preud'homme; Gerets, Grun, Demol, Clijsters, Dewolf, Van der Elst, Scifo, Versavel (Verwoort 107), Ceulemans, De Gryse (Claesen 64).

BOLOGNA/NAPLES
Wednesday, 27 June

Bed at 3.30, and the calls started at 8 a.m. FIFA wanted to know our requirements for Naples – stadium, hotel, training ground and the rest. Isn't it odd: the more important the games, the more tired we are, the shorter the gaps between games. The West German manager Franz Beckenbauer posed the question: why didn't we spread the games better to get a higher-quality tournament, give players time to recover from injuries and give the public more exciting matches? It is surely worth some thought.

A new friend from South Africa, Don Patel, telephoned to tell me he had watched on television and how pleased he was for me. Mick Wadsworth, who had watched Cameroon for me, rang and so did Dave Sexton, who was away to his next game before we played. The 'phone kept on ringing until BBC Radio linked me up with London to ask whether I or the Football Association would reconsider me leaving the job. The position, of course, was unaltered.

We tried to sort out our differences with the press, locking the doors to everyone but the English newspaper men. Views were aired on both sides, but the players, I knew, were not in a forgiving mood having been described that morning as 'yobs' by the *Star* and 'a disgrace' by the *Mirror* over the coach affair. But Platty came into the conference and did his bit for relations. He handles himself well.

Meanwhile outside, Jim Rosenthal of ITV mistakenly thought that it was Paul Gascoigne's birthday, thanks to an FA misprint, and bought him a big, gooey chocolate cake. Inevitably it finished up with the cake in Gazza's face, with ITV filming the slapstick they had set up. Rob Bonnet's BBC film crew also saw what was going on and tried to muscle in on the action and it ended with them all jostling and pushing each other. And the media call us hooligans!

More interviews, more calls, then off to Naples on our special charter and up to our hotel in the hills above Salerno to prepare ourselves for the task ahead, with a meeting after dinner to arrange our training schedules and consider the injuries.

The press were the next item on the agenda. They had suggested a sub-committee to talk to the players. The players, however, wouldn't wear it at any price. I said that we would have to try to work together to make life more comfortable for all of us, but they were determined to stick it out and not give in, listing the untrue stories to illustrate their point. They said: 'You won't change some reporters and you can't change their papers.' They said that they would continue to talk to the ones they wanted to talk to and not to the ones they thought had let them down. There was, they claimed, no rift and they agreed to make themselves available after training.

We didn't want to count our chickens but a semi-final place

was a distinct possibility and we had to talk about bringing out wives and families to watch, as promised. The practicalities were too involved to leave it until after the game so, as we had done four years earlier, we had to tempt fate again.

The next topic was discipline, not only on the field but off it as well. Cameroon had eight days' preparation. We had five, including a travelling day. The Belgian game had been punishing and if we were going to be ready it meant control. No tennis, no golf, no sightseeing, no Vesuvius, no Pompeii. Stick to the hotel, stick to the shade. Rest and recover. There was too much at stake to take chances.

Finally, I congratulated them but quickly added that this was only where we had expected to be and where we should be: in the last eight. If we hadn't got that far, we would have failed. From now on it was a different matter.

NAPLES
Thursday, 28 June

Very, very hot. Too hot even to sunbathe, never mind train. There was no Walker, no Lineker, no Barnes, no Hodge, but, amazingly, Butcher was fit to train. He believed that the leg had bent so much that it had actually helped to free it, and he claimed that it actually felt a lot better. We had to keep it light – relay races, competitive routines, all good fun. Everyone was in great spirits, with Waddle and Gazza superb. They were at the front when Don Howe told the players to keep walking while we set out the cones for the next routine. They did, but instead of continuing round the track they followed instructions to the letter and carried straight on. When we looked up they were all crowded against the wire mesh fence at the far end of the ground with the two daft Geordies climbing up. The spectators in the little ground couldn't believe what they were seeing.

But suddenly, both dropped out. The two who usually want to do the extra shooting practice, free-kicks and the rest, finished when the formal session ended. Both admitted they were tired. Their bodies were telling them they needed a rest. Should Chrissie have a complete break?

The players kept their promise and talked to the journalists they wanted to, while back at the hotel we gave a Spanish TV crew permission to film because they had missed the open session. I would call that cooperation plus.

I had dinner with Dick Wragg, chairman of the International Committee, who told me that he was going to quit when I did. Then there were three. I wondered who else was to follow. I appreciated that he had told me first. He wanted to arrange a little farewell party and asked me for one or two of the senior players. I suggested those with 50 caps and over, then he would have those he knew best.

I saw Peter Beardsley again. He wanted to tell me how thrilled he was and that, if needed, he was now fully fit and raring to go. He couldn't have been happy when I put Bull on instead of him, but he didn't show it.

I also had a chat with Gary Lineker – at his request. He had heard that I'd told the press that morning that he needed to start training if he was to keep his place. His bad toe, a really nasty injury, had meant a lot of rest and little training. I believe that if you don't train you lose that fine touch. Some of his hold-up play had not been good and I think that the lack of training was the cause. The other players had noticed, too. They were giving him a good-natured ribbing, telling him not to kick too hard in case he broke his lace and silly things like that. He took it all well and he was probably bright enough to know that I had no intention of dropping him, only to stir him up. You don't leave your best scorer out of a World Cup quarter-final. But I still felt he had reached the stage where he needed to make an effort.

NAPLES
Friday, 29 June

Breakfast these days had settled into a routine. I shared a table with Dick Wragg and Jack Wiseman while the players were represented as usual by Butcher, Woods, Parker and McMahon. After all that had happened I am sure that the gathered ranks of the media suspected I had kept them waiting in the broiling sun deliberately. I hadn't; it never crossed my mind. It was just that the team meeting had gone on a lot longer than I anticipated as we went through the Belgian match and the improvements that we needed against Cameroon.

I suppose I enjoy no more than a handful of cigars during the course of a year, but when Andrew Croker, son of former FA secretary Ted, approached me to do an advert for Hamlet I accepted. Quite frankly, the money on offer was too good to turn down. It opened my eyes to the sort of sums that can be earned if you chase them. I never have, and I'm not complaining.

I did a little more work on the arrangements to bring out the families for the semi-finals. I just hope it is not in vain, as it was in Mexico. Imagine the disappointment back home. We can't let them all down again.

No Barnes, no Walker for training in Naples. In fact, I was beginning to fret a little about Des. He seemed to take a whack on that bad leg every time he played and it was crumpling after an hour or so. It was a problem, but he never complained. Gary Lineker, at last, did a little training, much to my satisfaction. If anyone could shoot us through to the last four, it was the Tottenham man.

NAPLES
Saturday, 30 June

Dave Sexton telephoned to wish us luck as the telephone acted, once more, as my morning alarm call. Dave was followed by Don Patel from South Africa who wanted to know how our injured players were and to wish us luck.

We left for training just after 11 a.m. with the temperature soaring into the nineties. I gathered the team together on the pitch and told them who would play and how we would play. I had to tell Steve McMahon that I was sticking with Platt, which meant no place for him. He took it like the professional he is. Wright hurt his groin and didn't train. I wanted to work on the sweeper system but couldn't do it properly as we had no Wright and no Walker. Gary Stevens had to step in as emergency centre half, not for the first time. We trained for an hour, being careful to avoid injuries.

More and more pressmen were attending the conference every day and, again, the players handled it well. Turkish TV missed out and begged for permission to film at the hotel. We gave it.

Bless her, Mrs Porter rang again. Brian Gray, our liaison officer from Mexico four years earlier, arrived and I spent a pleasant hour with him and his wife.

But the day was dominated by quarter-finals, with Argentina squeezing past Yugoslavia 3–2 in a penalty shoot-out after a goal-less draw, in which Maradona missed his spot-kick. Again it was a good result for us because Yugoslavia were the better team and they were out. By this time my high opinion of Argentina had diminished. Maradona was no longer the same player, not even the best Argentinian player. I preferred the speedy Caniggia.

We had a team meeting planned for 7 p.m. but we cancelled it, had dinner early and let everyone watch the Irish take on the Italians in Rome. It was one everyone wanted to watch. The better team won but the Irish battled magnificently. It took a goal from the new Italian hero Schillaci to settle it but Jack's boys gave the hosts one hell of a fright and the Italians looked far from invincible. I did a live piece with Bob Wilson during the half-time break.

To add to my calls from around the globe I had another first during dinner when I was called away to take a call from the Albanian coach who rang to say he loved our team, loved our style and hoped we were going to win the World Cup. Amazing, isn't it! From Albania now. How on earth do they find out where we are staying?

I actually got to bed at 11.15 – the first time before midnight since we arrived in Italy. I wanted to be fresh for the first day of July.

BOLOGNA
Sunday, 1 July

My turn to make a telephone call. I rang the skipper Bryan Robson about his injury. He had undergone his operation and the surgeons found something which wouldn't have been cleared up without it. He was missing us as much as we were missing him. He said that having been away on the last three World Cups he had been unaware of the following and enthusiasm back in England. He was amazed and so was I. We just hadn't caught that sort of feedback from back home. The vibes we picked up were more negative. Bryan said that the whole country was singing. 'It was,' he said, 'lovely.'

Only a handful of players went training in the heat with Don Howe, Mike Kelly and Fred Street. But we needed to know about John Barnes. He would only play if he proved to me that he was fit. Some people seemed to think that we were creating a bit of a mystery, preparing to let him down lightly, using the injury as an excuse. Not true. I asked Fred to give him the most stringent of tests and he did, making John twist, turn, and smash the ball. Don came back to tell me: 'He has done everything.' With what I had seen the day before we were both convinced that he was ready.

We had a team meeting at noon and went through the Cameroon reports. Howard Wilkinson had seen them against Argentina, Romania, Colombia and the Soviet Union. Mick Wadsworth and John Lyall had also watched them, so we were well covered from that point of view. We also had the video highlights of their free-kicks and were able to show half an hour of their general shape. It was all valuable stuff. Everyone agrees they are physically tough and strong, although maybe a bit naive.

Howard Wilkinson rang me twice. He felt that this was a good time to play them; in fact he went as far as saying: 'Bobby, I think you have got a bye into the semi-finals. All you have to do is play like you did against the Belgians.'

He added that they would try and slow it down and reduce the 90 minutes to an hour by time-wasting. He reckoned we needed to up the pace, play for 80 minutes and make things happen. The Soviet Union had beaten them by four goals by playing quick, brisk football. But Cameroon knew they were already certain to qualify when they went out to play that game, and that might go a long way towards explaining that result – incidentally their first defeat in two World Cups! I told the team they would have to watch the Cameroon striker Roger Milla and forget that he is a 38-year old striker who has come out of

171

semi-retirement. He is electric quick and can do a lot of damage in 30 minutes. Their whole team becomes revitalised when he comes on.

Despite having received so much information on our African opponents, we didn't know what team their Soviet coach would pick because he had four suspensions, including N'dip and Onana who, according to our reports, were their best defenders. I honestly could not see us losing under the circumstances and my only discomfort was caused by my cracked rib which stopped me swimming and restricted me to a nap by the pool and a quiet read. It was a lazy afternoon.

We kept the same system and only one change, leaving substitute Platt in for McMahon. We were confident and had the bit between our teeth. We needed no motivation; after all we were playing for a place in the semi-finals of the World Cup, something no British team had ever achieved on foreign soil.

We discovered that our opponents if we won would be, as expected, West Germany. They played in the afternoon match and were not at their best as they beat the Czechs 1–0 with a Lothar Matthaus penalty after 24 minutes. Any chance of a late Czech come-back was scuppered by the strange sending off of Lubomir Moravcik 20 minutes from the end as yellow turned to red when he kicked off his loose boot.

The road from our hotel to the stadium in Naples was always busy, but our escort had us through in spectacular style on a hair-raising journey, shifting cars left and right to get us there in good time. And then the quarter-final. Where do you start in describing something like this? This is why ours is such a fantastic game – it is totally unpredictable. That is why the experts don't win the pools every week. The form book will always let you down when you least expect it.

It was nail-biting, heart-rending, like riding the roughest of roller coasters as it ebbed and flowed and changed course in crazy fashion. Everyone who wasn't English, in and out of the stadium, was on the side of the underdogs, just as we would have been had they been playing anyone else. For those next two hours we were probably the most disliked team in the world. What struck me most was their size and physical presence. Only Mfede was diminutive and he was replaced by another giant, Ekeke, after an hour or so. This was a different team from the one we had seen on television and which had been described to us by our 'spies'.

They might have taken the lead but for Shilton saving from the immensely talented Omam Biyik who had been put clean through by Makanaky. Some said it was our good luck. Wrong. It was a good save. That was why I picked Peter Shilton. But the Africans were a handful and I was relieved when, a few minutes later, we went in front with another superb goal from David Platt as he came in late down his favourite channel and connected with Stuart Pearce's perfect cross. A goal like so many he had scored for Aston Villa that season.

But Cameroon didn't succumb as I thought they would if we went in front. Far from it. It made them all the more determined. They had nothing to lose and had a real go at us and we were struggling to keep our lead. It was the first time that Gazza had a dodgy first half. He was all over the shop, not picking anyone up as they went through our midfield like a dose of salts. Paul got lost whenever Cameroon were in possession. Everyone had their hands full; even Des Walker was at full stretch against Biyik. It was a case of survival until half time. Frankly they were the better side.

At half-time I stormed into the dressing room and said: 'You may think you are one up and on the way into the semi-final but I'll tell you that if you carry on playing like that we are on our way out.' I had a word with Gazza, telling him to be solid and stop chasing the ball and to play off his man. He needed to be more of a midfield player and less of an ad-libber. Then Barnes came to see me about his groin. The injury had come back and he was not feeling good at all. We had all thought he was fit, himself included, but no matter how stringent the test, the match always finds you out. There was no way he was going to carry on and I had to make a swift decision. I had used Bull against Belgium but this was not a match for him. I thought Beardsley might give us more control – he had assured me of his fitness and I needed his experience.

But all the things I had worried about at half-time came horribly true. The game turned on two penalty decisions that could have been the end of us. Platt was brought down by 'keeper N'kono. It looked a penalty but referee Codesal Mendez of Mexico waved play–on, and seconds later Gascoigne stuck out a leg and down went half–time substitute Milla. The experienced old fox had played for the penalty and won it. After all my warnings! Even as I walked round the pitch at half-time and saw the shaved head of Milla I sounded the red alert, shouting a warning to both Butcher and Wright that he was on, preparing to start.

Kunde scored from the spot and it was all tied up. Worse was to follow as, only three minutes later, Ekeke, who had come on only a minute before, took a pass from Milla and put the outsiders in front. I thought then that it was going to be difficult to come back because they were the better side and had more cohesion. I could see now why they had done so well. As Omam Biyik almost added a third it flashed through my mind that my father, the kids, the players' wives were going to be let down again as they had been four years before. My poor dad. He had got his passport and was all ready to fly out. The underdogs were on top of the game and we were not penetrating their defence.

But the strange game was not finished yet. Gazza suddenly found his second wind and started to pose the opposition some questions. For an hour he had been insignificant – and he wasn't the only one. But this kid got us going. Whether they relaxed and thought they had it won I don't know. But the game began to swing our way. It was time to throw caution to the wind. I thought we might just as well go out 3–1 as 2–1, so I pulled off Butcher and sent on Trevor Steven. You have to be brave in this game. I take the decisions, no one else. I played with four up. But within five minutes Mark Wright had split his eye open and the world had caved in again. It was a real bad one and Fred Street waved across to the bench that there was no chance of him continuing. Fred was bringing him off and we had already used our substitutes. That was it; our chance had gone unless we could get Mark back on. But by the time he had been helped round to the bench the eye was completely closed. He was in no sort of shape to continue and both Fred and the doctor shook their heads. Suddenly Wright sat up and said he wanted to play. I told them to strap him up. We were down to ten men with Walker feeling his leg and limping again, little Parker at centre half struggling against the giants, and Beardsley not able to get into the game at all. It was a disaster. We were fighting for a share and couldn't get even that, nothing was going for us. We were in a hole and had I lost from their position I would have been very upset.

When the chance came, we missed it. We all jumped off the bench when Gazza split the two central defenders with a superb ball and Platty got through to steer the ball past their 'keeper, only for it to graze the post. We sent Wright back on. We couldn't stitch him, so he was padded and the eye covered and I hurried him back on, telling him to play in midfield to protect Trevor Steven, stop their left back and fill in on the overlap.

The one thing which kept us in it and gave us a bit of heart was our spirit. I looked around and saw clenched fists and players shouting to each other. It came when we were at our lowest. Suddenly Parker was leaping like a salmon and Walker discovered he could trust him and get on with his own job, while Trevor Steven looked like an international right back. Wright was involved and Lineker was chasing everything. But time was slipping away, I could almost see the minute hand move as I looked at my watch.

The come-back started with another great through-ball from Gazza. How Lineker loves to receive the ball in that way; he has built his career on it. He made a darting run, and then – chop! A penalty as clear as day. We had the penalty we had been dreaming and talking about for five years and it had come at exactly the right moment, just eight minutes from the end. The team had picked itself up – the spirit of adventure against adversity. They had done it themselves, not me. Now it was up to Gary and my biggest problem at that minute was whether nor not to look. Gary recovered, picked himself up and slotted the penalty home. He took it so well, keeping calm and coping with the situation. He said later he had been thinking of his brother Wayne in Tenerife.

Full-time came quickly and I was out onto the pitch like a flash. Cameroon had thought they had had it won but now they couldn't be so sure. It was down to fitness. Could we cope with the heat and another session of extra-time? I asked Peter Beardsley to get involved more, get busy, and then I turned to all of them and asked: 'Do you want to win? Do you want a place in the semi-final?' They did. The defence which had leaked for an hour-

and-a-half tightened up, Beardsley started to do all the things he is so good at and we looked solid again. It was the Cameroons, not us, who had run out of steam. Gazza was still on song and Platt ploughed through a tremendous quantity of work. Even so, we needed a wonderful clearance from Steven in our six-yard box, the sort only someone who has played in that position for years can usually execute.

We won it with a second penalty. Two penalties in eight years and now two in 23 minutes and, what is more, the second was a replica of the first. Gary was brought down again and the decision was fair and square; there was no gamesmanship on Gary's part, he had not played for it. I knew if we scored from the spot we would win. A little prayer as Gary got up and hit it straight as N'kono dived off in the direction Gary had struck the first penalty; 3–2. We were back from the dead. Not only did we see the game out but we almost scored another as Steven tore down the right and knocked in a great ball – but we couldn't finish off the move. This time it didn't matter. The whistle had gone and we were through, into the semi-final. That was special for me, the players and the whole country.

In the dressing room I told them: 'You know what's got us through. Not great football. It was fighting spirit. A little bit of football and a lot of heart. Your bottle was better than theirs. They couldn't cope with it. You could.' They deserved any credit that was going. There were no wild celebrations. They were too tired, absolutely back on their heels. I will never forget Chris Waddle and Peter Shilton sitting together, heads bowed, dripping with sweat when Waddle looked up and said: 'Some f*****g bye that was! Don't get us another bye like that one boss.' It was hilarious.

Doctor Crane asked me where Wright was. He wanted to get to work on the eye as quickly as possible. Neither he nor Gazza was anywhere to be found. They were doing television. I was furious and stormed into the studio, not caring whether it was live or recorded, grabbed them and dragged them away. Didn't they realise we had a semi-final against the Germans in three days time and I wanted Wright to be able to play? We needed every possible minute with him. When I calmed down it was a lovely feeling. We had made history. We were in the semi-finals. Everyone was aware of it. I consoled the Cameroon's Soviet coach, telling him he was unlucky. He surprised me by speaking enough English to say that we were too strong and too good in the end.

Bert Millichip, Dick Wragg and Colin Moynihan came in to congratulate us, bringing with them a high-ranking Foreign Office official who told me he had been enthralled with our spirit and was proud that we had shown the world what it meant. He added that it would do our country good throughout the world. He was so sincere about it, he had found himself caught up in it. I was near to tears.

The coach was dark but animated on the return to our hotel where there were a lot of people waiting for us. But there was no partying. We still had to see the job through. The big one was still to come and it was already almost 3 a.m.

Cameroon 2 (Kunde 63 (pen), Ekeke 67) *England* 3 (Platt 25, Lineker 82, 104 (both pens)).
HT: 0–1: Att: 55,000.
Ref: Codesal.
Cameroon: Nkono; Tataw, Massing, Kunde, Edwelle, Maboang (Milla 46), Libih, Pagal, Makanaky, Mfede (Ekeke 62), Omam Biyik.
England: Shilton; Parker, Butcher (Steven 74), Wright, Walker, Pearce, Waddle, Platt, Gascoigne, Barnes (Beardsley 46), Lineker.

NAPLES/TURIN
Monday, 2 July

Dave Sexton and Howard Wilkinson were first on the 'phone and I was quick to warn Howard that he had better watch his step when he went back into the First Division next season because he was in trouble. There were a few England internationals waiting to pounce. He was baffled until I explained that the players weren't too impressed with his idea of a bye into the semi-finals. He hadn't realised that I was going to pass on the message to the team.

ITV's Jim Rosenthal came to see me to apologise over the Mark Wright business. Apology accepted. Most of the players who had performed the night before stayed in bed as I did a succession of radio, television and press interviews, grateful that two-goal Gary Lineker was around to help me out.

We were waved away from the hotel as we set off yet again, this time heading for Turin and our date with destiny. We were staying at the Hasta Hotel where the Brazilians had lodged for 26 days and where England had stayed 10 years earlier in the European Championships under Ron Greenwood. It was a lovely hotel, a real football hotel, but there was no pool.

I was interested to hear that Brazil had not created the best of impressions during their long stay in this wine-growing region, and not just with their results. Apparently they had almost driven the staff mad with their indiscipline and their loud music. They still would be wandering round the hotel at 2 a.m., ordering room service in the early hours of the morning, with wives and kids coming and going all the time.

They had no such problem with us. Everyone was down for dinner promptly with a small meeting afterwards to discuss our training schedules and how to make the most of the little recovery time left. The problem was how to occupy that time with no pool to act as a diversion and with sunbathing banned. I even advised them not to train, to conserve all possible energy.

Then, at last, I allowed my mind to turn to the Germans. I was always aware of the strong possibility that we would have to play them eventually if we were going to have a serious crack at winning the Cup. There was no doubt that they had been the best side overall in the tournament but we needed to have no feelings of inferiority.

TURIN
Tuesday, 3 July

The vibes being transmitted in Italy were that we were a lucky lot but Mick Wadsworth 'phoned to tell me that back at home the nation was jumping for joy. Perhaps some of the journalists over here have missed the point, particularly the one who described us as a disgrace to the world game! Still, I suppose it is difficult to eat humble pie after writing us off after our opening game.

Peter Shilton joined those who hadn't played on Sunday in a

training session with Don Howe. I watched from the touchline and was thrilled at the attitude of all of them, especially that man Shilton. I wasn't the only one watching the training. Chris Waddle, Paul Gascoigne and Terry Butcher had also wandered over and their banter made the session not only useful but enjoyable as well. The spirit is tremendous.

Even the tedious press conference and television interviews had taken on a new dimension. With 20 teams out of the 24 gone, the world's media attention was on us, with the press conference spilling over the many chairs put out by the hotel on their lawn. Platt, Shilton and Wright shared the load with me. The adrenalin was flowing and that was how it should be.

Dave Sexton arrived, his work as a 'spy' finished. He was going to stay with us for the last week of the tournament, going over his comprehensive reports on the other three teams left in. Obviously we talked at length about the Germans. We felt they were there to be taken. That was also the feeling when Don and Mike joined us to discuss the team and formation. The problem lies in midfield where Franz Beckenbauer is certain to play three against my two. Do I keep our shape or do I throw in Steven or McMahon? I must say I am very tempted to pick Steven, the way he has been training and performing. For the first time since coming to Italy I have really had to ponder over selection. It is only in that one area, for I have decided I will stay with the sweeper for this one whether nor not Mark Wright is fit – and I expect he will be for this one. Should he take a turn for the worse I will shift Parker to mark and play Gary Stevens at right back. But what do I do about this midfield? I can't drop either Gazza or Platt, the way they are playing. If I changed it, Chris Waddle would have to be the one to go. That's the Germans' strength; maybe I will leave Chris out.

The Germans came under discussion yet again at the 5 p.m. team meeting as we watched selected phases of their exciting game against Holland. With the set-plays we were there for almost two hours before breaking off for an early dinner to allow us all to watch the live transmission of the semi-final between Italy and Argentina.

Once again we saw the favourites fall – but what a way to go. My heart went out to their manager Azeglio Vicini as the Italian dream ended not in honourable defeat but in the false light of a penalty shoot-out. I hope our game is settled before the end of extra-time and preferably in 90 minutes. Three successive sessions of extra-time is too much to ask of any team before a World Cup Final, emotionally as well as physically. The whole of Italy went into mourning. Being undefeated was not enough. The very least they expected was to play in the Final in Rome, but instead they had gone out with their poorest performance of the Championships.

Yet it had all begun so well with their new hero Schillaci scoring after just 17 minutes and everyone settling back to watch the slaughter of this ordinary Argentina side. But give credit where it is due. Argentina defended their crown with spirit – sometimes a little too much, for they will go into the final against ourselves or the Germans short of four suspended players, including their most dangerous, Caniggia. With Maradona little more than a shadow of his former glorious self, the champions are struggling.

It was Caniggia, stupidly booked for handball, who scored the equaliser to force the game into extra time, and even when Giusti was dismissed for an off-the-ball incident involving Baggio in over-time of the first half of extra-time the Italians could not get their game back together again. And when they did, the reserve goalkeeper Goycochea performed heroics. But he saved his best for last with an amazing 'double', saving first from Donadoni and then from Serena with Maradona scoring the penalty which mattered in between.

Amazingly Argentina were in their third final in 12 years and I was thrilled and delighted. I was now sure that our game against the Germans would decide who would win the World Cup. I was convinced that we could beat Argentina so that if we won the next day England would become World Champions. What a pleasant thought to go to bed with.

TURIN
Wednesday, 4 July

My wife Elsie . . . Don Patel from South Africa . . . Mrs Porter from Newcastle . . . Mike Shapow . . . it must be match day because the 'phone in my room is red hot with people wishing me well. We carry a lot of hopes on our shoulders today. I am ready for it. I need to make sure everyone else is.

Hence my first task that morning, once I escaped the telephone, was to go to Chris Waddle's room before breakfast where I asked to see him away from his room-mate Gascoigne. We made out way to the empty team room. He must have feared the worst. Chris was going to be my World Cup winner but he had been too much like the curate's egg, good in parts. His best game was against Belgium but he had been wildly up and down. But now we had come to the crunch because I had decided that I definitely wanted three in midfield but, against that, I didn't want to disturb the team any more than it needed. I was going to keep Beardsley in for the injured Barnes and I was hopeful that Wright would be fit enough to take Klinsmann, leaving Walker on Voller and, this time, Butcher, ever more versatile, as the free man.

But first we had to resolve the Waddle issue. Any doubts, any argument and he was out. I came straight out with it. I told Waddle I had a problem and that I was going to share it with him. I explained that I would have to leave him out unless I played him in midfield. That would mean extra work, a different role.

'That's my dilemma,' I told him, 'where will I get the best out of you for the team? Have you the heart and the capacity for that sort of midfield role? I have slept on it and if you assure me that you can do it I am going to keep the team and just change the formation. It will probably mean you taking Littbarski. It is a responsible job.'

He convinced me that he could do it and I decided to stick with this talented player instead of going for Trevor Steven, the most likely replacement, or Steve McMahon. Steven, after what he had shown me, would have done the job well. At training Mark Wright was cleared to play. He headed a few balls and said he was fine but, all the same, I took out insurance by playing Butcher to use his heading ability. In that area he is as good as anyone in the world. The die was cast. I told them the team.

McMahon came up to me afterwards and said that he thought I might have needed him for this one. I told him that he and others had been on my mind, pointing out how well Trevor Steven had played and yet he was out. But his point was a good one. With three in midfield he was entitled to think he had a chance as a specialist. I was still disconcerted but I was not going to let on.

But the question nagged – *had I picked the right team?*

I suppose every manager going to a game of this magnitude must harbour those doubts. There were no rehearsals, no replays, no such result as a draw. There was only one chance.

I had appreciated Steve McMahon coming to see me man-to-man instead of running to the newspapers. I kept it to myself as I went through a series of television interviews with ITN, BBC and ITV and took a call from my Ipswich barber Gino Palmeiri from Naples along with many more from well-wishers, friends and family.

I spent a large part of the afternoon with Dave Sexton who wanted to talk about his future. We had worked together for eight years but we had had little time to talk since it became public that I was leaving my job with England. He had been a great supporter and a great companion. He had done an outstanding job for the FA, particularly at the Lilleshall School, with the youth and the Under-21 side. The fact that I was leaving had upset him, he also felt that it put his own position up in the air. But even after I had explained how it had all happened he said that he was going as well and planned to write his letter of resignation to Graham Kelly.

I was appalled.

'Why?' I asked. 'Don't you like the job any more?'

'I love it.'

'Then wait and see, don't walk out. You know all about the Under-21s and the kids, Graham Taylor doesn't. He won't know about the 19-year-old at Halifax, the 18-year-old Middlesbrough reserve. It's a specialised job.'

That was no bull. Some clubs won't even acknowledge the letters we send. Others say they have nothing. What sort of state is a club in which has nothing worth talking about among their kids? What is its youth policy? Then there are others who simply don't tell you what they have because they don't want them put on show. And there are others who throw a couple of names at you to get you off their backs. You have to search, to find out for yourself. It doesn't just happen. There is time to be spent on the job. Dave has spent that time and has the experience. What is more everyone likes him. He is the original iron fist in a velvet glove. He is no softy and knows the game. I advised him to let the FA make the first move. He wisely decided to leave it. I knew that they would do what was right.

The kick-off was at 8 p.m., an hour earlier than we had been used to. Everything came forward an hour and we were on our way by 5.30.

The World Cup chief Luca di Montezemolo had sent a message saying that he would like to come into the dressing room an hour before the kick-off. You don't refuse your host but when he arrived he had with him the President of Juventus, Mr 'Football' (or some would have it Mr 'Italy') Agnelli. It was that limbo time before a game, some players were already in the dressing room and others were outside. Gazza walked in while he was there and said to one of the world's richest men: 'Hello mate – how are you?' putting his thumbs up as he said it. Agnelli was tickled pink. He was so used to people bowing and scraping that he found Gascoigne both refeshing and engaging.

Gascoigne was so confident. Before the game I had taken him to one side and told him that if he played like he did in the first hour against Cameroon we would be in trouble. I said: 'If you disappear, Matthaus will come through that gap like a cobra and put us out of the World Cup.'

It didn't faze Gazza at all. He answered: 'Boss – leave him to me.'

'Are you sure?' I asked.

'No problem. Don't worry.'

Lothar Matthaus; blistering pace, scorer of great goals, probably the player of the tournament. Gazza wasn't at all bothered and, on the day, he was absolutely right. On the day he did it. They were more worried about him than he was about them. Franz had clearly told his team to watch out for this boy called Gascoigne.

Gazza had caught the attention of one important man before the game but later he was to capture the hearts of the world as they watched an unbelievable climax on their televisions, a game most people described as the best in the entire competition. We were so even there was nothing to choose between us.

We had talked before about how the Germans liked to open up strongly and get an early goal, to dominate opponents right from the start. We decided that the best way to handle that was to be prepared and make the opprtunity to launch counter-attacks and to go at them with gusto. I told the boys that we would start positively. They took the idea on board, responded and gave me a brilliant first 35 minutes, when we were unlucky not to take the lead and control of the semi-final. We took a bit and gave a lot back. It was absorbing stuff.

Franz Beckenbauer had kept his secrets well. There was no Littbarski, no Bein. Instead little Olaf Thon and Thomas Hassler were in. It didn't change the shape or the pattern but it did surprise me when it was announced 50 minutes before the kick-off and it revived those nagging doubts. As I showed the sheet to Don I finally admitted out loud: 'Maybe I've picked the wrong team.' There was no sympathy or reassurance from Don, not that I expected or wanted any. He just looked at me and said: 'It's too late to worry about that now.'

I wasn't sure that Chrissie could contain Thon's attacking runs but, I suppose, when Franz saw my team, he must have been wondering the same sort of thing about Thon when Waddle would have possession. In the end we both have the same problems, the same doubts, the same fears and it is no use anyone who hasn't done the job telling me otherwise.

Waddle, as it happens, did a fine job and served some excellent long balls forward in that first, stunning half-an-hour. Gazza tested Illgner in the German goal in the early minutes while Pearce drove wide after Gascoigne had engineered the opening.

While we flowed they had some problems. Klinsmann and Voller had been shackled by Walker and Wright with Voller being replaced by Riedle after only 38 minutes. Voller was injured and it didn't look as though he fancied it too much. Funnily enough it was while he was off having treatment that the Germans had their best chance so far when Thon tested Shilton low to his left. When Riedle eventually restored the Germans' strength they began to surge forward and Shilts needed to be on his toes to save from Augenthaler and Thon.

Both teams came off to thunderous applause at the break. It was a great match, played in an excellent spirit with hardly a foul to spoil it. I told them how pleased they could be with themselves and that they had proved that there was nothing to be afraid of out there. I told them – and believed – that we could go on from here and win the World Cup outright. It was there to be won.

I knew that the first goal was going to be crucial but I was stunned when it was the Germans who scored it even though they had been on top for the first 15 minutes of the second half as those bouts of extra-time and the heat began to take their toll on us. An iffy foul by Pearce on the limping Hassler gave them a free-kick outside the box and when Brehme struck the ball it took a massive deflection off the boot of the advancing Parker and caught Shilton off his line as it squeezed in under the crossbar, maybe even touching it on the way.

My heart sank. Once again I was faced with the same problem, a goal down playing with a sweeper. On the Continent the normal practice under those circumstances is to keep the shape and bring on one forward for another. I needed more than that. I gambled again, exactly as I had done against Cameroon in the previous round. I took off Butcher, sent on Steven and shifted Chrissie Waddle wide, leaving us two against three in midfield. It paid off. Parker cancelled out his unfortunate own goal with his ball into the box which threw Kohler, Augenthaler and Berthold into a state of utter confusion. Lineker pounced the way only he can, wriggling between the three of them before turning and crashing a left foot shot beyond the reach of Illgner. Ten minutes remaining and it was anyone's game.

We saw out the remainder of normal time and left ourselves facing our third bout of extra-time in successive games. I gathered the players in a group again and told them that, once again, they had to do what they had already done twice before. Waddle surprised me by asking if he could go to outside right because he fancied a crack at Brehme who, he reckoned, had exhausted himself. He said: 'I can take him.' But it was Steven, only on for 20 minutes, who was fresher and I decided that Steven should run him in the first half of extra-time and Chrissie in the second.

Often, as players tire, extra-time slows to a careful exchange between teams afraid to make errors. Not this time. The excitement continued unabated. Waddle, the one I had worried about, was an inch from putting us in the final as he struck the inside of a post and saw the ball come straight out instead of rebounding into the net while Buchwald hit the outside of a post and Shilton made super saves from Matthaus and Klinsmann.

But perhaps the moment which captivated the world came just

eight minutes into extra time. Gascoigne, running his heart out for the team, chased Berthold to the sideline where he mistimed his challenge, bringing the full back down right in front of the German bench. They were instantly on their feet and I am sure that their reaction influenced referee José Ramiz Wright who handed the Spurs player his second caution of the tournament.

Realisation was immediate. Gazza knew that he would play no part in the final even if we did win. Tears streaming down his face, he pleaded in vain with the referee. He was distraught. It was a pity, for Berthold's reaction to the challenge and the concerted efforts of the West German bench were out of character with the rest of this sporting contest. Lineker ran towards me a few minutes later and shouted: 'Watch him . . . watch Gazza . . . He's gone.' Well done Gary. He knows Paul better than any of us. He is right. For five minutes Gascoigne ran about in his own cloud of purple mist. I was not tempted to bring him off but I watched him carefully. He gradually recovered his composure and I got the message to him at the turn-around that he might be out of the final but he could still make sure his mates got there and be the hero of his country.

'Get us to the final.'

'I can do it,' he said sniffing. 'Nay problem.'

But this time there were no penalties, no last-minute goals and we were into a shoot-out. What a blow. What a way to decide whether or not we should play in a World Cup Final. Still, I suppose it is better than tossing a coin or drawing lots but not as good as playing more extra time even though that would clearly have favoured our opponents.

We had talked about the possibility of penalties. There had been a good show of hands when we asked about penalty-takers. Plenty of takers even though we were without two of them, John Barnes and Bryan Robson. I wasn't too worried. Our name was on the World Cup. We had good penalty-takers and a great goalkeeper, the best in the World Cup. I was still a little concerned about Gazza but he indicated that he would rather take the sixth penalty if it came to a sudden-death situation after the first five. A brave choice.

We had a plan. Our regular penalty-taker Lineker would give us the start we needed and we would save our next best, Stuart Pearce, for the crucial fourth spot kick. I always reckoned that

Paul Parker, one of the great successes, against Egypt in Cagliari

Goalscorer Mark Wright earns the congratulations of the substitutes against Egypt

Senior professional Terry Butcher looks after Gazza after the youngster had given away a penalty against Cameroon

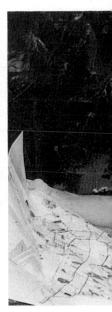

Above: Mark Wright climbs above Terry Butcher to keep out the Belgians

Right: David Platt can't contain his delight having grabbed a spectacular last gasp winner to beat Belgium

Below: Another team meeting

Peter Shilton and Terry Butcher both retired from international football after Italy

Mark Wright was never far away from Jurgen Klinsmann

Giving Paul Parker last minute instructions going into extra time against West Germany

Happy in defeat! Fourth place medals couldn't take away from what these boys had achieved in Italy

Left: Trying on the new PSV Eindhoven gear for size

Below: Graham Taylor can take England on to even greater heights

was a key penalty, particularly if you had missed one, because it kept the pressure on the opposition for their final penalty. We won the toss and took the first penalty, a good sign because it is like putting in golf, sink yours and your opponent is under pressure. Gary wants it, takes the ball and beats Illgner. So does Beardsley and a nervy young Platt. Shilton is unlucky. Every time he chooses the right way but Brehme, Matthaeus and Riedle hit scorching shots. If I had to back one player it would have been Pearce, cool and with the hardest shot in the business. Illgner saves with his feet and our world caves in. Pearce is distraught. What an unfair burden this is to put upon an individual in a team sport. Every professional footballer realises this and our players move to console him only to be beaten to it by the sporting Matthaeus.

Thon makes it 4–3 and then Waddle runs up and puts the ball into orbit. We are out. The Germans don't even need to take their fifth penalty. They are in the final against Argentina and we have the consolation prize of a third place play-off against Italy who had suffered the same fate.

It is heart-rending. My players are in tears. Pearce is inconsolable. Waddle shattered. Matthaus and one or two of the Germans delay their own celebrations to go among our players while Franz, heading for his fourth World Cup Final as player and manager, says: 'What a pity it has to come to this. They were two fine teams. You played so well.'

I choked back my own emotion to congratulate him, shake his hand and say: 'This was the real final. We have given so much entertainment in such a sporting game. Go on and win it now for us.'

All the time I am thinking – why, oh why does it have to happen to us? I have to bite my lip. I am so sad but I have to keep my smile, keep my dignity. What a shame. Just a penalty away from the dream. We were a whisker away. How wonderful it would have been to leave the job I loved so much with a World Cup Final. It was not to be.

The dressing room was awash with tears. Gazza was still upset. Poor kid. He was really wound up. I can't even remember my own reaction. For a few seconds it blew my mind; suddenly aware we are out. The dressing room is so quiet. It's best to say nowt. Suffer in silence. Others had the good grace to stay away.

I still had to show a brave face to the world's cameras and the press. That done I walked out of the stadium and up the slope to our full but silent bus, watching the TV crews crowd around the German players as they made their way towards their transport, their journey home and their celebrations. In that moment you could see the gulf between winning and losing.

We made our way back to the Hasta Hotel in Asti. We had a meal and it was not too much trouble getting the players and everyone else off to their beds. I told them at dinner that everyone here and at home was immensely proud of them. But we still had to finish the job. Italy were the hosts and now was not the time to let go and spoil it. We must behave professionally and play for third place and our still unbeaten record. There was still one more to go. Within half-an-hour everyone was in bed, all of us lost in our own thoughts. Sleep was a welcome friend that night, at least for those of us with no nightmares!

West Germany 1 (Brehme 59) *England* 1 (Lineker 80).
HT: 0–0. 90 mins: 1–1. Att: 62,628.
Ref: Wright (Brazil).
West Germany 4–3 on penalties.
Lineker 1–0, Brehme 1–1; Beardsley 2–1, Matthaeus 2–2; Platt 3–2, Riedle 3–3; Pearce saved 3–3, Thon 3–4; Waddle missed 3–4.
England: Shilton; Parker, Walker, Wright, Butcher (Steven 70), Pearce; Waddle, Gascoigne, Platt, Beardsley; Lineker.
West Germany: Illgner, Berthold, Brehme, Kohler, Augenthaler, Buchwald, Hassler (Reuter), Voller (Riedle), Thon, Matthaus, Klinsmann.

TURIN/BARI
Thursday, 5 July

For the first time we have been knocked out of a competition and no-one – well almost no-one – is demanding my head on a platter. Our own pride in our performance against the Germans has been reflected back at home where everyone is saying that it is the best performance for almost a quarter of a century and that we thrilled the nation and restored our battered pride.

It was good consolation at a time when I was at a very low ebb and having to keep on a brave face for the cameras and the interviews which continued unabated. To be honest I could have done without the game against Italy and the travelling but it was Italy we were playing and we still had a debt to pay. We couldn't let people down now by sulking and not giving of our best. But it was going to be difficult, no matter what I said to the contrary to the players and the media.

The manager of the hotel personally bade us farewell saying that it had been an honour and a privilege to host such sporting gentlemen. We were, he said, in a different class to the Brazilians. Another reason to feel good.

We flew to Bari and I took the opportunity to sit next to my secretary Michelle Rogers on the 'plane to catch up on work and to arrange to clear my desk. She was a bit low. So was I. The realisation that a job I loved was coming to an end began to sink in.

We had already had a press conference before we left our hotel in Asti but when we arrived in Bari there was a huge contingent of Italian journalists waiting for me. Oh well, what's one more?

I was touched when we arrived at our hotel in Truli, some hour's drive from Bari, because all the locals were out on the street to greet us. It seemed that we were very popular in defeat.

Strolling through the gardens of the hotel that night I came across Gazza and a stranger. 'It's my mate,' said Gazza, by way of introduction. It transpired that the *Sunday Mirror* had flown him over to cheer him up. The whole country, it seemed, was engulfed in Gazzamania, and why not?

BARI
Friday, 6 July

I rang Elsie from the hotel down the road. I felt empty, hollow, and needed to talk to her. She's great support.

Before training I told Terry Butcher, Stuart Pearce and Chris Waddle that they would not be starting against Italy tomorrow. Butcher's knee was bothering him again, in any case, while I wanted to give Tony Dorigo a game in place of Stuart and to play Trevor Steven for Waddle. Both Pearce and Waddle had suffered three successive periods of extra-time and played in every game. It was time for a rest.

Pearce was quite put out. He wanted to play, especially after that penalty miss but I explained to both that the decision had nothing at all to do with penalties, while adding to Pearce that he was the best left back and that is why I had picked him for every game. Waddle had worked well but was tired.

The other decision was whether to play Shilton. He had confided in Chris Woods, his long-suffering deputy, that he was retiring and offered to stand down if I wanted him to. I wanted to give him his 125th cap. It was a nice round figure and I thought that it would be fitting, in the absence of both Butcher and Robson, for him to skipper the side on his very last appearance. I told him: 'I am picking you because you are the best goalkeeper in the World Cup.' I said that I would speak to Chris and that he would understand. I was not in football to be nice and give everyone a game. I tried to persuade Shilts to announce his retirement to the press today but he wouldn't.

Mark Wright came up with a calf strain he had not mentioned before. Strange that it had taken a couple of days to emerge. I was cross because I had already told Butcher he was not playing and I told Mark: 'You're playing. You are fitter than him.' I was short of bodies, so I had to use Neil Webb as a sweeper in training that morning. I saw him later and explained again that I couldn't play everyone but that it was still important to see it out properly.

I added: 'You will be the number one substitute against Italy and I will bring you on if I can. I feel sorry for you. You have trained, kept your head up and not moaned. But that is what you are here for, just like Dave Beasant, Chris Woods and Steve Hodge.'

Shilton also came to see me again saying that he hadn't realised that I was leaving others out and as I was should he stand down as well to give Chris a game. I stood by everything I had said earlier: Chris's chance would come next season. Shilts said: 'You've convinced me. I will play.'

The whole world seemed to be at the press conference and I followed it with television interviews with crews from local Italian stations, the national channel RAI, English, Mexican, Spanish, Argentinian TV and Sky, one after another. It also looked as if the entire world had descended upon our hotel for we had all the wives and families round, a sort of open house. It was all very nice.

The hotel put on a lovely spread and the doc made sure that everyone was looked after. He's good at that. After the families had left the players met me for an hour for a signing session for each other organised by Terry Butcher. All the books, pennants, souvenirs they had promised to others and, of course, to themselves. After all they had something worth remembering. There was a great deal of friendship displayed in that hour.

I had the feeling it was all winding down even though we wanted to end the tournament on a high note. The local mayor came round for dinner and so did Roberto Pappalardo, a great friend and supporter of England long after we had left Sardinia.

I was in bed by midnight. Whacked.

BARI
Saturday, 7 July

My last game in charge of England and it was nice that, even though we were to all intents and purposes out of the World Cup, the routines of the past few weeks had not changed as I took the usual calls from Mr Patel in South Africa and Mrs Porter in Newcastle. The players' wives also made contact and asked if they could use the pool as their hotel did not have one. We said 'Yes' and allowed the players an hour in the shade and went through our usual pre-match programme.

We are professionals with a lot of pride to play for. I wanted to finish third, not fourth. We had to settle for fourth in the end – but didn't both sets of players emerge with fantastic credit? We were so unlucky to lose. We played too well and came back too bravely to be beaten by a poor penalty which was little more than a joke. What a part penalties had played in this competition for England and, come to that, everyone else.

But, for once, the result was secondary. If we had done ourselves proud against West Germany, shown our doggedness against Belgium and our character against Cameroon, we surely displayed our wonderful spirit against the Italians and, what is more, so did our supporters. I believe that this was a significant day in the history of our game, for the attitude of both our players and supporters, helped considerably by the Italians, must be a major influence in the return of our clubs to Europe in the coming season.

It was, in short, a day I will never forget even though, to many, the play-off for third and fourth place is as meaningless as a pre-season friendly and has no real place in the tournament. It never felt like that.

The atmosphere was superb in the brand new stadium in Bari; the football was of a high standard and the spirit of sportsmanship shone through in every minute of a high quality game of international football. The changed team did so well. Parker marked Baggio; Walker was tight on Toto Schillaci and Wright was the sweeper. Trevor Steven looked bright and perky and Tony Dorigo, despite a gashed eyebrow, looked every inch an international player.

The game was competitive. The Italians and their manager had taken a lot of stick since going out to Argentina and they were in no mood for an exhibition match. They wanted to do well in front of their own crowd. They had a lot to play for and we went with them to produce one of the finest games of the entire tournament with hardly a negative thought to disturb the enjoyment.

Our players on the bench helped the ambience by joining the crowd in the Mexican wave even before the kick-off although, I understand from the television people, that viewers at home did not see it because of the stuffy local director.

In fact the only thing to mar a memorable day was the officiating of French referee Joel Quiniou and his linesman Mohammed Hansal. The less said about them the better.

There were chances at both ends with Shilton distinguishing himself on his last appearance with several good saves from Baggio, and Lineker, hungry for goals, a constant menace at the other end – he had dreadful luck when a goalbound header bounced off the neck of the unsuspecting Vierchowod.

When the goal eventually came to break the deadlock I missed it – thanks to Mark Wright. He had been moaning about his calf injury at half time and had told me he didn't think he would last for three minutes of the second half, only to go back on and play superbly for half-an-hour without a sign of discomfort until he went down in a tackle and stayed down. I was watching physio Fred Street signalling me to prepare substitute Webb when I looked up to see Baggio crashing the ball into the net. I picked up the bits and pieces and it transpired that poor Peter Shilton had been caught napping as he rolled the ball in his box to win a little time while we were reduced to ten men.

What followed sounded like pure farce as Baggio stole the ball away from our captain, only to be brought down by Shilton's desperate challenge. The referee seemed to ignore the penalty claims just as he did the blatant offside position Baggio was in when Schillaci returned the ball to him.

That goal decided me to replace not only the injured Wright but also McMahon who seemed to be 30 yards behind the play, allowing Giannini to dominate him. I dispensed with the sweeper and sent on both Webb and Waddle. In for a penny, in for a pound. I moved Gary Stevens to centre half and Trevor Steven to right back and we had a go at them. These boys of mine do not know when to lie down even after the disappointment of the shoot-out and three periods of extra-time. Webb saw Zenga make a fine save from his volley and then, in the 80th minute, we did it again – or should I say David Platt did it again, scoring his third goal of the tournament.

Dorigo, who played so well, made the break and crossed for Platt to score with what I thought was one of the best headed goals of the entire tournament – in fact all three of his goals had been of the highest quality. I was now convinced that we were going to win it. We were up off the bench screaming for them to attack, win it, finish it off. We had Italy by the throat.

Then came the spot-kick. It was a weak, unfortunate penalty. Schillaci, tired and weary, lost the ball and collapsed over Parker's outstretched leg and scored from the spot to take him to six goals and become the tournament's top scorer, a well deserved honour but not with a goal like that.

I can only assume that the referee, with five minutes left, did not want the aggravation of extra time but I wish he knew what that did to us. It was a fine performance and we did not deserve to lose to a decision like that. They had won with a bizarre goal and a dodgy penalty to our classical goal.

With so little time left we piled forward and while we were stretched to the limit the Italians scored a magnificent goal as Berti ran half the length of the pitch to head a picture goal only to be brought back for a ludicrous offside, with television showing later that English players had kept him onside. But for once none of it mattered. There were no tears, only laughter. What an attitude. It was more like the closing ceremony of a Commonwealth Games as the players from both sides mingled, joining in the Mexican wave, disco dancing for the crowd, giving away their bunches of flowers and wearing their medals as proudly as if they were the winners. This game would not have been out of place as the final itself and as the television showed the world the sportsmanship of both sets of players it could have done us and our tarnished sport no harm at all.

What a lovely finish it was to my international career. I was full up when we eventually went to the dressing room and on for the after-match press conference.

Our travel officer Brian Scott found me to tell me that there were thousands of English fans still sitting in the stands, shouting my name. I thought he was winding me up. I didn't believe him for a minute. He persuaded me to have a look. If there were one or two waiting, I didn't want to appear sour. I walked back down the corridor and, sure enough, there they were. I was amazed. They chanted my name, clapped and cheered. What an emotional night this was turning out to be.

The players were in the same frame of mind. The two teams were still mingling in the dressing room area, changing shirts, and track suits, shaking hands. I found Vicini and we shook hands, both expressing the opinion that ours would be a better game than the final and that we were the two teams who deserved to be playing in Rome's Olympic Stadium next day.

It was all turning into a bit of a leaving party back at the Trulli Hotel. Dick Wragg and Jack Wiseman called the group to order, thanked me and presented me with a lovely painting. Then Terry Butcher got up and spoke on behalf of the players. This time giving me a Wedgwood dinner service. I was happy to respond because I also had a pleasant duty to perform. We had been given seven extra medals and I handed them over to Dave Sexton, Don Howe, Mike Kelly, Doc Crane, Norman Medhurst, Fred Street and kept the last one for myself. I am sure no-one minded. All the staff were thrilled. It was better than any bonus.

As the ceremonies finished I was suddenly aware that I was being surrounded and hemmed in from every side. I knew what was coming before I was hoisted in the air with just enough time to shout to Fred Street to take my watch and my medal. I was worried about my cracked rib but I could hardly complain as no one knew about it. They would have laughed. I was thrown bodily into the pool, missing the diving board by inches but making sure that I took a few of them with me. Butcher, Barnes and Walker were close but it is hard to tell when you are eight foot under.

I cut my foot on the way out of the pool and that seemed to cut through the euphoria and bring me back down to earth. Everyone was laughing and in great spirits as I changed into dry clothes. The players were having a ball, singing, having that promised drink. The time had come to leave them to it. Other than winning the World Cup this was the best way to go out. It was all very nostalgic after eight years.

Was there a trace of a tear or two? I am not telling.

Italy 2 (Baggio 71, Schillaci 84 pen) *England* 1 (Platt 80).
HT: 0–0 Att: 50,000.
Ref: Quiniou.
Italy: Zenga; Bergomi, Ferrara, Baresi, Vierchowod; De Agostini (Berti 67), Ancelotti, Giannini (Ferri 89), Maldini; Baggio, Schillaci.
England: Shilton; Stevens, Walker, Wright (Webb 72), Parker, Dorigo; McMahon (Waddle 72), Platt, Steven; Beardsley, Lineker.

BARI/ROME
Sunday, 8 July

It was the parting of the ways for England and Bobby Robson. The team were leaving for Luton on their private charter and I was heading off for Rome and the final we could so easily have been playing in.

Happily the two flights were taking off within minutes of each other and I was able to walk across the tarmac to the Britannia jet and say my last farewells to the players, their wives and the officials in the 'plane itself. It was a good way but I confess that I did not turn back to watch it take off. I heard later that day that they returned to a tumultuous reception, with 100,000 people in the streets of Luton to welcome them back. They deserved it. I am told that the nation stopped when we played and that they were ecstatic over our performances. We had got on with our jobs to the best of our ability.

One of the players' rewards was the Fair Play Trophy which was to be presented at the Olympic Stadium. That was a magnificent achievement when you consider the intensity of our seven games and the fact that we played three bouts of extra-time and still finished with fewer fouls and cautions than any other team. The award was a great tribute. We had told the players how crucial it was to our game and the country. We didn't feign injury, there was no gamesmanship, we didn't try to get anyone sent off; we had been hard but fair in our tackling, we had never retaliated and we had left the referees alone. Considering that FIFA had instructed a clampdown by officials resulting in more cautions and sendings-off than ever before, the fact that we had only five yellow cards – three of them ludicrous – was a source of pleasure.

I haven't liked what I have seen from some of the other teams. The diving, the cheating. I abhor the histrionics and the brutality, especially the elbow in the face. I won't have cowards or cheats in my teams and as a result we weren't prepared to kick our grandmothers to win the Cup. We tried to do everything within the rules laid down by FIFA.

That was not the case with the World Cup Final between West Germany and Argentina. Much of it was the opposite of what we believed in. Argentina were to blame.

I cannot believe that it was manager Carlos Bilardo who dictated the way the holders played – or didn't play as it transpired. They hadn't been a good team during the tournament; Maradona was no longer the inspiration he had been four years earlier and they had lost four players through suspension. They were in the World Cup Final without a team and it looked as though they had not even considered trying to win. They played so negatively that they did not have a direct shot at goal in 90 minutes. Illgner was little more than a spectator in the German goal and probably a very bored one at that. It looked as though Argentina's sole intention was to survive and try to win the world's most important football trophy in another penalty shoot-out.

It left the Germans to do all the attacking, and take all the initiative. They tried to create goals but missed their chances. In the end they won it with yet another penalty and another disputed one at that as Voller fell over under a challenge from Sensini as he raced onto Matthaus' pass. It didn't look a penalty to me.

We also witnessed the first ever sendings-off in a World Cup final, both Argentinians and both decisions with question marks against them. Monzon went first for a flying tackle on Klinsmann which may or may not have connected, while Dezotti followed him for grabbing Kohler by the neck as he tried to retrieve the ball.

An ugly game, not worthy of a final and certainly nowhere near the class of our games against West Germany and Italy, both of which would have given the final the distinction and quality that this one lacked. That was not just my opinion either but one expressed by almost everyone I talked to that night as I said my goodbyes at the various farewell parties at Rome's Hilton Hotel.

ROME/LONDON
Monday, 9 July

The party's over. It really is time to call it a day. I left Rome, Italy and the England management as I flew home to Heathrow. Everyone was very pleasant to me on the 'plane and I was greeted by a lot of photographers when we disembarked. As we walked up the ramp a young lady came to me for my autograph and after I had signed she asked if she could walk alongside me so that she would be in the newspapers next day.

'Certainly,' I said, 'If you fancy being on the front page of the *Sun* tomorrow.'

She was off like a scared rabbit.

I was amazed, as I walked past the various departure areas, at the welcome I received, and again in the luggage carousel when the people waiting for friends and relatives burst out into spontaneous applause. I was quite embarrassed but it was very touching. It was a nice way to go but I had to put it all behind me. I had two days to clear my office and pack for a two-year visit to Holland.

9

Retrospectively

England can go on and win the World Cup in the United States in 1994 and my only regret is that I will not be the manager when they do it. But I am delighted that I not only left behind the legacy of a team rich in talent and with a flexible choice of systems but that I have also left it in the charge of a man with the qualities to carry it through to its conclusion.

Graham Taylor, I have no doubt, is the right man for the right moment. A strong character and a very good coach who will bring the best out of his players. If ever he should need me I will be available. I shan't get in his hair and I can promise now that he will not pick up the newspapers every other day to read me telling him how to do the job or criticising him in any way at all. I know from my own experiences the pain and anguish that that can cause, and if I jumped on that particular bandwagon I would not be able to look at myself in the mirror in the morning.

I understand his appointment of Lawrie McMenemy as his assistant because there is no question that you need someone to take some of the weight off you. I asked for Don Howe in a similar full-time role but the FA decided at the time that they could not afford a second big wage and continued to employ him on a match-to-match basis for what amounted to little more than pin money. Presumably we made enough money in Italy for Lancaster Gate to agree to Graham's request and, together, they can make the job considerably easier. It is a heavy burden for one man, both mentally and physically, and in this case a trouble shared may well be a trouble halved. I hope Graham has asked for and got all he wants at the start because, as in any job, that is the time to make your demands. It is difficult to make any major changes after that.

It is a tough job but the best there is in football and, despite reports to the contrary, the Football Association are good employers who, once the appointment is made, keep any interference to an absolute minimum. They were incredibly supportive of me during my personal difficulties created by the tabloid press and resisted all outside efforts to get me out, backing me right to the finish.

I knew by early May that Italy was going to be my last chance to make an impact on the World Cup and I needed all the help I could get. I would never get another opportunity to have a tilt at the biggest prize in football and I knew that I had at my disposal a squad rich in talent and with greater depth than I ever had before. The minimum target was a place in the last eight to justify ourselves and our seeding when we set out, but by the end we were disappointed that we should go out in the semi-finals and not go all the way to the title itself. We felt we were the best team left in the competition when we went into that semi-final with West Germany in Turin.

The strange thing is that the fact that I knew I was leaving possibly helped me. I was not conscious of it at the time but in retrospect I was a lot more comfortable about the tactical changes I made and the substitutions at critical moments. It was never going to make any difference to my energy or enthusiasm but mentally I was probably more relaxed than at any other time in my eight years at the helm. Staying or leaving, I was going to give this my best possible shot and I believe that I did exactly that.

Once you reach this level there is an awful lot of luck involved with injuries, refereeing decisions, the draw, who you play against. It was the same in Mexico when we started slowly and built up, only losing in the quarter-finals because we were unlucky enough to come up against the favourites Argentina with Maradona in truly world-class form. This time we would have welcomed Argentina at any stage, but especially in the final in Rome's Olympic Stadium on 8 July because I am certain that we could have beaten them.

We were close in Mexico and I knew that we could go even

closer this time as Butcher, Robson, Shilton, Lineker, Beardsley, Waddle and Barnes could only be better players with their experience, while there were also promising youngsters like Wright, Walker, Parker and Pearce.

Gascoigne and Platt were in a different category when we went out. They were the unproven players with potential, the ones who came through to earn themselves international reputations and multi-million pound transfer values. The shape and style of the team evolved as the weeks unfolded. There is nothing fortunate or lucky when that happens; it goes on with every successful team, even the Germans who finished with a slightly different team from the one they began with.

I always went out with the firm plan of playing Mark Wright as a sweeper against Holland but even after the success of the ploy I was not going to be railroaded into playing that system all of the time. In the end we were flexible and adaptable and able to counter every eventuality until we fell foul of that awful lottery against the Germans in Turin.

I knew that our goalkeeping situation was good, having Shilton and three other excellent goalkeepers competing for three places, although in the end we had all four with us because of the injury sustained by David Seaman which saw us send an S.O.S. for Chelsea's Dave Beasant. In fact the whole defence was sound. We didn't concede a single goal in the qualifying competition and of the eight goals we lost in 18 games in the two years since the European Championships, there were two in each of the games against Uruguay and Czechoslovakia.

My only real area of doubt was whether we could score enough goals. It's always going to be tight if you score only one but with our defence I knew that if we could score two or more we were not going to lose. It was not a new problem. I had looked through the League all season and, even now, I am convinced that I didn't leave a single striker at home who should have been with us; in fact I remain convinced that I took the right 22 players. There are no regrets in that direction at all. David Rocastle and Michael Thomas, two players I really like, had lost their international form, while the Arsenal club captain, Tony Adams, had his best ever season only to miss out because of my decision on Mark Wright. I don't think that even Tony would quibble after seeing Wright establish himself as one of our outstanding and most versatile defenders. He even scored one of our goals and my concern over the problem proved to be justified. We did not score enough goals and it meant that every game was tight for us with little or no breathing space. Goals were a worry prior to departure, during the World Cup, and it will be in the immediate future when Graham Taylor sits down and studies what options he has available to him in that department. We are not simply talking about goalscorers in the First Division but strikers who can score consistently at international level against the best defences and goalkeepers there are. Even the weakest countries are now well coached and carefully organised. Most international teams are based on a defence–first system. How often do the Germans, Italians, Spaniards, Brazilians or Argentinians concede more than two, even on their worst days. We were and are a little short on fire power. That was one of the reasons why Bryan Robson was always so important to me and why David Platt will be just as critical to Graham Taylor. Robson, and Lineker often carried us in that respect with Barnes, Beardsley and Waddle not contributing as many goals as either I, or they, would have liked. No doubt Graham, like me, will look closely at the younger goalscorers, Ian Wright, Nigel Clough, Dalian Atkinson, Paul Williams and maybe even his young Aston Villa striker Ian Olney, as well as at more established strikers like Alan Smith who was a contender until I opted for Steve Bull for the final vacant spot.

It was suggested in some dark corners that I ignored young Nigel Clough because of some sort of war with Brian Clough. Absolutely untrue and totally without foundation. I didn't speak to Brian enough to fall out with him and I would not have bitten off my nose to spite my face. If Clough had been good enough he would have gone to Italy. Quite simply, I wasn't looking for his type of player. I was looking for a goalscorer at international level, someone of high repute. Nigel is an intelligent player with a football brain who likes to send other people in to score goals. He lacked the sharpness of pace for that front position and had I taken him he would have been a duplication of Peter Beardsley. Had he been the right player I would have had no hesitation in selecting him because, like all Forest players Clough sent to me over the years, he was not a scrap of trouble. Nigel is a lovely, quiet boy. Certainly Brian has been one of the great providers for me over my eight years. He produced good players who trained well, were good to work with and who knew how to behave on and off the field. I never had to tell a Forest player to go to bed or to be on the coach for 10 a.m. because they were always there.

No, I had no doubts then and have no doubts now that England had her strongest 22 players in Italy, but I also knew that to achieve an absolute maximum I needed a fit Bryan Robson; a rejuvenated Lineker; a fit Peter Beardsley; and either Steve Bull or John Barnes to emerge as a frequent goalscorer. We did remarkably well considering so few of those factors came into play!

I knew that Steve Bull would provide us with a little added dash and enthusiasm but was aware at the same time that he had technical deficiencies – only to be expected for someone yet to play First Division football. I wavered once or twice after watching him before we left, particularly at West Ham, but he is a good character and very single-minded about scoring goals. It was a treat just to have him around and it was always my intention to use him only as a substitute. It says a lot for him that he was able, largely through his own efforts, to convince me to start with him against Egypt. I even gave him two wingers so that he should have the best possible crack at it but he was short on touch. Coming on as a substitute when others were tiring compensated and that's when he looked his best. However, Bull could still be the answer for Graham Taylor. He certainly has the ambition and the appetite to reach the top if he can maintain his progress, and if Wolves manager Graham Turner can help him to develop the technical expertise he will need at international level he could be the answer at the next World Cup.

It is interesting that we squeezed through against Egypt that day I played Bully through the middle with Lineker. We also struggled against Cameroon and when drawing with an Irish side we should have beaten. It was the same in Mexico, and frequently through my England years we did not always do ourselves justice against the so-called minnows but performed well and with skill against the best sides, as we did in Italy where we were more comfortable against Holland, Belgium and West Germany than we were against the other three. The minnows do tend to raise their game against England because of our history and who we are. They often play better on the day than they do against other opponents. It is very similar to Liverpool going to York and drawing 1–1 and then three days later winning 7–0 at Anfield. Teams lift themselves and are able to raise their games on a specific day with nothing to lose, as they do with England. Egypt, for example, did not attack against us the way they had done against the European Champions Holland. They pulled everyone back and were not disgraced by a 1–0 defeat even though they expected and hoped for a draw. But they gained out of the defeat while it was looked upon as a bad result for England.

I must admit that I felt easier in myself when we were pitting our wits against the best teams in the world. There is a genuine fear in losing to the lesser teams that disappears when we play the best. Lose in a World Cup to Egypt or Cameroon and it looks bad, lose to Brazil or West Germany and no one minds so much. Also, as the tournament progressed, we reaped the benefits of having the squad together for so long, and by the time we played Cameroon we had shared the highs and lows and built a bond. By then we were more like a club side and I am certain that played a major part in our fighting back when all seemed lost against the Africans.

On a long trip like that – we were away for seven weeks and together well before that – it is just as important to develop that spirit as it is to develop football skills. Taking the wives for that first week helped. Little things like days off, playing golf, even losing the skipper had a positive aspect. I remember telling them that he had gone and that it was no use them wearing their hearts on their sleeves. They would have to do it without him. The garbage printed in some of the papers also saw them pull a protective shell around themselves and draw in to each other. We saw the togetherness and spirit improve throughout those seven weeks and when we got out onto the pitch they were really working for each other with total support from those on the bench. That's why we never knew when we were beaten.

Don Howe and I also learned from our past experiences, modifying the training and always making sure that something was kept in reserve as a game approached. Playing three sessions of extra-time in succession showed that we were amongst the fittest, if not *the* fittest, teams in the competition. West Germany looked good early on as did the Italians. But we improved and by the end we were as good as anyone in the competition as we proved in those last two games.

The standards of discipline were extremely high. They trained right, got to bed early; there was no boozing. In short everyone went for the World Cup. Never once did I hear money mentioned before or after the tournament. All of that commercial side vanished completely once we stepped aboard our 'plane at Luton airport. They were a wonderful squad and gave me and their country everything they could.

If I had been fortunate enough to stay on, I would have kept them together. There would have been no Shilton, of course, and no Butcher but there are not many of the others who will not be in contention for the European Championships in two years' time and for the World Cup two years after that. In fact I believe that I could have taken this side on to win the Europeans in Sweden in two years – what wonderful compensation that would have been for what happened to us in West Germany! I was delighted to see that Graham Taylor had kept the squad together for the first game against Hungary.

That is the sort of quality we have left behind, proof that there are players in the squad with world-class ability who can handle the big occasion on the biggest stage. They also defied the critics by proving they can match the best in technical terms as well, despite that five-year absence from competitive European football. We now know we have nothing to fear from anyone. Every player will have come back from Italy richer for the experience on and off the pitch. They have returned with a higher education and with no feelings of failure, having gone out in such a freakish way. They also know that other sides fear them and can never be certain of victory against them until the final whistle blows. Most important of all is that England now have a new engine room in Gascoigne and Platt, groomed and ready to play. Graham Taylor doesn't need to give them experience, they already have it. They are almost the finished product – not quite, but not far off.

Not that I need to tell the new England manager anything about Platt. He was the one who pulled him out of lower-grade football after he had been rejected by Manchester United. I spoke to Graham often about him after he had signed him from Crewe and brought him along. He stressed what a great squad player Platt would be in Italy, able to play a number of roles. He went one better, he became a World Cup player with three goals under his belt. The fact that the Arsenal boys suffered a loss of form opened the door but it was his unselfish performance against Brazil at Wembley which clinched his place, particularly in the final 20 minutes when the South Americans raised their game and tried to pull the goal back. He showed defensive qualities I had not previously been aware of. It displayed great heart from a great team man and I did not need to look at him again after that night. He was in. I was also impressed with his sheer professionalism. His whole demeanour and attitude was spot on. He was outstanding at the training ground, impeccable around the hotel and more often than not first to bed. He is a strong, firm character with obvious qualities of leadership and I would be surprised, even a little disappointed, if he did not develop into a future England captain. With Graham knowing him so well it would help him too for it is always good to have a first lieutenant on the pitch whom you can trust. I was lucky; I had two – Terry Butcher to begin with while the relationship with Bryan Robson developed. The value of these relationships lies in having senior players on the park and in the dressing room who believe in you, who trust you, who will work with you. They can then persuade and influence the others to go in that direction.

I always saw Platt as a midfield player rather than a striker. When I first selected him for the squad he had been scoring a lot of goals from a front position for Villa. It was his ability to time those late runs into the penalty area which impressed me initially and I was not so sure that he could play as well with his back to goal as he did when he was playing off people. He is a great runner with the ball. He is also very good in the air, coming in late against both Cameroon and Italy to score with text-book headers. Robson is undoubtedly the classical player in that role but Platt has some of it along with his own individual talents. But like Robson he is prepared to roll up his sleeves and work, challenge and hustle to win the ball back. I used him on Gullit against Holland when he showed he had the physical capacity to break off and get involved as an attacking player as well. He is not yet the finished article. His pass selection still needs a little polishing and his first touch can still improve. But he has the character, the engine and the temperament to go all the way, and in David Platt England not only have a long-term player but also a future captain.

If Graham Taylor wants he can pick the quickest back four in Europe, maybe the world if he played Paul Parker, Des Walker, Mark Wright and Tony Dorigo. None would beat them for pace in a one versus one situation. If pace is a prerequisite then we have the best. What is more it does not end there; try getting past Gary Stevens or Stuart Pearce with pace and you would be disappointed.

They all showed that they can hold their own in world-class company in terms of ability and experience, but it will depend on what system he plays at the back as to whom he selects. It is his decision, he must decide which way he wants to play. For more than 90 games I played with a flat back four, not always with that sort of pace. We played a way we all understand; but in the World Cup against the highest quality opponents with the best forwards in the world, the Gullits, Van Bastens, Romarios, Vollers and Caniggias, I knew it might not be enough. I finally decided we needed the extra defender – but not in every match and not all of the time. I learned adaptability and flexibility.

We had conceded five goals in two games against Holland and I had to make certain we did not leak goals like that once more. That was why I took Mark Wright with me. He was used to the sweeper system and I always planned to pick him against the Dutch. I also had cover for him in little Paul Parker but while the QPR defender has great defensive qualities, Wright is so much better at bringing the ball out. That's why I took Wright out to Italy unfit and waited and waited for him. I knew I could not risk Butcher and Walker against Marco van Basten and Ruud Gullit without help.

The adaptability of the players to switch so easily from one style to another pleased me immensely. The difference is not so much for the markers but for the full backs who have to adjust from playing in a line to playing in a shell formation, a curve of five. Parker and Pearce had never played that way before. I am sure Trevor Steven could have done it but I was concerned about his lack of experience in defensive play, although when it came to the crunch against Cameroon in that position he was outstanding and probably kept us in the World Cup with one spectacular goal-line clearance. He is yet another option for Graham Taylor and Steven could become a world-class performer in that position.

Graham, I am sure, will find all these alternatives with high quality players intriguing. However, the problem with England is that when you want to try something new during the normal season and it goes wrong you have to wait for a month before you can put it right. In that four weeks all sorts of things happen to your mind and your thoughts.

At one of the final press conferences I was asked what I hoped to be remembered for. It was a question which demanded more time and thought than I could give it then. I had hoped that it would have been as the first England manager to lead the country to a World Championship on foreign soil. I will have to settle for being the first to get the team into the last four, but I have thought about the question since and I am proud to have kept our international head above water and our pride intact during a most difficult period.

At the risk of labouring the point, we are the only country in the world whose players were banned from performing anywhere else at club level. They have had no chance of testing themselves or learning to play against different styles, players, pace and formations. We were even robbed of international experience away to countries like Italy, West Germany and Holland because of the government's fears of more hooligan problems. We took players to Italy whose greatest experience of playing foreign football was in friendlies. That is why I restarted the B internationals.

Yet we were still able to compete with the best at the highest level. It is hypothetical how much better we would have been had those players had five years' benefit of playing the top European sides. We came out of Italy with our pride, our heads held high and our reputation fully restored in the most prestigious tournament of them all when, for the first time, even the teams from other continents were competing on terms because they now have so many players in the rich leagues of Europe. The Brazilians, for example, were almost playing at home!

I also believe that our good behaviour on the field which led to the Fair Play Award, in which FIFA put so much faith, helped more than a little in our clubs' return to European club competition. I am delighted for Graham Taylor but the points system for entry means that it will be a long time before we are fully restored in terms of numbers.

Without our attitude, if we had sustained lots of bookings and had dismissals it would have damaged our credibility and might have provoked off-field trouble.

It meant a lot to all of us winning that award, but especially me. I place a lot of stock in fair play. Before we went to Italy I heard all sorts of dire warnings about how Pearce, Butcher and others would give away fatal free kicks around the penalty area, but it didn't happen. Ask Stuart Pearce if he would prefer a fillet steak or a good tackle and he would go for the tackle every time. He loves a tackle that boy, but he stayed on his feet, as did the rest of our defence, and tackled low and fair. He, like all of our defenders, had an excellent World Cup.

That is what I leave behind, along with an infrastructure for the future with our centres of excellence and the National School, and an international record which stands with the best, especially at Wembley and in qualifying competitions where I have lost only one match which cost us a place in the European Championships in France in 1984. We have only conceded three goals in a game three times, all away from home and all 3–1 results. We have always been difficult to beat wherever we have gone. But the most important aspect of the job, certainly at public level, is to qualify for the major finals every two years. You can only get your reputation for team and players from the big stage, that is where the interest is.

It is all in the past now but if I had the opportunity to do it all again I would, and I wouldn't change anything. I did everything that I thought was right. I gave it every consideration and I would grasp the England job again if it were offered. Definitely. No question. In many ways it is frustrating and high pressured, and whatever you do criticism is bound to follow because you cannot be everything to every man.

It is the job every football manager should aspire to. It is the pinnacle and if you don't reach it you will never know. Only a few men can ever boast that they have been there, England's manager. We are not talking about going to Leicester or Liverpool, or even Barcelona for a European tie, but to Brazil, Albania, Australia, Uruguay and all corners of the globe and you discover it can be as difficult in Finland as it is in Brazil. Go to a country thinking you should win by five goals and you might come back with your tail between your legs.

Every game is a test of your football knowledge, stretching the brain; and all of the time you have to keep your head and be a diplomat. It wouldn't suit some high-profile managers I know who supplement their wages by adversely criticising others in their profession.

There will be many things Graham Taylor will want but won't get because club football will always be put ahead of the country. If England's results are important in the World Cup they should be important all of the time and the national manager should be given consideration and time to prepare his teams whatever the opposition. But even more than an extra day before a game I would have loved to see the players on a Thursday after a mid-week game to debrief them. By the time we meet again the match has lost its impact, it is irrelevant, and it may be different players a month later anyway because of injuries and club commitments.

But there is not a lot else I would have changed. It was interesting to hear Graham Taylor say how he wanted to go out and about working with the players. I had the same enthusiasm and tried to set up gatherings around the country. Sadly the club managers did not share my enthusiasm and the idea withered and died. I found I had to leave the clubs to get on with it. The only real time you can work with players is on the rare occasion that it is your turn – and then it is not always guaranteed.

Enough of Bobby Robson's past . . . what of his future? If my first few months as coach to the Dutch side PSV Eindhoven are anything to go by I am going to be a happy man indeed. I have signed a two-year contract, but it does not mean I am going to leave at the end of that time. I have not gone to Holland to take the money and run. I am hungry for success. I won the UEFA and FA Cups at Ipswich and went close to the English title several times but I have never won a championship and that is what we all want at PSV.

Not that everyone thinks I will flourish and survive in the Netherlands. In one of my first television interviews, in the pretty town of Volendam where I addressed the other Dutch coaches, the interview opened with the TV man saying: 'Many critics say that you will bring English football into Holland and that you will not survive until Christmas. What have you to say about that?' Not a lot.

What PSV offered me was not just financial security but a top job. Where do you go after managing England? It is like asking the Prime Minister what she will do when her term of office finally ends. There was no question of me retiring to my Ipswich home and putting my feet up. For a start I couldn't afford to do so.

I have never been a commercial animal. Money has not been a major motivating factor in my life – if it had I would have accepted one of the offers which came my way over the years from Barcelona, Bilbao, Everton, Aston Villa, Manchester United, Leeds, Wolves or Sunderland. Barcelona, in particular, has always intrigued me, it is one of the biggest and most challenging jobs in world football but I had the chances to go and turned them down. I believe I have the same opportunities at PSV but without the attendant pressures. At this stage of my life I don't need those sorts of pressures.

In that respect PSV are the perfect club. There are no language problems because everyone speaks English. I cannot imagine managing a side where no one understands what you are saying and you cannot understand them. The whole atmosphere is relaxed and comfortable. It is a big, big club but it is well organised and run by nice people. No club I have been to in England has the same training facilities, and we run 13 teams ranging from eight-year olds to the first team with its players drawn from all over the world. I have full responsibilities with the coaching of the first team but I don't have to worry about office work, contracts, transfer fees, staffing; it is all done for me so I can get on with the day-to-day business with the senior players.

It was perfect going straight in from the World Cup because I had got back into the daily routine over the two months instead of being with the players for three days every month or so. It was no effort to slip back into the club routine. I am under no illusions. There is more than a hint of success about this club. Finishing second in their League is considered a failure and, indeed, their eyes are on recapturing the European crown they conceded to Milan. They badly want to win the silverware; that's why they went for an experienced manager and, if I may be permitted, a big coach, a big name who was not afraid of working with star players.

It is hard to foretell the future but if I like it here who knows? How much of a lure would the World Cup be if another country came in for my experience? It would have to be a team with a chance or a team, like the United States or Cameroon, with a challenge.

Having had two large bites of the World Cup cherry it would always attract me because it has all the excitement, the drama — and with major decisions thrown in. It seems my England days have long gone but I am a patriot and if there was ever an emergency there is no doubt at all I would answer the call. After all managing England has given me something I could never have had anywhere else: eight memorable years which changed my life.

I don't regret a minute of it.

10
A Dutch treat

PSV Eindhoven is an international club in every sense of the word. It is a veritable League of Nations with players not only from all over Europe but also from Africa and, of course, South America.

The most talented of all these imports is, without question, the brilliant Brazilian Romario, a player who had caught my eye long before I agreed to take on the challenge of managing Holland's top team. I had watched him with considerable admiration during the build up to the World Cup, well aware of his club record of a goal-a-game in his first season in the Dutch League.

It was a pity that a broken leg curtailed his appearances in Italy to a bare minimum but I was more concerned about having him fit and healthy for the start of my new career. A goalscorer like him is rare to say the very least.

Not only is he an outstanding performer – when he wants to be – but he is also a nice man. Yet he presented me with problems I had never experienced in my life before.

At times during my career I have heard the expression 'Player Power'. I even heard it aimed at England when we modified our tactics in Italy on our way to the semi-finals. It was something which never really affected me. I was the boss. I survived or fell by the results and that meant I had to make the decisions, all of them.

Romario immediately presented a new problem. When I arrived he was the biggest thing at the club and understandably so. He was popular with the crowd in spite of inactive periods during a game, but his sudden explosions in the penalty area more than made up for that. The club had a little gem in Romario and everyone knew it.

He is, quite simply, a goalscorer. Nothing more. He doesn't need to be. He scores clever goals, simple goals and goals that look completely impossible. There are days when he doesn't touch the ball so much, or tackle, or chase defenders. Just when you are getting exasperated with him he suddenly delivers. He scores goals out of nothing, a genuine match winner. He conserves all his energy for the moment when the ball comes to him and then he becomes something completely different. In the penalty area he is lethal.

In any case you can't stay cross with him for long. He has an angelic face. One look can melt you. He is a bright boy and I like him and love his talent. When he is on top of his game he is great to have around.

He speaks a little English – and understands what he wants to understand. He comes from a different culture and has a different mentality, but he knows his potential and he knows his value – and he uses that to the full.

Over the years I have learned to become something of a psychologist, as every manager has to be if he is to get the best out of his players. During my time in the game I have come across all sorts and everyone has to be handled differently.

Romario was something special and was to become one of my biggest tests.

It became quite apparent that, in many eyes, a coach is easily replaced – a goalscorer of the unique talents of Romario is not. I had a two-year contract. He had a six-year contract. I quickly made up my mind that I would do everything possible not to put that theory to the test.

Half way through that first season the Dutch League closed down for the winter break and we had arranged an important tour to India where we were to be watched by vast crowds. Naturally they wanted to see our best players and none comes better than Romario.

But he was recovering from an injury which had kept him out since early in the season and he didn't want to go to India. It wasn't me he was fighting, it was the club. He knew that if he didn't go he would be fined. He simply said 'So what?' I don't know what he earns because contracts aren't part of my side of the business, but it was clear that he was willing to fork out a few thousand pounds in return for going home to Brazil where he would be with his own people in the warm and where he could train and get fit.

It wasn't the only time he went back to Brazil during that season. One Friday I went to the training ground to prepare the team for an important game on the following Monday, only to be told by club manager Kees Ploegsma that Romario had returned home again because his daughter was sick and had been taken to hospital as a precaution. He said he would be back for the game.

He was. By the time he had flown half way round the world his daughter was out of hospital and well on the mend. He turned round and flew home in time for the game. Naturally he was so knocked out by all that travelling in such a short space of time that he was dead on his feet. He hardly touched the ball and we lost only our second league game of the season to Den Haag, a game we should have won.

That sort of thing is difficult for an English manager to comprehend but, fortunately, many of the things I had to do in my years at Ipswich are not my responsibility at Eindhoven. My job is to prepare the players for games while contractual and other untechnical matters are left to Kees Ploegsma who handles them so well.

It is up to me to ensure that Romario is fit mentally and physically for our games. His goals and his short bursts of high activity make him the best. I was told that before I arrived the club had turned down £5 million for him from a top Italian club. If England's Paul Gascoigne is valued at around £8 million, I suppose that Romario must have been worth £10 million at that moment in time.

But then it was always going to be a challenge. That was one of the reasons I took on the job in the first place. I had enjoyed eight years with England and now I was back with the day-to-day involvement of a club and club footballers although I had a host of international footballers to work with.

Arriving at Eindhoven there was no time to contemplate whether I had made the right decision or even to reflect on the emotion of the World Cup. The weather was as good as it had been in Italy and I was still flush with our success. It did me no harm that England had played well and gone beyond expectations while the Dutch most certainly had not.

I was feeling good and having finished on a high I was looking forward to the new job, the fresh surroundings, different people and a total change in my way of life.

I knew players like Romario by sight, as I did most of the PSV players. I knew considerably less about the forthcoming opposition, and I couldn't speak the language. It was going to test me to the full.

But there was no fear involved. The club had shown that they wanted me and from my own point of view I was well aware of the strength of the club and its standing in world football. I couldn't wait to start.

There was certainly no time at all to settle in. I arrived on Friday and started work on Saturday morning, meeting Chairman Jacques Ruts and my Dutch assistant Hans Dorjee that first morning. I spent an hour and a half with Mr Ruts and then another 90 minutes with Hans. One of the first things I had to do in that second conversation was to put my assistant's mind to rest and assure him that I was not, as most of the papers had suggested, going to appoint Mick Mills or anyone else from England to take his place.

He was on an option but as far as I was concerned he was part of the club. I told him quite sincerely that I needed someone with a wide knowledge of Dutch football as I was going in almost blind.

With that settled, I was able to get down to the real nitty-gritty. I needed to know about my players, how we played, what system we used and whether we played with a sweeper against the smaller clubs as well as the bigger teams.

Hans was more than helpful and not at all secretive. He felt that with all the comings and goings we were still one class player short of a title winning side. There was no one of the quality we needed in Holland but we did need another player. Before I arrived, the club had bought striker Johnny Bosman and midfielder Erwin Koeman and when I joined I became involved in the latest transaction to secure the tall and elegant Romanian Gica Popescu, a player I had watched and admired during my travels around Europe.

Hans had been to see him play in the World Cup and liked what he saw. He was available but the Chairman wouldn't move until I had joined and given my sanction. That was apparently one of the reasons why they wanted me over so quickly, with the start of the season only five weeks away.

We were talking a lot of money and a big contract and before I gave my approval I wanted to check him out. As England manager I had both Micky Wadsworth and Howard Wilkinson watching the Romanian group for me in Italy. I not only had their reports but also videos of their games against Colombia and Jack Charlton's Irish team.

The team needed someone who could head the ball and I needed to confirm that he was as competent in this area as he was in other departments. My 'spies' were able to tell me that the Romanian coach had Popescu heading the ball before the kick-off against the Republic of Ireland, well aware of what he was going to have to face in the next couple of hours. He had him attacking the ball and the video of the drawn game – decided by penalties – proved the point. I told the Chairman we should take up the option.

The alternative would have been to bring in an English player. The idea was very attractive and I would have been prepared to gamble heavily on both David Platt and Mark Wright after their showings in the World Cup. I thought about it very carefully before coming to the conclusion that it might not look right to surround myself with English players.

With hindsight, I made the right decision to pick Popescu. He is a truly outstanding and gifted player, quite able to play either at the back or in an attacking midfield role. There is nothing I dislike about this young man, either as a footballer or as a person. He has a wonderful attitude and temperament. He is a coach's dream. He listens, learns, and obeys instructions like the good professional he is.

Popescu loves the country and loves the club. The day he signed we went to the stadium restaurant for dinner and he was asked why he had chosen to sign for PSV instead of going to Italy. He told the Chairman it was partly because of the appointment of Mr Robson. He said that he respected the way England had played in the World Cup and that had helped persuade him to join. It was a much appreciated compliment so early on.

Popescu was just one of a whole group of helpful people around me. I was put under the wing of Cor Sprengers, a long time employee of both the club and their sponsors, Philips. He, his wife

Marjan and daughters Corine and Patricia not only looked after me but became family friends.

It helped that they made me feel instantly at home. Holland is a lovely country and football is the main sport. Everywhere you look there are pitches and the facilities for youngsters who wish to take up the game are fabulous at every level. Football dominates the country in sporting terms, as they don't have the many alternatives that are offered to our own youngsters at home. That is probably why they have done so well for a country of their size at both club and international level over the years.

I couldn't believe the facilities at PSV when I arrived. The first team and the reserves have their own training grounds with choice of pitches, all kept immaculately. Thousands came to watch the team train pre-season and I took to it all straightaway. The people and the newspapers were responsive although I almost thought I was back home when one of the papers suggested I would be gone by Christmas.

The argument was over the style of football I would bring to Holland. They thought it would be too English but against that a lot of people *expected* me to bring some English qualities to the Dutch game.

I was still taking some stick from back home but what I found disrespectful was the attitude of some that I had gone to manage a team in a Mickey Mouse League. Of course the Dutch First Division is not as strong as the English First Division nor is there as much chance as there is at home of a bottom team beating a top team.

But then where in the world is the quality as high as in England? Only Spain, West Germany and Italy can match it.

The standard in my first season in Holland has been good. I haven't been able to take anything for granted and there have been difficult games at places like Roda JC, FC Twente, FC Utrecht, Vitesse, Fortuna Sittard and against the surprise team of the season Groningen, as well as the traditional tough fixtures at Ajax and Feyenoord.

With 15 internationals gathered from around the globe I was, quite rightly, expected to do well but I didn't realise how well until we got under way with a 1–1 draw with NEC in Nijmegen in the second game of the season. With two points from our opening game I thought that was a satisfactory start but I quickly discovered that PSV were expected to beat teams like NEC 3–0, home or away. I had to change my philosophy and lift my targets.

Every defeat is greeted like a disaster and even when we went six months between defeats the pressure was on, albeit from the outside. Our next game after that 3–0 defeat by Den Haag was at home to the champions Ajax and it was suggested quite strongly that my job was on the line.

We won 4–1 but I missed the last few minutes because I was so surrounded by television crews and cameras. I had to ask myself what was going on and, more to the point, what would be happening if we were losing 4–1?

The fact that we had lost so many star players through injury hardly seemed to matter to other people. In fact it was not until 2 March that I managed to play what I considered to be my best team when we beat Feyenoord 6–0, followed by RKC and Roda, both by 3–0 margins. Then the injuries hit us again and we went down 1–0 to Feyenoord in the semi-final of the Dutch Cup on our own ground, just a couple of weeks after our big victory against them.

But injuries are a fact of football life. You expect them and get on with it.

The Cup defeat was one of the most disappointing performances of the season. We played without passion and despite the prospect of the 'Double' looming strong, we simply didn't play. Even the crowd was quiet and low key. After tasting the joys and sorrows of the English FA Cup it was hard to understand the almost couldn't-care-less attitude.

But the greatest pressure came when we went out of Europe at the first hurdle to French cup winners Montpellier. We went out on a 1–0 aggregate and immediately the *English* newspapers suggested that I was in danger of losing my job after a month. When we then lost 3–1 at Ajax the English press seemed to take delight in putting my livelihood on the line.

There was a lot of interest from England in what I was doing with PSV, with regular visits from all branches of the media. I was under no illusions and was well aware that everything could turn sour if the team or I did not come up to scratch.

It doesn't matter how big a name you are in the international soccer arena. You are only as good as your last result. Look at Rinus Michels who won the European Championship for Holland and then lasted only a few months with West German Bundesliga side Bayern Leverkusen. If it can happen to him it can happen to anyone. I knew that Bobby Robson was not fireproof. I was concerned for the club and wanted to do well both for them and for myself.

I had left England probably more popular than at any time in my international managerial career and I had hoped that the people back home would have wanted me to succeed for the reputation of our country and our football. But the same people who wanted me sacked while I was at the FA now seemed to be taking great delight in putting my head on the block again and what made it worse was that the reports were being followed up by the Dutch media.

The defeat at Ajax was as unlucky as it was annoying. We were so much on top that their goalkeeper Stanley Menzo was named man-of-the-match. We were 1–1 with five minutes to go when our Dutch international goalkeeper Hans van Breukelen and Danish international defender Jan Heintze got themselves in a tangle to give away a goal. The third came while we were chasing an equaliser.

It looked to be a heavy defeat but it wasn't. As Ajax manager Leo Beenhakker said afterwards: 'PSV made the match. We got the result.'

But the flak was intense. Our chairman Mr Ruts had spoken to me briefly after the game in Amsterdam, saying what bad luck we'd had and that sort of thing, but the criticism was so intense that the press went to him and asked what the position was with Bobby Robson. He responded by saying that I had a two-year contract with the club. End of statement.

He felt the need to call me to his office to talk about the situation a couple of days later to reassure me that none of the aggravation stemmed from the club. Indeed, he was surprised and shocked at how the English press had reacted. I knew better.

I got on well with the other coaches in Holland and while there was huge rivalry between Ajax and ourselves I had a particularly good relationship with Beenhakker. Leo, like myself, has been through it all as manager of his national side as well as having the difficult, if rewarding, task of coping with the huge demands of

Real Madrid in Spain. I like him a lot. He is an honest and fair man. We are similar in many ways and we have been able to have a joke and a laugh after defeats at the hands of the other.

Three years ago the cash dried up at Ajax. They couldn't afford to buy the big names and told their public the truth. They put their faith in a crop of good young players and warned everyone that it would be three or four years before the side came to maturity and they could think of winning Championships again. They did it far quicker than they had dared to hope.

They have an advantage over us in terms of young players in that we cannot poach from their territory for the important 12 and 13 year olds. It means they draw on a population of around three million while we are restricted to 200,000.

As well as Beenhakker, other coaches also treated me with great respect. Most speak English and most took time out to have a chat after games. Even so it is not quite like it is at home where managers are on the move all the time watching other games in other divisions and meeting up in board rooms and tea bars.

I went to a couple of meetings held by the coaches and enjoyed being with them and talking to them as a group. All of them were courteous and none indulged in slagging each other off in public.

But there was a feeling about working abroad. I often wondered how the attitude would change if there was a string of bad results or if there really was an undercurrent of jealousy at a foreigner coming in and taking one of the top jobs in the country. I also considered how fickle the fans might be if the results did not suit them. But then that's probably true of fans the world over.

I enjoy being in Eindhoven. It is very much like Ipswich in that although it is dominated by Philips it is still a rural town. If the fans from Amsterdam or Rotterdam want to insult our supporters they chant things like 'Farmers, farmers.'

The big difference was that at Portman Road I had to be involved in selling the club and everything else that went on. I was even involved with the negotiations with the sponsors Pioneer. At Eindhoven it is the opposite. I don't even know what Philips put into the club each year, I just know that it is an awful lot.

Philips, in fact, had just had what was a bad year for them when I arrived and I was well aware that there was not a bottomless pit of guilders I could draw on whenever I wanted to buy a new player. The money comes in once a year and that is that.

There is no interference from Philips and no one ever comes to me making demands. I have to be self sufficient.

But if I want anything from them for myself I have access. My home in Eindhoven is full of their electrical appliances and through television and teletext I am able to keep in minute-by-minute contact with everything that is going on at home.

Not that I have a lot of time to miss home. I am absorbed in my job, enthralled with it.

The only heartache to start with was when England played. In the days before the game I would look at my watch and imagine what the squad would be doing at that moment, training at Bisham Abbey, having dinner together at the Bull Inn at Bisham, wondering what Gazza was up to.

I was careful not to put Graham Taylor under any undue pressure by being high profile. I kept away from both of the games against the Irish and only went to those against Cameroon and Poland.

He knew that he would get no criticism from me. In return he has not been critical of my years in charge. He appreciated the work I put in and I am backing him all the way. I felt for him when the supporters and the press attacked him after the win in Turkey even though the win meant that England went top of their qualifying group and extended their unbeaten run to six games.

I knew how he must be feeling. Imagine what it was going to be like when he lost one.

As a spectator at Wembley I tried to enjoy the games but it was hard. I found myself wondering what I would say at half-time. But I am getting over that now.

I haven't been on the telephone to Graham. He knows my number if he wants me. I have 'phoned Gascoigne a couple of times, Peter Beardsley when he was going through a bad time, and I sent Gary Lineker a telegram when he was made captain.

I have different players to concern me now, not just the talented Romario and Popescu but a whole group of top players.

I read while I was in Italy how van Breukelen was supposedly going to walk out on the club and how Eric Gerets was going to run the team, not Bobby Robson. It was all without foundation. In Gerets, the veteran Belgian international, I couldn't have had a more responsible, respectful or disciplined captain. We never even spoke about that story and although he is a very strong character I did not find him in anyway difficult. In fact at the age of 37 I found him to be a remarkable player.

Van Breukelen is a character and a good goalkeeper. He speaks good English and far from walking out on me and the club he signed a new two-year contract on our return from the tour of India.

There are others like Berry van Aerle, a bit of a Kenny Sansom in that he has a great personality, keeping everyone laughing while being an outstanding player. He would be a great success in English football, as would many of the team. Popescu would be a revelation and Gerets, central defender Stan Valckx, Erwin Koeman, Jan Heintze and, of course, Romario could all make their mark in English football without too much bother. I have no doubt that PSV would be good enough to finish in the top four of the English First Division.

Someone had remarked that on the two occasions Ipswich had finished runners-up in the First Division, the issue had not been decided until the final day of the season . . . and here we were again.

Would it be third time lucky? Was I jinxed? These were the questions being bandied about by the media as the Dutch Championships came to the final dramatic day, with ourselves and the defending champions, Ajax, on level points with one home game left apiece: Eindhoven taking on Volendam and Ajax meeting Vitesse in Amsterdam.

Fortunately, and despite the few slips in the final weeks of the season – not least of all an horrendous 4–1 defeat at Groningen the week before – we still had a two-goal cushion. So we knew exactly what we had to do. We had to win and win by enough goals to keep Ajax at bay.

Football is full of coincidences. Not only was this the third time I had found myself sweating on the last day of the season for the greatest domestic prize in football and a chance at the European Cup itself, but exactly a year earlier, on June 16 in Sardinia, as

England manager, I had pitted my wits against Holland and their manager Leo Beenhakker.

Here we were at it again, albeit in different cities, with me managing PSV and Leo in charge of Ajax.

It may have been nerve wracking for the two managers but for the people of Holland it was tremendous. They were agog. Ajax were forced to move their game to the larger national stadium and you couldn't find a seat in our Eindhoven stadium. You could have cut the tension with a knife, particularly when the news came through that Ajax were two up against Vitesse when we were holding a one goal advantage against Volendam.

The Dutch handled it very well. They not only ensured that we played our final games on the same day – games in Holland can be on Friday, Saturday or Sunday – but they also had officials with walkie-talkies on the touchlines to be sure that we both kicked off at the same time.

At that moment I was more than aware that had we given a goal away we could have chucked away the title. But, to be fair, we never looked like we would. Volendam were restricted to just two shots. We gave a thoroughly professional performance and scored our goals at regular intervals, thirty minutes, sixty minutes and eighty minutes.

We had done our job and done it well, although Ajax must take great credit. They did everything they could to hang on to that title and in the end it came down to our two games against each other. They won the first 3–1 but the difference lay in our 4–1 win at home.

This is how tight it was and what that result meant:

	P	W	D	L	F	A	Pts
PSV	34	23	7	4	84	28	53
Ajax	34	22	9	3	75	21	53

It was a day I will never forget. My first Championship and the prospect of a tilt at the European Cup, and not just any European Cup but the first with the new League format of the last eight teams playing off in two groups before a big final.

Let's face it, we are talking fortunes for the clubs concerned and the new format adds spice to the first two rounds which can sometimes be mere formalities. Now, suddenly, those two rounds alone are like a semi-final and a final.

Maybe this is why my old friends back home were suggesting that I would be on my way if I didn't win this final match and a place in the European Cup. As far as I know it wasn't true. The chairman didn't discuss it with me, but then he doesn't have to if he is going to sack you. It was up to me, by winning the League, to be sure that he was never put in that position.

We did so by winning more points than the previous year when Ajax pipped us at the post and with bigger attendances. Even had we missed out in that final game I would have been disappointed to have been sacked after leading the League for the entire season. I knew, and so did everyone else, that had we enjoyed a full squad all season we would have won it much earlier.

Had that happened we would probably have been happy with the squad we had, but if we were going to challenge seriously for the big one we knew that we would need to add to and improve the squad. PSV are a big enough club to realise that, and they immediately made it clear that the finance would be available for new players. I was already looking forward to my second season in Dutch football.

I had a gut feeling that to compete in and have a realistic chance at winning the European Cup we needed to buy and sell.

But that was still to come. For the time being it was a good feeling to win that first title. We had won it fair and square and I was pleased for myself, the club, the players and most of all for our spectators. I felt a great rapport with them after that game and even more so when we boarded an open top bus at our ground and headed for the town hall.

As we left the ground the heavens opened. It was a real cloud-burst and within minutes we were drenched. But all along the way the streets were crowded with supporters and you couldn't see an inch of pavement in the square.

It was a lovely feeling of great warmth and at that moment I hoped that back home in England the football fans would feel proud that an Englishman had won a title in a foreign country. I was happy to do it for PSV but I was also glad to be flying the flag for England.

There was just time after the celebrations for a quick few days of holiday in Italy before returning to my home in Ipswich for the tenth anniversary celebrations of our UEFA Cup success, and to watch a bit of cricket for two weeks, and then back for the second year of my contract with PSV Eindhoven. That may have surprised a few back home but not me. That was what I had always intended.

11
England

Goodness only knows what would have happened in the twelve months after the World Cup had Chris Waddle's shot gone in instead of coming back off the post in the semi-final against West Germany. Had it done so England would surely have been the defending champions in the USA in 1994.

I have been honoured with a series of awards, none bigger nor more gratefully received than the CBE.

It was a great honour to a patriot like myself. I have always been conscious that my old Ipswich neighbour Alf Ramsey became a knight after winning the World Cup for England in 1966, but no one ever works with a gong in mind and until I took a telephone call asking me if I would accept it, I hadn't even thought of the prospect.

That day at Buckingham Palace was unforgettable. I attended with my wife Elsie and two of my sons, Mark and Paul. I was certainly in good company with others like Peter Shilton, Esther Rantzen, Raman Subba Row, Dame Mary Gow and the Editor of the *Daily Star*, Brian Hitchen. I was awestruck by the Palace, it was all so regal, lovely, just as you think a Palace should be with guardsmen, sumptuous decor, deep carpets and the magnificent ballroom.

Everyone made me feel at my ease and although we saw only a small part of Buckingham Palace it was a real thrill.

The Queen was clearly well briefed for she said to me: 'I understand that you are in a very tough game.'

I answered: 'Yes I am ma'am, but it is most enjoyable.'

The Queen responded: 'I am sure it is but you have done very well.'

I picked up an ITV award at the Café Royal in London but had to turn down the invitation to present BBC's Sports Personality of the Year award, which would have been a considerable honour.

I also went back to Italy twice, flying to Treviso to Diadora's Golden Gala where I was presented with another Fair Play Award. That was also the theme of a very special presentation in Frisinone, 30 miles outside Rome when I became the first recipient of the Gaetano Scirea award and was given a fabulous gold and crystal sculpture created by Nevio De Zolt for the way I had conducted myself during the World Cup Finals.

Scirea was the first gentleman of Italian football, surviving its most cynical period for 25 years without a blemish on his character, only to be tragically killed in a car crash in Poland while on a scouting trip for Juventus. I was not always the best of losers but Johnny Cobbold at Ipswich showed me how you could lose with dignity and being in such a responsible role with England did the rest.

It was a great honour, with the Cameroon striker Roger Milla and former Italian goalkeeper Dino Zoff also picking up awards. What a pity that Milla should have spoiled what he achieved in Italy with his behaviour when Cameroon came to England. I suspect that he will always regret never having played at Wembley because of his demands.

I was also thrilled after the World Cup with the way football boomed back home because of the interest we had created in Italy.

But I was deeply disturbed when the top chairmen decided to take the First Division back to 22 teams. After all we had done in Italy it did seem to be a massive step backwards. Don't people in football ever learn how important it is to have a successful national team? The knock on effect is felt throughout the game, as more people come through the turnstiles, and the market value of the players increases, yet still obstacles are thrown in the way of England.

That is one of the reasons why I was delighted when the Football Association, backed by the top clubs, came up with the 18 team Super League designed, in part, to assist the England manager with free dates for him to prepare his team.

Going back to 22 clubs, particularly now that English clubs are back in Europe, is a retrograde step. It stands to reason that the successful clubs have the best players who will be wanted internationally and those are also the players and the clubs who will be involved in long runs in Cup competitions. It puts a huge strain on the physical and mental resources of the international players.

No country in the world has the kind of intensive programme faced by professionals in the English First Division and by the end of a long, tiring season they are hardly in shape to play a major tournament like the European Championships or the World Cup.

Of course football in Britain should be run by one body with one voice – just as every other country runs its football. Too many people involved in the administration of the game wear two hats, looking for the best of both worlds.

The Football League like a successful England team but could do more to help it. They are happy to jump on the bandwagon but if they were serious in their aims they would have never considered going back to a 22 team First Division.

They should all be worried about the future for, compared with Holland, we are a long way behind. PSV, for example, have 13 teams, starting with boys aged 8 to 10 and going right through to the seniors. They control the training, coaching and playing from eight years upwards.

At Ipswich we ran only three teams. The youngest players are 14 by which time they are set in their ways. That was fine when football was part of every schoolboy's curriculum, under the eye of a games teacher with a good knowledge of football. But now football has been shoved to one side, competing with all sorts of other activities. School playing fields are being sold off and the day of the geography master taking the boys for soccer after school seems to be long past.

While I was head of coaching at the FA I worked long and hard with Charles Hughes to set up our centres of excellence for boys aged 11 to 14 but the restrictions devalued it. The boys were allowed just an hour a week. What good is that? Would you restrict a promising swimmer or a pianist to an hour a week? Of course not.

Education has changed and at some stage people will have to admit that and hand the game over to the major football clubs to run. Many think that eight is too young. It might be. But I would like to see boys of 10 and upwards introduced to the skills and concept of playing.

If the FA and the Football League want the game to retain its status they must work to find the money to fund it with the right sort of coaches, facilities, pitches, kit and everything else that is needed. Managers like Alan Brown, Stan Cullis, Joe Mercer, Bill Shankly, Harry Catterick, Bertie Mee, Ron Greenwood, Bill Nicholson and the rest were fighting for this years ago. They were men of vision who knew what was required all those years ago. But they, like those who followed, were stifled by the English Schools Football Association. I came in at the end of it and I had the same frustrations. All I wanted was for the game to go forward and to prosper. I believe it can prosper under the Premier League.

Sponsorship will be vast as will television fees. But some of this must be used to help the Halifaxs and the Scunthorpes of this world because they are still and will remain the breeding ground for talent. Our game shouldn't be struggling for money with the pools and everything else that feeds off its popularity and success. That cash should be spread throughout the game to keep it strong at every level. That is the strength of English football.

England is blessed with a fine League and super players but that does not mean we should sit back and rest on our laurels. English players still need to work on their technique. We produce 100-per-cent triers and fighters in a game played at 100 miles per hour but the faster the game goes the more skill will be required. That first touch has to be ever better.

Because English clubs play high velocity football twice a week there is simply not enough time to train between rest and recovery. When Ipswich won the UEFA Cup we played 70 games. We didn't train, we simply played and tried to keep ourselves fit and fresh. The tendency is to fiddle about for half an hour. That's not training.

In Italy they play on Saturday and train twice a day. Here in Holland we train all day on Monday and Tuesday and stretch our season out to June with a big mid-winter break. Games are cancelled before internationals to help the team prepare.

The test is international and European football. If we can survive that then English football can say that they are up there with the best. It can't be judged on the first season back even though United went all the way to the Final and beat Barcelona 2–1 to win the

European Cup Winners' Cup. Look at the lesson Aston Villa learned. It will take two or three more seasons to judge where England stand from a club point of view. But it is nice to be in a position to judge after the years in the wilderness.

From an international point of view we've held our heads up in the most difficult of circumstances but it can give a false impression because it only takes into account the top players.

Graham Taylor has already shown that he is the right man to assume control of the international scene. He has done the right thing to divorce himself from everything other than running the national team.

I tried to take on everything from presenting certificates to schoolboys to setting up the schools of excellence. Graham seems to be confining his energy to the England team just as Alf Ramsey did – good luck to him because we need a successful England team for the game to develop and prosper.

He certainly has quality players to work with. David Seaman, Chris Woods and Nigel Martyn are in the world category of goalkeeping and you could say the same about defenders like Mark Wright, Des Walker, Paul Parker and Stuart Pearce, with others like Tony Dorigo, Gary Pallister, Earl Barrett, Trevor Steven and Gary Stevens to back them up.

In David Platt and Paul Gascoigne we unearthed two exceptional midfield players.

But the area we still need to develop is our next selection of front players, people who can score goals regularly at international level. I was lucky. I always had Gary Lineker, Peter Beardsley, Chris Waddle and John Barnes to shuffle about to suit the occasion, but they will need replacing as they get older. We will soon have to see how players like Ian Wright, Stuart Slater, Paul Merson and Kevin Campbell shape up at the top level.

I am delighted to see Graham carrying on where I left off. He will put up with all the problems as I and managers before me had to and he will learn as he goes on.

I was upset for him when he was insulted by the fans and attacked by the papers after the 1–0 win against Turkey in Izmir, but I suspect those who were chanting my name after the game were the same ones who wanted my head a year or so earlier.

The important thing in Turkey, especially after the earlier results, was to win. England did exactly that and from what I saw David Seaman did not have a single save to make.

For years West Germany have qualified however they could and then developed their teams afterwards, gaining strength by the experience of playing in so many finals. We are now developing the same qualities and the benefits are already being felt.

It is not all gloom and doom. The game in England is in a healthy state. Hooliganism is on the wane and our stature in the world is high once more.

But the burning question is what is to come in the future. How many clubs can look at their 14-year-olds and say they have a group that excites them? The chances are that there aren't many. The game at grass roots is crucial. We can't have an apex if we don't look after the base. This is in the hands of the FA and if that is the case then obviously they are the ones who should have the main voice in the game.

In England we have the best infrastructure in the world to bring on the youngsters, with 93 clubs providing natural breeding grounds for ten-year-olds and upwards. I would hate to see it wasted.

Fact File

Born: Sacriston, Co. Durham – 18 February, 1933. A miner's son, one o
five brothers.

Playing details

Club	Signed	Apps	Gls
Fulham	1950	152	68
WBA	1956	239	56
Fulham	1962–67	193	9
England		20	4

Robson's England Reign

Date	Venue	Comp.	Versus	Result	1	2	3	4	5
1982–83 Season									
22 Sept 82	Copenhagen	ECQ	Denmark	2–2	Shilton	Neal	Sansom	Wilkins *	Osma
13 Oct 82	Wembley		West Germany	1–2	Shilton	Mabbutt	Sansom	Thompson	Butch
17 Nov 82	Salonika	ECQ	Greece	3–0	Shilton	Neal	Sansom	Thompson	Marti
15 Dec 82	Wembley	ECQ	Luxembourg	9–0	Clemence	Neal [1]	Sansom	Robson *	Marti
23 Feb 83	Wembley		Wales	2–1	Shilton *	Neal [1]	Statham	Lee	Marti
30 Mar 83	Wembley	ECQ	Greece	0–0	Shilton *	Neal	Sansom	Lee	Marti
27 Apr 83	Wembley	ECQ	Hungary	2–0	Shilton *	Neal	Sansom	Lee	Marti
28 May 83	Belfast		Northern Ireland	0–0	Shilton *	Neal	Sansom	Hoddle	Robe
1 June 83	Wembley		Scotland	2–0	Shilton	Neal	Sansom	Lee	Robe
12 June 83	Sydney		Australia	0–0	Shilton *	Thomas	Statham	Williams	Osma
15 June 83	Brisbane		Australia	1–0	Shilton *	Neal	Statham	Barham	Osma
19 June 83	Melbourne		Australia	1–1	Shilton *	Neal	Pickering	Lee	Osma
1983–84 Season									
21 Sept 83	Wembley	ECQ	Denmark	0–1	Shilton	Neal	Sansom	Lee	Osma
12 Oct 83	Budapest	ECQ	Hungary	3–0	Shilton	Gregory	Sansom	Lee [1]	Marti
16 Nov 83	Luxembourg	ECQ	Luxembourg	4–0	Clemence	Duxbury	Sansom	Lee	Mart
29 Feb 84	Paris		France	0–2	Shilton	Duxbury	Sansom	Lee	Robe
4 Apr 84	Wembley		Northern Ireland	1–0	Shilton	Anderson	Kennedy	Lee	Robe
2 May 84	Wrexham		Wales	0–1	Shilton	Duxbury	Kennedy	Lee	Mart
26 May 84	Glasgow		Scotland	1–1	Shilton	Duxbury	Sansom	Wilkins	Robe
2 June 84	Wembley		USSR	0–2	Shilton	Duxbury	Sansom	Wilkins	Robe
10 June 84	Rio de Janeiro		Brazil	2–0	Shilton	Duxbury	Sansom	Wilkins	Wats
13 June 84	Montevideo		Uruguay	0–2	Shilton	Duxbury	Sansom	Wilkins	Wats
17 June 84	Santiago		Chile	0–0	Shilton	Duxbury	Sansom	Wilkins	Wats
1984–85 Season									
12 Sept 84	Wembley		East Germany	1–0	Shilton	Duxbury	Sansom	Williams	Wrig
17 Oct 84	Wembley	WCQ	Finland	5–0	Shilton	Duxbury	Sansom [1]	Williams	Wrig
14 Nov 84	Istanbul	WCQ	Turkey	8–0	Shilton	Anderson [1]	Sansom	Williams	Wrig
27 Feb 85	Belfast	WCQ	Northern Ireland	1–0	Shilton	Anderson	Sansom	Stevens	Marti
26 Mar 85	Wembley		Rep. of Ireland	2–1	Bailey	Anderson	Sansom	Steven [1]	Wrig
1 May 85	Bucharest	WCQ	Romania	0–0	Shilton	Anderson	Sansom	Steven	Wrig

Managerial
Signed   *Club*
1967   Vancouver Royals
Jan. 1968 (sacked Nov)   Fulham
Jan. 1969   Ipswich

England (July 1982–July 1990)
P   W   D   L   F   A
95 47 38 10 154 60

Since July 1990   PSV Eindhoven

Honours With Ipswich: FA Cup winners 1978, UEFA Cup winners 1981, First Division runners up 1980–81, 1981–82. With PSV Eindhoven: Dutch Division One Champions 1990–91.

	7	8	9	10	11	Substitutes	Match No.
cher	Morley	Robson	Mariner	Francis²	Rix	Hill(7)	1
ilkins*	Hill	Regis	Mariner	Armstrong	Devonshire	Woodcock(8)¹ Blissett(9) Rix(10)	2
bson*	Lee¹	Mabbutt	Mariner	Woodcock²	Morley		3
cher	Coppell¹	Lee	Woodcock¹	Blissett³	Mabbutt¹	Chamberlain(7)¹ Hoddle(11)¹	4
cher¹	Mabbutt	Blissett	Mariner	Cowans	Devonshire		5
cher	Coppell	Mabbutt	Francis	Blissett	Devonshire	Blissett(10) Rix(11)	6
cher	Mabbutt	Francis¹	Withe¹	Blissett	Cowans		7
cher	Mabbutt	Francis	Withe	Blissett	Cowans	Barnes(10)	8
cher	Robson*¹	Francis	Withe	Hoddle	Cowans¹	Mabbutt(7) Blissett(9)	9
cher	Barham	Gregory	Blissett	Francis	Cowans	Barnes(3) Walsh(9)	10
cher	Gregory	Francis	Walsh¹	Cowans	Barnes	Williams(3)	11
cher	Gregory	Francis¹	Walsh	Cowans	Barnes	Spink(1) Thomas(2) Blissett(9)	12
cher	Wilkins*	Gregory	Mariner	Francis	Barnes	Blissett(4) Chamberlain(11)	13
cher	Robson*	Hoddle¹	Mariner¹	Blissett	Mabbutt	Withe(10)	14
cher¹	Robson*²	Hoddle	Mariner¹	Woodcock	Devonshire	Barnes(10)	15
cher	Robson*	Stein	Walsh	Hoddle	Williams	Barnes(4) Woodcock(8)	16
cher	Robson*	Wilkins	Woodcock¹	Francis	Rix		17
ight	Wilkins*	Gregory	Walsh	Woodcock	Armstrong	Fenwick(5) Blissett(11)	18
wick	Chamberlain	Robson*	Woodcock¹	Blissett	Barnes	Hunt(7) Lineker(9)	19
wick	Chamberlain	Robson*	Francis	Blissett	Barnes	Hateley(9) Hunt(11)	20
wick	Robson*	Chamberlain	Hateley¹	Woodcock	Barnes¹	Allen(10)	21
wick	Robson*	Chamberlain	Hately	Allen	Barnes	Woodcock(10)	22
wick	Robson*	Chamberlain	Hately	Allen	Barnes	Lee(8)	23
cher	Robson*¹	Wilkins	Mariner	Woodcock	Barnes	Hateley(9) Francis(10)	24
cher	Robson*¹	Wilkins	Hateley²	Woodcock¹	Barnes	Stevens(2) Chamberlain(7)	25
cher	Robson*³	Wilkins	Withe	Woodcock²	Barnes²	Stevens(4) Francis(10)	26
cher	Steven	Wilkins*	Hateley¹	Woodcock	Barnes	Francis(10)	27
cher	Robson*	Wilkins	Hateley	Lineker¹	Waddle	Hoddle(7) Davenport(9)	28
cher	Robson*	Wilkins	Mariner	Francis	Barnes	Lineker(9) Waddle(11)	29

Date	Venue	Comp.	Versus	Result	1	2	3	4	5
22 May 85	Helsinki	WCQ	Finland	1–1	Shilton	Anderson	Sansom	Steven	Fenw
25 May 85	Glasgow		Scotland	0–1	Shilton	Anderson	Sansom	Hoddle	Fenw
6 June 85	Mexico City		Italy	1–2	Shilton	Stevens	Sansom	Steven	Wrig
9 June 85	Mexico City		Mexico	0–1	Bailey	Anderson	Sansom	Hoddle	Fenw
12 June 85	Mexico City		West Germany	3–0	Shilton	Stevens	Sansom	Hoddle	Wrig
16 June 85	Los Angeles		USA	5–0	Woods	Anderson	Sansom	Hoddle	Fenw

1985–86 Season

Date	Venue	Comp.	Versus	Result	1	2	3	4	5
11 Sept 85	Wembley	WCQ	Romania	1–1	Shilton	Stevens	Sansom	Reid	Wrig
16 Oct 85	Wembley	WCQ	Turkey	5–0	Shilton	Stevens	Sansom	Hoddle	Wrig
13 Nov 85	Wembley	WCQ	Northern Ireland	0–0	Shilton	Stevens	Sansom	Hoddle	Wrig
29 Jan 86	Cairo		Egypt	4–0	Shilton	Stevens	Sansom	Cowans [1]	Wrig
26 Feb 86	Tel Aviv		Israel	2–1	Shilton	Stevens	Sansom	Hoddle	Marti
26 Mar 86	Tbilisi		USSR	1–0	Shilton	Anderson	Sansom	Hoddle	Wrig
23 Apr 86	Wembley		Scotland	2–1	Shilton	Stevens	Sansom	Hoddle [1]	Wats
17 May 86	Los Angeles		Mexico	3–0	Shilton	Anderson	Sansom	Hoddle	Fenw
24 May 86	Vancouver		Canada	1–0	Shilton	Stevens	Sansom	Hoddle	Marti
3 June 86	Monterrey	WCF	Portugal	0–1	Shilton	Stevens	Sansom	Hoddle	Fenw
6 June 86	Monterrey	WCF	Morocco	0–0	Shilton	Stevens	Sansom	Hoddle	Fenw
11 June 86	Monterrey	WCF	Poland	3–0	Shilton *	Stevens	Sansom	Hoddle	Fenw
18 June 86	Mexico City	WCF	Paraguay	3–0	Shilton *	Stevens	Sansom	Hoddle	Marti
22 June 86	Mexico City	WCF	Argentina	1–2	Shilton *	Stevens	Sansom	Hoddle	Fenw

1986–87 Season

Date	Venue	Comp.	Versus	Result	1	2	3	4	5
10 Sept 86	Stockholm		Sweden	0–1	Shilton *	Anderson	Sansom	Hoddle	Marti
15 Oct 86	Wembley	ECQ	Northern Ireland	3–0	Shilton	Anderson	Sansom	Hoddle	Wats
12 Nov 86	Wembley	ECQ	Yugoslavia	2–0	Woods	Anderson [1]	Sansom	Hoddle	Wrig
18 Feb 87	Madrid		Spain	4–2	Shilton	Anderson	Sansom	Hoddle	Adam
1 Apr 87	Belfast	ECQ	Northern Ireland	2–0	Shilton	Anderson	Sansom	Mabbutt	Wrigh
29 Apr 87	Wembley	ECQ	Turkey	0–0	Woods	Anderson	Sansom	Hoddle	Adam
19 May 87	Wembley		Brazil	1–1	Shilton	Stevens	Pearce	Reid	Adam
23 May 87	Glasgow		Scotland	0–0	Woods	Stevens	Pearce	Hoddle	Wrigh

1987–88 Season

Date	Venue	Comp.	Versus	Result	1	2	3	4	5
9 Sept 87	Dusseldorf		West Germany	1–3	Shilton *	Anderson	Sansom	Hoddle	Adam
14 Oct 87	Wembley	ECQ	Turkey	8–0	Shilton	Stevens	Sansom	Steven	Adam
11 Nov 87	Belgrade	ECQ	Yugoslavia	4–1	Shilton	Stevens	Sansom	Steven	Adam
17 Feb 88	Tel Aviv		Israel	0–0	Woods	Stevens	Pearce	Webb	Wats
23 Mar 88	Wembley		Holland	2–2	Shilton	Stevens	Sansom	Steven	Adam
27 Apr 88	Budapest		Hungary	0–0	Woods	Anderson	Pearce	Steven	Adam
21 May 88	Wembley		Scotland	1–0	Shilton	Stevens	Sansom	Webb	Wats
24 May 88	Wembley		Colombia	1–1	Shilton	Anderson	Sansom	McMahon	Wrigh
28 May 88	Lausanne		Switzerland	1–0	Shilton	Stevens	Sansom	Webb	Wrigh
12 June 88	Stuttgart	ECF	Rep. of Ireland	0–1	Shilton	Stevens	Sansom	Webb	Wrigh
15 June 88	Dusseldorf	ECF	Holland	1–3	Shilton *	Stevens	Sansom	Hoddle	Wrigh
18 June 88	Frankfurt	ECF	USSR	1–3	Woods	Stevens	Sansom	Hoddle	Wats

1988–89 Season

Date	Venue	Comp.	Versus	Result	1	2	3	4	5
14 Sept 88	Wembley		Denmark	1–0	Shilton	Stevens	Pearce	Rocastle	Adam
19 Oct 88	Wembley	WCQ	Sweden	0–0	Shilton	Stevens	Pearce	Webb	Adam
16 Nov 88	Riyadh		Saudi Arabia	1–1	Seaman	Sterland	Pearce	Thomas	Adam
8 Feb 89	Athens		Greece	2–1	Shilton	Stevens	Pearce	Webb	Walk
8 Mar 89	Tirana	WCQ	Albania	2–0	Shilton	Stevens	Pearce	Webb	Walk
26 Apr 89	Wembley	WCQ	Albania	5–0	Shilton	Stevens	Pearce	Webb	Walk
23 May 89	Wembley		Chile	0–0	Shilton	Parker	Pearce	Webb	Walk
27 May 89	Glasgow		Scotland	2–0	Shilton	Stevens	Pearce	Webb	Walk
3 June 89	Wembley	WCQ	Poland	3–0	Shilton	Stevens	Pearce	Webb [1]	Walk
7 June 89	Copenhagen		Denmark	1–1	Shilton	Parker	Pearce	Webb	Walk

1989–90 Season

Date	Venue	Comp.	Versus	Result	1	2	3	4	5
6 Sept 89	Stockholm	WCQ	Sweden	0–0	Shilton	Stevens	Pearce	Webb	Walk

	7	8	9	10	11	Substitutes	Match No.
utcher	Robson*	Wilkins	Hateley[1]	Francis	Barnes	Waddle(4)	30
iutcher	Robson*	Wilkins	Hateley	Francis	Barnes	Lineker(4) Waddle(11)	31
butcher	Robson*	Wilkins	Hateley[1]	Francis	Waddle	Hoddle(4) Lineker(10) Barnes(11)	32
Vatson	Robson*	Wilkins	Hateley	Francis	Barnes	Dixon(4) Reid(8) Waddle(11)	33
iutcher	Robson*[1]	Reid	Dixon[2]	Lineker	Waddle	Bracewell(7) Barnes(10)	34
iutcher	Robson*	Bracewell	Dixon[2]	Lineker[2]	Waddle	Watson(3) Stevens(4)[1] Reid(7) Barnes(11)	35
enwick	Robson*	Hoddle[1]	Hateley	Lineker	Waddle	Woodcock(10) Barnes(11)	36
enwick	Robson*[1]	Wilkins	Hateley	Lineker[3]	Waddle[1]	Steven(7) Woodcock(9)	37
enwick	Bracewell	Wilkins*	Dixon	Lineker	Waddle		38
enwick	Steven[1]	Wilkins*	Hateley	Lineker	Wallace[1]	Woods(1) Hill(7) Beardsley(10) (+o.g.)	39
utcher	Robson*[2]	Wilkins	Dixon	Beardsley	Waddle	Woods(1) Woodcock(9) Barnes(11)	40
utcher	Cowans	Wilkins*	Beardsley	Lineker	Waddle[1]	Hodge(7) Steven(11)	41
utcher[1]	Wilkins*	Francis	Hateley	Hodge	Waddle	Reid(7) Stevens(10)	42
utcher	Robson*	Wilkins	Hateley[2]	Beardsley[1]	Waddle	Stevens(7) Steven(8) Dixon(9) Barnes(11)	43
utcher	Hodge	Wilkins*	Hateley[1]	Lineker	Waddle	Woods(1) Reid(8) Beardsley(10) Barnes(11)	44
utcher	Robson*	Wilkins	Hateley	Lineker	Waddle	Hodge(7) Beardsley(11)	45
utcher	Robson*	Wilkins	Hateley	Lineker	Waddle	Hodge(7) Stevens(9)	46
utcher	Hodge	Reid	Beardsley	Lineker[3]	Steven	Waddle(9) Dixon(10)	47
utcher	Hodge	Reid	Beardsley[1]	Lineker[2]	Steven	Stevens(8) Hateley(9)	48
utcher	Hodge	Reid	Beardsley	Lineker[1]	Steven	Waddle(8) Barnes(11)	49
utcher	Steven	Wilkins	Dixon	Hodge	Barnes	Cottee(7) Waddle(11)	50
utcher	Robson*	Hodge	Beardsley	Lineker[2]	Waddle[1]	Cottee(9)	51
utcher*	Mabbutt[1]	Hodge	Beardsley	Lineker	Waddle	Wilkins(8) Steven(11)	52
utcher	Robson*	Hodge	Beardsley	Lineker[4]	Waddle	Woods(1) Steven(11)	53
utcher	Robson*[1]	Hodge	Beardsley	Lineker	Waddle[1]	Woods(1)	54
Mabbutt	Robson*	Hodge	Allen	Lineker	Waddle	Barnes(8) Hateley(9)	55
utcher	Robson*	Barnes	Beardsley	Lineker[1]	Waddle	Hateley(10)	56
utcher	Robson*	Hodge	Beardsley	Hateley	Waddle		57
Mabbutt	Reid	Barnes	Beardsley	Lineker[1]	Waddle	Pearce(3) Webb(4) Hateley(11)	58
utcher	Robson*[1]	Webb[1]	Beardsley[1]	Lineker[3]	Barnes[2]	Hoddle(4) Regis(9)	59
atcher	Robson*[1]	Webb	Beardsley[1]	Lineker	Barnes[1]	Reid(7) Hoddle(8)	60
Vright	Allen	McMahon	Beardsley*	Barnes	Waddle	Fenwick(6) Harford(7)	61
Vatson	Robson*	Webb	Beardsley	Lineker[1]	Barnes	Wright(6) Hoddle(8) Hateley(9)	62
allister	Robson*	McMahon	Beardsley	Lineker	Waddle	Stevens(3) Hateley(9) Cottee(10) Hoddle(11)	63
dams	Robson*	Steven	Beardsley[1]	Lineker	Barnes	Waddle(8)	64
dams	Robson*	Waddle	Beardsley	Lineker[1]	Barnes	Hoddle(8) Hateley(9)	65
dams	Robson*	Steven	Beardsley	Lineker[1]	Barnes	Woods(1) Watson(6) Reid(7) Waddle(8)	66
dams	Robson*	Waddle	Beardsley	Lineker	Barnes	Hoddle(4) Hateley(9)	67
dams	Robson*[1]	Steven	Beardsley	Lineker	Barnes	Waddle(8) Hateley(9)	68
dams[1]	Robson*	Steven	McMahon	Lineker	Barnes	Webb(9) Hateley(10)	69
utcher	Robson*	Webb[1]	Harford	Beardsley	Hodge	Woods(1) Walker(5) Cottee(9) Gascoigne(10)	70
utcher	Robson*	Beardsley	Waddle	Lineker	Barnes	Walker(5) Cottee(11)	71
allister	Robson*	Rocastle	Beardsley	Lineker	Waddle	Gascoigne(4) Smith(9) Marwood(11)	72
utcher	Robson*[1]	Rocastle	Smith	Lineker	Barnes[1]	Beardsley(9)	73
atcher	Robson*[1]	Rocastle	Waddle	Lineker	Barnes[1]	Beardsley(9) Smith(10)	74
atcher	Robson*	Rocastle	Beardsley[2]	Lineker[1]	Waddle[1]	Parker(2) Gascoigne(8)[1]	75
atcher	Robson*	Gascoigne	Clough	Fashanu	Waddle	Cottee(10)	76
atcher	Robson*	Steven	Fashanu	Cottee	Waddle[1]	Bull(9)[1] Gascoigne(10)	77
atcher	Robson*	Waddle	Beardsley	Lineker[1]	Barnes[1]	Rocastle(8) Smith(9)	78
atcher	Robson*	Rocastle	Beardsley	Lineker[1]	Barnes	Seaman(1) McMahon(4) Bull(9) Waddle(11)	79
atcher*	Beardsley	McMahon	Waddle	Lineker	Barnes	Gascoigne(4) Rocastle(11)	80

235

Date	Venue	Comp.	Versus	Result	1	2	3	4	5
11 Oct 89	Katowice	WCQ	Poland	0–0	Shilton	Stevens	Pearce	McMahon	Walker
15 Nov 89	Wembley		Italy	0–0	Shilton	Stevens	Pearce	McMahon	Walker
13 Dec 89	Wembley		Yugoslavia	2–1	Shilton	Parker	Pearce	Thomas	Walker
28 Mar 90	Wembley		Brazil	1–0	Shilton	Stevens	Pearce	McMahon	Walker
25 Apr 90	Wembley		Czechoslovakia	4–2	Shilton	Dixon	Pearce [1]	Steven	Walker
15 May 90	Wembley		Denmark	1–0	Shilton	Stevens	Pearce	McMahon	Walker
22 May 90	Wembley		Uruguay	1–2	Shilton	Parker	Pearce	Hodge	Walker
2 June 90	Tunis		Tunisia	1–1	Shilton	Stevens	Pearce	Hodge	Walker
11 June 90	Cagliari	WCF	Rep. of Ireland	1–1	Shilton	Stevens	Pearce	Gascoigne	Walker
16 June 90	Cagliari	WCF	Holland	0–0	Shilton	Parker	Pearce	Wright	Walker
21 June 90	Cagliari	WCF	Egypt	1–0	Shilton *	Parker	Pearce	Gascoigne	Walker
26 June 90	Bologna	WCF	Belgium	1–0	Shilton	Parker	Pearce	Wright	Walker
1 July 90	Naples	WCF	Cameroon	3–2	Shilton	Parker	Pearce	Wright	Walker
4 July 90	Turin	WCF	West Germany	1–1	Shilton	Parker	Pearce	Wright	Walker
7 July 90	Bari	WCF	Italy	1–2	Shilton *	Stevens	Dorigo	Parker	Walker

	P	W	D	L	F	A
Total	95	47	29	19	154	60

Key		
	ECQ	European Championship Qualifying match
	ECF	European Championship Finals match
	WCQ	World Cup Qualifying match
	WCF	World Cup Finals match
	*	Captain

Numbers by player's name indicate number of goals scored in match

Numbers by substitute players indicate player replaced

	7	8	9	10	11	Substitutes	Match No.
Butcher	Robson *	Rocastle	Beardsley	Lineker	Waddle		81
Butcher	Robson *	Waddle	Beardsley	Lineker	Barnes	Beasant(1) Winterburn(3) Hodge(4) Phelan(7) Platt(9)	82
Butcher	Robson *2	Rocastle	Bull	Lineker	Waddle	Beasant(1) Dorigo(3) Platt(4) McMahon(7) Hodge(8)	83
Butcher *	Platt	Waddle	Beardsley	Lineker [1]	Barnes	Woods(1) Gascoigne(9)	84
Butcher	Robson *	Gascoigne [1]	Bull [2]	Lineker	Hodge	Seaman(1) Dorigo(3) Wright(5) McMahon(7)	85
Butcher *	Hodge	Gascoigne	Waddle	Lineker [1]	Barnes	Woods(1) Dorigo(3) Platt(4) Rocastle(9) Bull(10)	86
Butcher	Robson *	Gascoigne	Waddle	Lineker	Barnes [1]	Beardsley(4) Bull(10)	87
Butcher	Robson *	Waddle	Gascoigne	Lineker	Barnes	Beardsley(4) Wright(6) Platt(8) Bull(10) [1]	88
Butcher *	Robson *	Waddle	Beardsley	Lineker [1]	Barnes	McMahon(9) Bull(10)	89
Butcher *	Robson *	Waddle	Gascoigne	Lineker	Barnes	Platt(7) Bull(8)	90
Wright [1]	McMahon	Waddle	Bull	Lineker	Barnes	Platt(8) Beardsley(9)	91
Butcher *	McMahon	Waddle	Gascoigne	Lineker	Barnes	Platt(7) [1] Bull(11)	92
Butcher *	Platt [1]	Waddle	Gascoigne	Lineker [2]	Barnes	Steven(6) Beardsley(11)	93
Butcher *	Platt	Waddle	Gascoigne	Lineker [1]	Beardsley	Steven(6)	94
Wright	Platt [1]	Steven	McMahon	Lineker	Beardsley	Waddle(6) Webb(9)	95

237